Political Perspectives

Essays on Government and Politics

Kenneth L. Manning
John Fobanjong

University of Massachusetts–Dartmouth

KENDALL/HUNT PUBLISHING COMPANY
4050 Westmark Drive   Dubuque, Iowa 52002

Cover photo supplied by Corel.

Copyright © 2003 by Kenneth L. Manning and John Fobanjong

ISBN 0-7575-0507-4

Printed in the United States of America
10 9 8 7 6 5 4 3 2 1

Contents

People and Politics: Political Behavior

Preface

Political Perspectives provides readers with a selection of contemporary and classic readings on political issues that contribute to the discussion of American politics.

The selections in this text have been assembled from a variety of sources. The original essays have been written for an undergraduate audience by both well-established and up-and-coming scholars. These academics have drawn upon their professional knowledge and classroom experience to offer enlightening views in their fields. As such, this volume is able to combine a wealth of academic expertise with the experience of classroom perspectives to offer readers a diverse assortment of interesting political insights. Each article brings the author's own views to a timely issue. Agreement with the authors' perspectives, or lack thereof, can thus be the inspiration for classroom discussion.

But rather than focus exclusively upon academic work, this volume brings in "real-world" readings, too. Some pieces are selections from modern political actors, their own words providing the best way of conveying their ideas. And to round off this mix, a few classics have been added. The goal here is diversity— of opinion, of style, of perspective

The text has been divided into three general sections. After an introduction to the study of politics, readers are presented essays that touch upon the fundamental constitutional principles of liberty and equality. In keeping with the aim of this book to complement rather than duplicate introductory texts, each article brings an illuminating perspective to a fundamental constitutional principle or debate. Following the section on constitutional principles is a segment that pertains to key governmental institutions. Readers will note a particular emphasis upon the president's involvement in international affairs and current issues in that area, matters that have recently been of increased interest to students and the public. Of course, it goes without saying that the legislative and judicial branches also merit discussion, and these areas are complemented by informative writings as well. Finally, in a section on political behavior, we present an array of articles which address pertinent issues concerning public opinion, elections and voting, group participation, and political parties.

The articles have been purposefully kept brief; as teachers of introductory courses, we've found that students tend to be more receptive of pieces that are informative yet concise. The ultimate goal of this book is to provide readers with an engaging review that complements American politics textbooks with timely and interesting articles that may be the catalyst for stimulating dialogues.

Insights on the Discipline of Political Science

An Introduction

JOHN FOBANJONG

Very few students enter college knowing what major to pursue. Even for students who come in with a declared major, it is not uncommon to see them switch in the middle of their college career. To help students make informed decisions early in their college career, the following reading discusses political science as an academic discipline. If you are reading this, it is probably because you are enrolled in an introductory level course in the social sciences. Not only is this reading going to be useful to students who are yet to declare a major, students who have already picked out a major are going to find it useful as well. Even in an introductory course, it is important that we look at the big picture in order to gain some familiarity with what economists often refer to as the *macro-level* understanding of the discipline. This would help us determine if this is what we want to pursue as a field of study. An understanding of what political science is, who political scientists are, what they study, how they study it, and why they study what they study can place a course in politics into better perspective. It will also help us think critically about the subject matter. It is necessary, therefore, to begin by defining political science.

Defining Political Science

Many of the social realities that are studied in the social sciences are frequently all so evident that we often wonder if we should belabor ourselves defining them. For many, there is the general assumption that political science studies politics, sociology studies society, and historians study history, so why bother to define it. Generally, however, what may initially appear all too evident at first thought, particularly to the layperson, may not always be exactly how professionals who study the discipline see their work. Whereas the nonprofessional or college freshman is more likely to see political science as the study of politics, political scientists tend to see their field as an intellectual discipline that is more engulfing. For the nonprofessional, people who study political science go on to become politicians. It is not unusual to hear a grandparent warn their grandchild who has come from college to say that she is contemplating majoring in political science that "I don't want you to go into politics." Nothing could be more distorted. Few people who are educated in political science go directly into politics. This is because the skills that they have acquired in the study of political science are in demand in many more careers than just politics. Just as agronomists (plant and soil engineers) who study agriculture do not always go on to become farmers, people who study political science do not necessarily go on to become politicians. It is equally true that not every student who majors in business graduates to become a business man or woman. What political scientists do is develop scientific theories that enable them to learn and understand how political society is organized, what politicians do, how they do what they do, and why they do what they do.

If it were true that people who study political science automatically go on to become politicians, then many of our politicians would be people with political science degrees. But that is not the case. The U.S. presidency, for example, is generally seen as the highest political office in the nation. Yet, since the founding of the United States, only one person educated in political science has been elected to this political office. The rest have either been farmers, lawyers, or businessmen. The only political scientist who has occupied the office was Woodrow Wilson. Elected in 1913, Wilson was president during the First World War. Under his presidency, the Nineteenth Amendment to the U.S. Constitution was passed, granting women the right to vote. If education in political science can be credited with transforming people into visionaries, Woodrow Wilson was certainly transformed into one. Besides carrying through with the women's vote and presiding over World War I, Wilson conceptualized the legal framework that defined the international system in which we live today. He was the mind behind the League of Nations—the forebearer of today's United Nations. He sought to universalize democracy by proselytizing the principle of self-determination for the colonized peoples of the Third World. As appealing as such thoughts may sound today, in Woodrow Wilson's era, his views were radical and very much the antiestablishment. Much of the Third World at the time was under the colonial rule of Western Europe. His appeal for the self-determination of these people was therefore not received kindly by Western colonial powers. For the colonized peoples of the Third World, however, Wilson was a hero.

In many more ways than one, this political scientist turned president was way ahead of his time. So far, we cannot tell whether his visionary insights should be attributed to his skills as a politician or to his education in political science. What we can tell is that when you place individuals who are educated in political science in political positions where they are able to put their political science knowledge to work, they will in most cases articulate public policies that are visionary. Thus, although laypersons see political science as a major for people who want to go into politics, political scientists generally see the discipline as a major that prepares students to become problem solvers and better decision makers.

So What Exactly Is Political Science?

Although we have seen that politics and political science are two very distinct pursuits, it is still not enough to tell us what political science is. To get a precise understanding of political science therefore, we need to come up with a working definition. Even as we see that political science, like most social science disciplines, needs defining, it is often difficult to come up with a universally accepted definition. As a result, some disciplines develop more than one definition—all of them correctly describing their field of study. This is the case with political science. It is a discipline that has been defined at various times by various scholars, in various ways.

One of the most popular of such definitions is from the political scientist Harold Lasswell, who defines political science as the study of "who gets what, when, and how."[1] Just as an economist observes the various activities that are involved in the production, distribution, and consumption of goods to formulate his theories, the political scientist observes the various processes that are involved in the acquisition and control of political power to formulate his theories. The interpretation given to this definition by some political scientists is that politics is a struggle for power. Matthew Holden, Jr., for example, sees political science as the study of "the organization of power." For him and for a growing number of political scientists, the discipline's master concept is not democracy, the state, or liberalism, it is power.[2] Power in this sense is seen not as an end, but as a means to an end. It allows groups or nation-states that have it to control the allocation and distribution of resources within a state, or in the international system. This is what Lasswell means when he informs us that politics determines who gets what, when, and how.

What does this definition mean to the student who is studying political science? It means that political science is a discipline that allows him or her to gain a systematic understanding of power, participation, and authority as they influence the structures and workings of governments, political conflict, cooperation, and public policy. In most group settings, there is no value more widely sought after than power. It is a value that political scientists spend their lives studying.

The Breadth of Political Science

More than one thousand years ago, the Greek philosopher, Aristotle, stated that man is in essence a political animal. By that he meant politics is involved in every aspect of our lives. Combining Aristotle's thoughts with Lasswell's definition of politics as the determinant of who gets what, when, and how, we are brought to the realization that political science is a discipline that touches every aspect of society, from business and economics, to social systems, private lives, and ethics. As you study political science, you are going to learn that everything in life is political. Every newscast, election, group interaction, political scandal, or even religious rift—here or around the world—has its roots in the ideologies and policies that shape our governments and societies. Even within the smallest unit of society—the family—politics is at play. When two or more children within the family compete to outperform one another or win their parents' favor, in what sociologists call "sibling rivalry," they are actually playing politics. Harold Lasswell would see such rivalry as a struggle among siblings to determine "who gets what, when, and how."

The breadth of political science as a discipline, therefore, is extensive and growing. Among other things, political scientists study how human beings share or fight for power and authority, what forms of governments or political structures are conducive to stability and human welfare, and how people are organized to live and get along harmoniously in society. Political scientists study ideas and ideological concepts—both new and old—that are key to political organization and political action, including ideas like representation, democracy, justice, equality, liberty, rights, and emancipation. The field of political science is also expanding to address the politics of knowledge production, gender, race, religion, ethnicity, terrorism, human rights, social movements, environmentalism, colonialism, war, peace, conflict resolution, international organizations, globalization, and postmodernism.

The Organization of the Study of Political Science

From what we have seen so far, it would appear that political scientists study almost every behavior that has to do with the quest for, and control of, power. Although this may be true, it is also true that to facilitate the study of the discipline, political science is divided into various subfields. They include political theory, international relations, comparative politics, political institutions, political behavior, and public policy. Most undergraduate programs in political science require their majors to take courses in a variety of different subfields. For students who go on to graduate school, however, they are required to specialize in one of these areas, and minor in one or two of them as subfields. Whether one intends to go on to graduate school or not, it is important to know what the distinctions among the various political science subfields are, and what one would learn if one decides to specialize in any of them.

Political Philosophy

This is the area of political science that produces the grand theories that define and guide the growth of the discipline. For this reason, it is also often referred to as political theory. As a subfield, political philosophy offers courses on political thinkers, their ideas and theories—from the classics to modern political theory. Indeed, political science can be rightly seen as the stepchild of philosophy, because the first formal study of the discipline was in philosophy. When scholars such as Socrates, Plato, John Locke, Thomas Hobbes, Thomas Jefferson, and James Madison carried intellectual debates on the political organization of society, these debates were conducted within the discipline of philosophy. It was not until about 100 years ago that the discipline weaned itself from philosophy and became known as political science. As an organized academic discipline, therefore, political science has been around only for a century.[3] Since then, much of the new knowledge that develops in the discipline is referred to not as political philosophy, but as political theory. In the study of the ideology of politics, for example, the opposite ends of the spectrum are often referred to today as liberal and conservative theories. A hundred years ago, they would have been referred to as liberal and conservative philosophies. And people who teach and study political science today would be referred as philosophers rather than as political scientists.

International Relations

With the birth of the modern nation-state system and the development of warfare, there was the need to carve out a subfield in political science that focuses on the study of conflict, peace, and various other forms of interactions among nation-states. This led to the growth and development of theories that were distinctively directed at the study of international relations, international organization, the international political economy, and foreign policy. Since the Second World War, international relations has become the fastest growing and most innovative subfield in political science. It uses highly sophisticated statistical methods to study and predict the likelihood of warfare and to evaluate national capabilities, diplomatic brinkmanship, and peace and conflict resolution. Among some of its analytical tools are simulation, game theory and the prisoner's dilemma. We are reminded by recent changes in the international system that international relations is, for the foreseeable future, going to continue to remain the fastest growing subfield in the discipline. Some of the most visible changes that we are already noticing today include the end of the Cold War and the transformation of the international system, as well as the growing interdependence of the international system, multinational business networks, regional trade groupings, terrorism, globalization, and the global environment.

Political Behavior

This is a political science subfield that studies how people behave in political society. From voting behavior to lobbying, political campaigns, public opinion, and decision making, political scientists seek to understand and explain underlying motivations that surround political action and political activities. In the study of public opinion, for example, scholars gather citizens' views on a variety of key issues of the day and statistically analyze the results to help guide politicians and policymakers in their decision making. In the area of voting behavior, for example, political scientists develop models that explain elections, political campaigns, and voting behavior.

Political Institutions

This is the subfield in political science that is most familiar to college students. It focuses on the study of the Constitution, Congress, the presidency, the judiciary, federalism, and the bureaucracy. The field of political institutions concentrates its study on the structures of government—how they're arranged and how well they work. In most political science degree programs, American Government is usually the introductory course to this subfield. Some of the enduring controversies that are studied by American institutional scholars include interest groups and political action committees, political parties, the electoral college, proportional representation vs. the winner-take-all system, the judicial nomination process, presidential power, and civil liberties and rights.

Courses that are offered within the subfield of political institutions allow us to study and understand the institutions of the political society in which we live. Unlike in nondemocratic societies, citizens of democratic states are expected to be active participants in the political process. To become informed consumers, therefore, it is important that we understand how our political system functions, how we can influence it, and what we can do to make sure that our best interest is served. In a recent American Political Science Association publication marking the 100th anniversary of the discipline, Ira Katznelson highlights the point that American political scientists have the responsibility to educate the citizenry to overcome the lack of information on matters of public life in order for them to become thoughtful participants. This is particularly so in this age of skepticism about the hazards of mass political participation.[4]

Just as we study our political system, people in other countries are also studying theirs. Thus, the study of political institutions does not exclusively focus upon American politics. Sometimes, to find out how our political system is faring, we may want to stretch our necks out and examine how other political systems doing. Through comparative politics, another key subfield in political science, we are able to study other political systems.

Comparative Politics

This is a subfield that deals with the politics of countries and regions such as Africa, Asia, Europe, Latin America, and North America. This field also covers approaches that study politics and ways of thinking about and comparing nation-states. Among the methodologies used in the study of the subfield are quantitative statistical methods. It is easier and more meaningful to compare different political systems using quantitative rather than qualitative techniques. Among some of the things studied in the subfield are: regime type and regime stability, modernization, political development, political socialization and political culture, revolutionary change, interest groups and interest articulation, political parties and interest aggregation.

As in international relations, comparative politics is another political science subfield that is currently going through rapid changes. There has been a proliferation of new nation-states in the international system since World War II (before World War II there were less than 45 nation-states in the world). Today, there are more than 193 countries in the world. Thus, comparativists—as the scholars in this field describe themselves—now have many more political systems to study. With the underling assumption that different countries have different political systems, studying each of the 193 countries that are in the world today could be quite daunting. At the same time, with the collapse of the communist world and the growing appeal of democratic forms of government, the political systems of the world may actually be growing increasingly homogenous rather than heterogeneous. In other words, today's comparativists may have less to compare than they had in the pre–World War II era, when there were only some 45 countries in the world to study.

At the same time, we know dissimilarities can be found even among political systems that are similar. Empirically, this is the case even with Western democracies. The structures of American democracy are very different from the structures of European democracies. Even among two neighboring democracies such as Canada and the United States, there are vast differences in how the two political systems are organized. Thus, even if every country in the world today became democratic, it will not necessarily put the comparativist out of business. The comparativist will continue to study other political systems to determine how democracies differ from one another.

Public Policy

Public policy is ultimately what government does. It may also be what government does not do. That is to say, public policy is the government's response (or nonresponse) to the needs and concerns of the public. People who specialize in the field of public policy work in the developing, implementing, and evaluating of public policies. Of course, public policies are found in a wide range of areas. Welfare policy, for example, deals with government programs that provide public assistance to a wide range of individuals, ranging from social security to veteran's benefits. Economic policy concerns itself with issues of employment, job creation and job training, interest rates, inflation, and money supply. Those who specialize in the study of public policy often go beyond developing and recommending policies to lawmakers, to evaluating the impact and effectiveness of existing policies.

Other Areas of Specialization

The major subfields discussed in the previous sections are core areas that provide scholars with the opportunity for academic concentration within the discipline. A variety of other more highly specialized or noncore areas provides scholars with more opportunities for concentration. In comparative politics, they would include regional specialization in such areas as Western democracies, Africa, Asia, Latin America, and the Middle East. In international relations, political scientists can choose to specialize in the study of conflict resolution, war, trade, human rights, arms race, terrorism, foreign policy, international law, and international organizations. In American political institutions, scholars can specialize in the study of Congress, the presidency, the judiciary, federalism, or state and local politics. Behaviorists can become experts in fields like minority politics or campaigns and elections, just to name two. In the political theory subfield, scholars can choose to specialize in the study of conservative or liberal theory. Thus each subfield has even more specialized areas of academic interest in which political scientists may develop expertise.

What Do Political Scientists Study and How Do They Study It?

Political scientists study almost everything, from decision making to war, to state and interstate relations, budgeting, the environment, gender, race, religion, gambling, wealth, sex, and sexual orientation. The scope of field is limited only by one's imagination. The typical political scientist is a person who is open-minded. He or she is intellectually curious, and reads and explores a wide variety of materials and views, frequently interacting and listening to the opinions of both conservatives and liberals. Every new opinion, idea, or controversy is a potential subject for research. In essence, the political scientist has the unenviable task of attempting to make order out of disorder, certainty out of uncertainty. This person's work would sometimes lend to predictions. Sometimes, it will simply clarify or explain a certain phenomenon that happened, how it happened, and why it happened.

Because society is constantly changing, political scientists are in many ways, lifelong students. To stay on top of their discipline, political scientists must always be learning. Whether they are home or at work, on a train or airplane, the mind of the typical political scientist is constantly at work—observing, examining, exploring, and studying. Indeed, what is considered "work" in other professions, political scientists consider "study." Wherever there is an assembly of people or groups of people, the political scientist will probably want to study them.

Professionally, political science work is largely carried out through teaching, research, consulting, administration, management, advising, leadership, diplomacy, and international negotiations. In the next section, we are going to take a much closer look at select career opportunities in political science.

The Political Scientist as Diplomat

One of the most popular employment opportunities for persons with degrees in political science is a career in diplomacy. Nation-states frequently interact. With the growing globalization of the international community, many more fronts for interaction are opening up everyday. At the official level, individuals working on behalf of their nations are charged with the responsibility of facilitating these interactions. These individuals are known as diplomats. They represent their nation in foreign countries, and conduct negotiations that are aimed at advancing their national interest.

There are basically two types of diplomats—the appointed diplomat and the career diplomat. Appointed diplomats are usually senior diplomats, with the rank of ambassador or consul. Appointed by the governments of "sending" states, the appointments are generally influenced by political considerations. The career diplomat is a trained professional whose recruitment is based strictly on merit rather than on political considerations. Although one does not necessarily have to be a political scientist to become a diplomat, in reality, one's chances of becoming a successful diplomat are enhanced with an academic background in the discipline. It is for this reason that one of the subfields in political science specializes in the development of skills in diplomacy, international relations, and international organizations.

For career diplomats, the United States Department of State administers a foreign officer recruitment exam every year. The exam is usually for candidates with college degrees. A majority of the candidates who apply are individuals with degrees in political science. Candidates who successfully pass the exam are given specialized training in language, diplomacy, and culture. Anyone who enjoys travel and foreign cultures will enjoy a career in diplomacy.

The Political Scientist as Consultant

Various career opportunities are open to political scientists in consulting, both in the public and private sector as well as in domestic and international affairs. In domestic politics, political scientists frequently work as lobbyists, fund-raisers, public opinion pollsters, newspaper columnists, television news analysts, campaign mangers, and advisers. At the international level, political scientists with expertise in comparative politics often work as mediators, foreign policy analysts, investment risk analysts, or international security analysts. One of the most famous consultants on investment risk analysis is former U.S. Secretary of State, Henry Kissinger. He provides various public and private sector investors with the advice that would help them assess the risks that are involved in doing business in foreign countries.

Various public and private sector organizations also turn to national think-tanks for decision-making advice. There are hundreds of think tanks in the United States that employ political scientists. They include the Brookings Institution, Council on Foreign Relations, the Hoover Institute, the Heritage Foundation, among others.

Teaching as a Career in Political Science

Political science offers career opportunities in teaching that go from elementary school through college and beyond. There is a very good chance that your social studies teacher in elementary or high school studied political science in college, because political science is one of the contributing disciplines to social studies. To be certified as a social studies teacher, therefore, a teacher is expected to have either earned a degree in political science or in any of the social science disciplines.

Generally, political science teaching at the elementary and secondary school levels is largely descriptive, and focuses mainly on the study of national institutions and political processes. Here, students learn about the structure of our national government, the three branches of government, how the president and national leaders are elected, and their terms of office and powers.

At the college level, political science teaching is much more highly specialized. Unlike in elementary and high school, not only is it a field that stands on its own, it is also a discipline that is taught by professionals with postgraduate degrees in the discipline. Teaching here is both descriptive and theoretical, and goes beyond the study of national institutions to the study of comparative politics, international relations, public policy, and political theory.

Whether it is at the elementary school, secondary school, or college level, political science teaching is quite a lively experience. Our world is constantly changing. Public policies are made everyday, in the form of new laws. Expected and unexpected events occur daily around the world. The political science teacher or professor has to stay informed and alert to all of these changes. He or she has to be an avid reader of new developments in this field. The political science teacher also has to be an avid reader and watcher of news, a participant in public events, a contributor to professional conferences, and a critical observer of social change. For the political science teacher, the world is the lab. It is from staying active and staying involved that this teacher is able to find materials for research and collect ideas help make his or her teaching exciting and alive.

The Political Scientist as Researcher

Besides teaching, another important responsibility of the college professor is research. To keep their jobs, professors at most institutions of higher learning are required to constantly carry out research and publication. It is a responsibility that professors often enjoy referring to in academic parlance as "publish or perish." It is also one of the key distinctions between college professors and schoolteachers.

As with all academic disciplines, political science research requires both descriptive and theoretical knowledge. It serves no purpose to simply describe events without being able to theorize or draw general lessons from them. Neither does it do any good to formulate purely abstract theories without being able to apply them to the real world. Although political scientists conduct both basic and applied research, researchers who are closer to the academic ivory tower tend to be interested in more theoretical research. Here, they contribute to the growth of knowledge in the discipline by building theories through an inductive process, whereby theory is formulated from the careful observation of real-world events. They can also build highly statistical theoretical models that can be used to make real-world predictions. Known as the deductive model, it is a process that goes from theory to fact, because it enables the prediction of fact from theory.

Theory building and the growth of knowledge in political science frequently begin with an idea that is developed either through critical thinking or by closely observing society. The idea is then developed into a theme or research topic. For a political science researcher, the first rule of thumb in choosing an idea or research topic is that it should be interesting. Nothing could be more frustrating as to conduct research on a topic that is boring and uninteresting. The second rule of thumb is to identify sufficient resources on the topic. Prior to embarking on a research topic on "Democratic Transition in Kazakhstan," for example, a political science researcher must first make sure that there are sufficient primary and secondary source materials available through libraries, the Internet, academic archives, or fellow scholars. This usually involves a "literature review, " which is simply the reading and understanding of major published works relating to the research topic. If insufficient material is available, then the researcher may have to gather the resources on their own. In the above instance noted, the scholar may have to travel to Kazakhstan to interview people in order to gather information for his or her study.

With an interesting topic at hand and the adequacy of resource materials ascertained, the political science researcher can now proceed to developing his or her thesis. A thesis statement is usually a brief outline, usually a paragraph long, stating what the researcher plans to study. It is a statement that is going to guide the scholar through the rest of the research, and therefore, it must be very clear and precise. In practical terms, it is often good to sound off an idea, topic, or thesis to a friend and colleague to get their feedback. Indeed, there is no better way to test the soundness of the idea behind one's proposed research than to discuss it with others.

Once the political science researcher is satisfied with the research thesis, he or she can then proceed to developing a hypothesis. A hypothesis is an assumption that the researcher wants to test in order to prove or disprove it. Having more than one hypothesis allows the researcher to move on to the testing of other hypotheses once the first ones have been proved or disproved. As with the thesis statement, hypotheses must be very clear and precise.

The question in testing a hypothesis boils down to one key question: do the data support what I hypothesized? If, for example, I hypothesized that "as individuals become older, they are more likely to vote in a election," I must ask: Is this confirmed by the data I gathered? If so, then I may accept my hypothesis and state with confidence that a person's age predicts their likelihood of voting. If not, then I may reject my hypothesis and say that age does not predict one's probability of voting. This is admittedly a simplistic example but it is nonetheless an illustration of the basic function of conducting social science research.

With the thesis formulated, the literature and data gathered, and the hypotheses tested, the political scientist is now ready to begin writing to report about what he or she found. It is a process that requires patience, perseverance, and concentration. Before it gets to the final product, it will have to go through several readings and corrections. As with the thesis statement, the political science researcher might have a friend or colleague read the final product before it gets sent out to a publisher, policymaker, or research institute. These are but a few of some of the primary recipients of political science research.

The Political Scientist as Global Citizen

Besides research, political science graduates can find work in almost every field that requires creativity, leadership, and innovation—from military leadership, to business manager, bureaucrat, diplomat, news consultant, campaign adviser, lawmaker, and elected official. Students who study politics go on to careers in law, interest groups, media, consulting, international organizations, governmental and nongovernmental organizations. Political science students often pursue careers in government service in such diverse jobs as foreign service with the State Department, intelligence experts with the CIA, lobbyists for groups like Amnesty International, or conducting applied research for research institutes. Of course, some go on to be professional educators at the elementary or secondary school level and enjoy the lively experience of teaching.

Indeed, career opportunities in political science are limited only by one's imagination. A good example is the case of George Gallup, the founder of the Gallup Poll Corporation. As a political science student in the 1940s, he came up with the rather abstract and unheard of idea that he was going to write his thesis on the methods of gathering and evaluating public opinion. He followed the various research processes discussed here, and developed a method for measuring public opinion that has, in more than half a century, proven much more accurate in predicting political results than the science of meteorology is at predicting weather trends.

As an undergraduate major, political science is one of the paths more often chosen by students interested in going to law school, or to graduate school in political science or other postgraduate programs in the humanities and social sciences. This is because political science develops skills that are essential both for advanced studies as well as for the job market. They include writing and reading skills, public speaking, critical analytical and conceptual skills, and teamwork. Anyone who enjoys reading, writing, socializing, and organizing people will certainly enjoy studying political science.

Endnotes

1. Harold Lasswell, *Politics Who Gets What, When and How* (New York: Peter Smith Pub, January 1990).
2. Matthew Holden, Jr., "The Competence of Political Science: 'Progress in Political Research Revisited,'" *American Political Science Review*, 94 (1):1–20.
3. Ira Katznelson and Helen V. Milner, *Political Science: State of the Discipline* (New York: W.W. Norton Co., 2002) 1.
4. *Ibid.*, p. 10fn.

Political and Constitutional Foundations:

Liberty and Equality

Tyranny of the Majority
ALEXIS DE TOCQUEVILLE (1805—1859)

Majority rule is often associated with democratic traditions. A study that sets out to examine the tyranny of the majority may therefore seem out of place and consequently easily dismissed as having nothing to do with the study of democracy. Yet, tyranny of the majority is a reality that is lived in majoritarian democratic systems. In the study that follows, Alexis de Tocqueville examines the intricacies and nuances of majority rule in the early years of the American democratic experiment, and laments its iniquitous underpinnings. He notices a system in which there are no institutional or constitutional barriers against the ironclad rule of the majority, and foresees a day when the politically disenfranchised may resort to physical force to challenge such exclusive authority. Thirty years after de Tocqueville's prophesy, American democracy had its first true test in a civil war that sought to challenge the status quo.

The author was a French aristocrat who was fascinated by American democracy in the early years of its founding. He traveled to the United States, where he spent four years observing and meticulously documenting its development. His findings ended up in a two-volume publication that went on to become a classic in the halls of academia. Entitled Democracy in America, *it has become required reading in most advanced political science programs. This text is from Volume I, Chapter XV of his classic work.*

. . . In my opinion the main evil of the present democratic institutions of the United States does not arise, as is often asserted in Europe, from their weakness, but from their overpowering strength; and I am not so much alarmed at the excessive liberty which reigns in that country as at the very inadequate securities which exist against tyranny.

When an individual or a party is wronged in the United States, to whom can he apply for redress? If to public opinion, public opinion constitutes the majority; if to the legislature, it represents the majority, and implicitly obeys its injunctions; if to the executive power, it is appointed by the majority, and remains a passive tool in its hands; the public troops consist of the majority under arms; the jury is the majority invested with the right of hearing judicial cases; and in certain States even the judges are elected by the majority. However iniquitous or absurd the evil of which you complain may be, you must submit to it as well as you can.

I said one day to an inhabitant of Pennsylvania, "Be so good as to explain to me how it happens that in a State founded by Quakers, and celebrated for its toleration, freed blacks are not allowed to exercise civil rights. They pay the taxes; is it not fair that they should have a vote?"

Democracy in America by Alexis de Tocqueville. Translated by Henry Reeve (1839).

"You insult us," replied my informant, "if you imagine that our legislators could have committed so gross an act of injustice and intolerance."

"What! then the blacks possess the right of voting in this county?"

"Without the smallest doubt."

"How comes it, then, that at the polling-booth this morning I did not perceive a single negro in the whole meeting?"

"This is not the fault of the law: the negroes have an undisputed right of voting, but they voluntarily abstain from making their appearance."

"A very pretty piece of modesty on their parts!" rejoined I.

"Why, the truth is, that they are not disinclined to vote, but they are afraid of being maltreated; in this country the law is sometimes unable to maintain its authority without the support of the majority. But in this case the majority entertains very strong prejudices against the blacks, and the magistrates are unable to protect them in the exercise of their legal privileges."

"What! then the majority claims the right not only of making the laws, but of breaking the laws it has made?"

If, on the other hand, a legislative power could be so constituted as to represent the majority without necessarily being the slave of its passions; an executive, so as to retain a certain degree of uncontrolled authority; and a judiciary, so as to remain independent of the two other powers; a government would be formed which would still be democratic without incurring any risk of tyrannical abuse.

I do not say that tyrannical abuses frequently occur in America at the present day, but I maintain that no sure barrier is established against them, and that the causes which mitigate the government are to be found in the circumstances and the manners of the country more than in its laws . . .

A distinction must be drawn between tyranny and arbitrary power. Tyranny may be exercised by means of the law, and in that case it is not arbitrary; arbitrary power may be exercised for the good of the community at large, in which case it is not tyrannical. Tyranny usually employs arbitrary means, but, if necessary, it can rule without them.

In the United States the unbounded power of the majority, which is favorable to the legal despotism of the legislature, is likewise favorable to the arbitrary authority of the magistrate. The majority has an entire control over the law when it is made and when it is executed; and as it possesses an equal authority over those who are in power and the community at large, it considers public officers as its passive agents, and readily confides the task of serving its designs to their vigilance. The details of their office and the privileges which they are to enjoy are rarely defined beforehand; but the majority treats them as a master does his servants when they are always at work in his sight, and he has the power of directing or reprimanding them at every instant.

In general the American functionaries are far more independent than the French civil officers within the sphere which is prescribed to them. Sometimes, even, they are allowed by the popular authority to exceed those bounds; and as they are protected by the opinion, and backed by the co-operation, of the majority, they venture upon such manifestations of their power as astonish a European. By this means habits are formed in the heart of a free country which may some day prove fatal to its liberties. . . .

It is in the examination of the display of public opinion in the United States that we clearly perceive how far the power of the majority surpasses all the powers with which we are acquainted in Europe. Intellectual principles exercise an influence which is so invisible, and often so inappreciable, that they baffle the toils of oppression. At the present time the most absolute monarchs in Europe are unable to prevent certain notions, which are opposed to their authority, from circulating in secret throughout their dominions, and even in their courts. Such is not the case in America; as long as the majority is still undecided, discussion is carried on; but as soon as its decision is irrevocably pronounced, a submissive silence is observed, and the friends, as well as the opponents, of the measure unite in assenting to its propriety. The reason of this is perfectly clear: no monarch is so absolute as to combine all the powers of society in his own hands, and to conquer all opposition with the energy of a majority which is invested with the right of making and of executing the laws.

. . . I know no country in which there is so little true independence of mind and freedom of discussion as in America. In any constitutional state in Europe every sort of religious and political theory may be advocated and propagated abroad; for there is no country in Europe so subdued by any single authority as not to contain citizens who are ready to protect the man who raises his voice in the cause of truth from the consequences of his hardihood. If he is unfortunate enough to live under an absolute government, the people is upon his side; if he inhabits a free country, he may find a shelter behind the authority of the throne, if he require one. The aristocratic part of society supports him in some countries, and the democracy in others. But in a nation where democratic institutions exist, organized like those of the United States, there is but one sole authority, one single element of strength and of success, with nothing beyond it.

In America the majority raises very formidable barriers to the liberty of opinion: within these barriers an author may write whatever he pleases, but he will repent it if he ever step beyond them. Not that he is exposed to the terrors of an auto-da-fe, but he is tormented by the slights and persecutions of daily obloquy. His political career is closed forever, since he has offended the only authority which is able to promote his success. Every sort of compensation, even that of celebrity, is refused to him. Before he published his opinions he imagined that he held them in common with many others; but no sooner has he declared them openly than he is loudly censured by his overbearing opponents, whilst those who think without having the courage to speak, like him, abandon him in silence. He yields at length, oppressed by the daily efforts he has been making, and he subsides into silence, as if he was tormented by remorse for having spoken the truth. . . .

If great writers have not at present existed in America, the reason is very simply given in these facts; there can be no literary genius without freedom of opinion, and freedom of opinion does not exist in America. The Inquisition has never been able to prevent a vast number of anti-religious books from circulating in Spain. The empire of the majority succeeds much better in the United States, since it actually removes the wish of publishing them. Unbelievers are to be met with in America, but, to say the truth, there is no public organ of infidelity. Attempts have been made by some governments to protect the morality of nations by prohibiting licentious books. In the United States no one is punished for this sort of works, but no one is induced to write them; not because all the citizens are immaculate in their manners, but because the majority of the community is decent and orderly. . . .

The tendencies which I have just alluded to are as yet very slightly perceptible in political society, but they already begin to exercise an unfavorable influence upon the national character of the Americans. I am inclined to attribute the singular paucity of distinguished political characters to the ever-increasing activity of the despotism of the majority in the United States. When the American Revolution broke out they arose in great numbers, for public opinion then served, not to tyrannize over, but to direct the exertions of individuals. Those celebrated men took a full part in the general agitation of mind common at that period, and they attained a high degree of personal fame, which was reflected back upon the nation, but which was by no means borrowed from it. . . .

In that immense crowd which throngs the avenues to power in the United States I found very few men who displayed any of that manly candor and that masculine independence of opinion which frequently distinguished the Americans in former times, and which constitutes the leading feature in distinguished characters, wheresoever they may be found. It seems, at first sight, as if all the minds of the Americans were formed upon one model, so accurately do they correspond in their manner of judging. A stranger does, indeed, sometimes meet with Americans who dissent from these rigorous formularies; with men who deplore the defects of the laws, the mutability and the ignorance of democracy; who even go so far as to observe the evil tendencies which impair the national character, and to point out such remedies as it might be possible to apply; but no one is there to hear these things besides yourself, and you, to whom these secret reflections are confided, are a stranger and a bird of passage. They are very ready to communicate truths which are useless to you, but they continue to hold a different language in public.

If ever these lines are read in America, I am well assured of two things: in the first place, that all who peruse them will raise their voices to condemn me; and in the second place, that very many of them will acquit me at the bottom of their conscience. . . .

If ever the free institutions of America are destroyed, that event may be attributed to the unlimited authority of the majority, which may at some future time urge the minorities to desperation, and oblige them to have recourse to physical force. Anarchy will then be the result, but it will have been brought about by despotism. . . .

U.S. Constitutional Theory and Religious Freedom

JOHN J. CARROLL

Religion and the Constitution are two fundamental institutions in American politics. Behind some of the most protracted and devastating wars in human history have been differences over religious beliefs. Conscious of this, the framers of the U.S. Constitution enacted, through the Establishment Clause, the separation of Church and State. In the text that follows, John Carroll examines the evolution of the two institutions in the past century. Noticing the rather amazing transformation of America from a monolithic Protestant society to a pluralist mosaic of religious denominations, Carroll attributes the transformation to the multiplicity of immigrant and ethnic minorities whose religious practices have enjoyed the tolerance and freedoms that are enshrined in the U.S. Constitution. Although the Supreme Court's interpretation of the Establishment Clause is frequently controversial, it is this very interpretation that has made such religious plurality possible. Carroll discusses the theories of religious freedoms and tolerance that are identified and interpreted by the Supreme Court, as it seeks to fence out the state from entanglement in religious controversies.

Introduction

In the past century the United States became an increasingly pluralistic religious state. The country has been transformed from a dominant Protestant state intolerant of other persuasions to a highly complex religious society, reflecting the diversity of its waves of immigrants. Ironically, some of the most difficult recent constitutional questions have arisen in the context of claims made by Native Americans asserting their rights to practice free of majoritarian (Christian) imposed limits.[1] Similar claims are beginning to be heard from other non-Christian groups, including persons of Asian, Latin American, and African extraction, as such claims had been made earlier by Jews, Mormons, and other dissenters.

The U.S. law of religious freedom is governed by two principal provisions in the First Amendment to the Constitution known as the free exercise and establishment clauses. The language reads: "Congress shall make no law respecting an establishment of religion, or prohibiting the free exercise thereof. . . ." A third clause is found in Article VI of the Constitution. It states that ". . . no religious Test shall ever be required as a Qualification to any Office or public Trust under the United States," and has rarely been invoked.[2]

While the language of the First Amendment is directed to the Congress, it has been held to apply to the states of the Union as well as to Washington.[3]

Religious rights raise particularly complex and delicate questions, pitting as they do the claims of conscience against those of the state. The demands of Caesar may be made as loudly as those of God but in the Christian tradition religion may hold the trump with its promise of salvation and threat of eternal damnation. Consequently, the interpretation of the clauses has posed exceptionally delicate problems, and controversy has followed the Supreme Court whenever it has interpreted them.

Compounding the difficulty in interpreting the religious clauses has been the lack of consensus about the intention of the Framers of the First Amendment. It should be no surprise that given the incomplete record from 1791 and before, and the multiplicity of groups and individuals active in ratification campaigns, scholars are unable to agree on what was originally intended.[4] Furthermore, the nation has been transformed by the influx of immigrants, first Catholics and Jews, now Muslims, Buddhists, Hindus, and others, so the context within which the clauses are interpreted has been drastically changed. One reaction to the new pluralism on the part of the old-line Christian churches, especially those holding membership in the National Council of Churches, has been to embrace theories of religious tolerance and request the courts in *amicus curiae* briefs to interpret the Constitution in their light. But these positions are controversial, especially so when fundamentalist churches who believe in a literal interpretation of the Christian Bible become active. Some fundamentalist groups argue the United States is a Christian nation and Christian traditions should be reflected in U.S. law and morals. These groups reject the mainstream ideas of religious tolerance and crusade for public prayers, prayers in government schools, and other symbolic and substantive recognition of their Christian doctrine.

Since the 1940s, a group of justices on the U.S. Supreme Court have worked out a theory of religious tolerance and interpreted the Constitution in its light. These judges held a majority of the nine seats on the Court for about three decades, starting in the late 1940s. During that period, they broke new ground in developing a theory of religious toleration that they conceptualized as the goals or purposes of the clauses. Among these members of the Warren Court, Justices Hugo Black and William Brennan took the lead in rethinking the constitutional issues and giving the problems associated with church-state relations a fresh look.

Since the Republican presidencies of Richard Nixon (1969–1974), Gerald Ford (1974–1977), Ronald Regan (1981–1989), George Bush (1989–93), and George W. Bush, justices skeptical of the Warren Court formulations have been appointed to the Court and challenged the application of the Warren era doctrines. Nonetheless, the Warren Court theories retain much of their currency because they present a coherent theory of religious freedom, respond to many of the legal and social problems posed by country's growing religious diversity, and have attracted influential religious and legal adherents.

Freedom of Conscience

In *Everson v. Board of Education,*[5] Justice Hugo Black traced the origin of the religious clauses to the experiences of the colonists with persecution by established and dominant sects in Britain and the American colonies. The *Everson* opinion laid great stress on the oppression that resulted when an established church enforced its authority against other groups, and concluded that a major purpose of the religious clauses was to assure that conscience be completely free from government coercion. Protection of religious conscience has been the primary liberty interest in the line of free exercise decisions, which have dealt with the claims of religious minorities, most commonly Mormons in the nineteenth century, Jehovah's Witnesses through the Second World War, and, more recently, Native Americans, Jews, and Muslims. Black's views were influential and the Court became more receptive to claims of conscience after *Everson*.

Thus, a major goal of the clauses, and perhaps its most obvious is to secure religious freedom for persons of faith and official tolerance for those without, positions that are now counted among the most basic of international human rights. Deeply felt religious and ethical beliefs can place tremendous demands on the individuals who hold them. Such beliefs can dictate an individual's behavior in ways that might bring him or her into direct conflict with the state. Religious beliefs may require a person to abstain from war, even in the face of national peril, to refuse to pay taxes, to resist public schooling for their children, or to engage in civil disobedience.

Furthermore, religious belief and practice lend meaning to some people's lives and, thus, have value as forms of self-expression and modes for the exploration of existence. As a matter of public policy under this formulation, the state does not dictate the terms of individual belief, which belong to the private sphere. Individuals should be free to adopt whatever faith they choose, to preach their religion in public, and to practice openly within the limits of public morality and order.[6] In this way, it can be argued, religious pluralism strengthens the nation by providing alternative life models from which citizens can choose, and by enriching the public policy debate by bringing to bear diverse perspectives on issues of morality and justice. As a consequence, the state may draw substantial benefits by fostering a rich cultural and religious life marked by diversity.

Protecting the State from Instability

A second major argument in favor of religious freedom flows from the disputatious and highly emotional nature of the subject matter. Religious freedom helps protect the state from instability that might follow from its entanglement in religious controversies. For this reason, "separation" of church and state is an inviting theory around which to organize religion-state relationships because it claims to minimize the political divisiveness that could result from intensely contested doctrinal disputes. This may be particularly important to a highly pluralistic modern society, where the numbers and variety of religious beliefs are extraordinary.

When government enters the religious arena in a pluralistic religious society, it places itself on ground where everything is contested. There is no agreement on whether God exists among persons of faith, let alone between believers and nonbelievers. The various religious groups disagree about the characteristics of God, if there is one or many, who God is or was, what God requires of people to be saved, whether salvation is possible for all or some of mankind, whether life exists after death and the form that life might take, the relationship between God and human beings, the definition of ritual, how God can be known, how God can or must be worshiped or served, and so on. While some persons take the position that what you believe is less important than belief itself, others strongly disagree. Some firmly believe there is a religious truth, of which they or their group are the keepers, and the beliefs of others are erroneous, even sinful.

Because everything is subject to controversy, it is not possible for government to take *any* action of a religious nature without offending the religious views of some of its citizens. Even efforts by the American states to sponsor public prayer of a "nondenominational" or ecumenical nature was offensive to some.[7] Some argued the official prayer violated a biblical injunction to pray to God in private, while others believed that the platitudinous quality of nondenominational prayer is offensive to God. Even seemingly trivial governmental involvement may give offense. For example, some object to the motto "In God We Trust" appearing on U.S. coins because money may be used for profane purposes, for example, to buy prostitutes or for gambling.

When the state involves itself in religious matters, religious groups come to see the government as an arena for struggle, in which each seeks official endorsement for its own brand of religious orthodoxy. Citizen is set against citizen and efforts are made to draw in the government as a partisan of each side. The desire to politicize religious differences is readily observable in American life. It can be illustrated by contemporary debates over the place of religion in the public schools, including such controversies as the teaching of "creationism" (the idea that God created the world complete as we know it) as an alternative to Darwinism, bitter battles over school prayer and what that prayer should be, and campaigns for and against sex education. Outside the schools, disagreements over religious displays on public property, and the continuing debates over abortion, living wills, and the "right to die," all involve conceptions that flow from religious perspectives on life and personal duty. Even in a state with relatively well-developed boundaries between the governmental and religious spheres, controversies of this sort are common. Imagine how it might be if the government regularly sponsored religious exercises and involved itself in disputes between religious groups. The results of such competition could be destabilizing to the state if losing groups came to believe that the state was allied with the winners, and hence, was operating without legitimacy and beyond the sanction of faith.

To avoid such dangers, the state stands aloof from religious controversy: It does not enter disputes over religious dogma, avoids intrusion into the internal affairs of religious groups, and avoids the appearance of partiality toward one sectarian group or another.

As a constitutional goal, fencing out the state from entanglements in religious controversies through policies of toleration and abstention is both a logical extension of the religious clauses and an extension of the general constitutional interest in national security. Justice Robert H. Jackson argued in *West Virginia v. Barnette* that "Assurance that rights are secure tends to diminish fear and jealousy of strong government, and by making us feel safe to live under it makes for its better support."[8] Jackson's observation on the utility of the Bill of Rights was more persuasive to the Court's majority than Justice Felix Frankfurter's counterargument that a school board should be allowed to expel pupils for their refusal on religious grounds to salute the flag, a practice reasonably designed, in Frankfurter's view, to achieve the legitimate objective of inculcating patriotism and national unity.

Protecting Religion from Debasement by the State

A third goal of the clauses is to protect religion from debasement by the state. Under this rationale, religion is not relegated to the private sphere in order to marginalize it, but to protect it.

Clearly the temptation of politicians to wrap themselves in their national flag is exceeded only by the urge to adorn themselves with holy scripture. Religion lends legitimacy to government and its actions and, because of this, religious associations are eagerly sought by political leaders hoping to improve their public standing or that of their party. In so doing, politicians adapt religion to political needs and may distort and misuse it, offending those who believe their sacred doctrine, rituals, or images have been profaned. An example of this is the recurring controversies in the United States over the display of Christian nativity scenes under government sponsorship, particularly when the purpose of the display is an inducement to commerce. The mayor of Pawtucket, Rhode Island, for example, defended the nativity scene in his town as a primarily secular display erected to improve the downtown Christmas shopping season. For some of the clergy who sued to remove the crèche, the mayor's vulgar purpose was a misuse of a holy symbol, and they believed the town debased the image of the birth of Christ by placing it alongside cartoon figures of Jumbo the Elephant and Mickey Mouse.

This goal that aims to protect religion from the profane raises an important distinction often missed by critics of modern church-state jurisprudence. That distinction is between a secular society and a secular state. The idea of a secular society is one in which religion is absent from the life of the people. Secularists of this type may be hostile to religion. They may view religion as corrupt, an agency by which the advantaged exploit the disadvantaged, an obstacle to social and economic reform, or misguided superstition.

In contrast, the idea of a secular state, which is associated with the arguments being developed by the Court, assumes no hostility toward religion. Persons who believe in the secular state may be religious or not. They argue that beyond its obligation to guarantee citizens the right to practice their faiths, governments should avoid entanglements in religious matters. Advocates of the secular state, unlike those of the secular society, recognize that religion plays an important role in civil society and that religious freedom is a basic human right.

Another alternative to the secular state, besides officially establishing a religion, is *accommodation,* in which government seeks to work cooperatively with religious groups and may even advocate religiosity among its citizens. The difficulty with this approach, as we have seen, is that it requires government to take sides, to choose among alternative modes of worship or ritual. This will usually mean that the religious views of the dominant groups within society will be advantaged over others. Under such circumstances, there is a danger that some religious groups will benefit while others will not; religious freedom for minorities may be curtailed, even while it is enhanced for the orthodoxy receiving official support.

Protect the Autonomy of Religious Life

The fourth goal that the Court has identified for the religious clauses is to prevent state interference with the autonomy of religious life. In the contemporary state where government programs reach every aspect of life, there is a danger that government aid to religious institutions, whether they be educational or charitable, will carry with it regulations that direct or frustrate the religious mission of the grantee. Justice Harry Blackmun observed in *Bowen v. Kendrick* that "The First Amendment protects not only the State from being captured by the Church, but also protects the Church from being corrupted by the State and adapted to its purposes."[9] This constitutional purpose, which is primarily achieved through the establishment rather than free exercise clause, is also designed to keep government from entering religious controversies as a partisan of one side or another, as when church factions compete for control of church property.[10] The constitutional objective is to allow religious groups to maintain their independence and the integrity of their doctrine and practice, free from state sanctions or inducements. It requires religious groups to prosper or fail in the free marketplace of ideas without support or opposition from the state.

Discussion

These are the main outlines of the theory of religious freedom as it has been developed by scholars and judges. There are alternative perspectives, such as the accommodationist view, which have substantial followings. In general, accommodationists believe that religion is so intertwined with everyday life that it cannot reasonably be closed out of the nation's political and governmental life. They argue that political leaders often act from religious motives, that government officials attend church and bring the political arena in with them, and that the public display by government of religious symbols is unavoidable, or even desirable.

Accommodationists also argue that religion has an important moral role in shaping the society and protecting its values. For this reason, they argue, school children should pray each morning before classes begin, presidents and other public officeholders should lead the nation in prayer and call on God to guide us. From this perspective, national recognition and reliance on God will help us create a better moral order, which will bring a good measure of security and peace to our national life.

Some accommodationists also believe that the United States is a Christian nation and the government merely recognizes its traditions when it recognizes Christianity and encourages its support. None of these arguments is consistent with the theory of religious freedom, outlined above, but all have had their advocates in the society and on the Supreme Court bench.[11]

The meaning of the religious clauses has emerged through a great debate, a struggle between persons holding accommodationist and secular state perspectives. Very often the result has been compromise, and a rule of law that shifts and turns depending who is doing the judging and the particular interests in the case at hand.

The theory of secularism, as developed by members of the U.S. Supreme Court and others, is in many ways an American construction with its emphasis on individual autonomy and conscience, and its insistence that private entities be largely independent of government support. As such, it is a theory that will have limited utility in nations with differing traditions, national experiences, and contemporary problems. Nonetheless, it offers a challenging conception of how religious freedom might be secured and the constitutional regime that might guarantee it.

Endnotes

1. See *Employment Division v. Smith,* 494 U.S. 872 (1990) rejecting a free exercise right to use peyote, an hallucinogen, as part of an American Indian ritual.
2. But see *Torcaso v. Watkins,* 367 U.S. 488 (1961), holding the government may not require affirmations of religious belief.
3. *Cantwell v. Connecticut,* 310 U.S. 296 (1940).
4. For a general treatment of the difficulties inherent in divining the original intentions of the framers, see H. Jefferson Powell, "The Original Understanding of Original Intent," 98 *Harvard Law Review* 885 (1985); on the religious clauses in particular see, among others, Leonard Levy,

The Establishment Clause: Religion and the First Amendment (New York: Macmillan, 1986), and Michael W. McConnell, "The Origins and Historical Understanding of Free Exercise of Religion," 103 *Harvard Law Review* 1409 (1990).

5. *Everson v. Board of Education,* 330 U.S. 1 (1947).

6. See *Cantwell v. Connecticut,* 310 U.S. 296 (1940) protecting the right of Jehovah's Witnesses to preach and broadcast religious doctrine on the streets.

7. *Engel v. Vitale,* 370 U.S. 421 (1962) holding the recitation of nondenominational prayers in government schools to be unconstitutional; and *Lee v. Weisman,* 505 U.S. 577 (1992) holding that religious invocations at public school graduation exercises are unconstitutional.

8. *West Virginia v. Barnette,* 319 U.S. 624 (1943).

9. *Bowen v. Kendrick,* 108 S.CT. 2590 (1988).

10. *Kedroff v. St. Nicholas Cathedral,* 344 U.S. 94 (1952), *Presbyterian Church v. Hull Presbyterian Church,* 393 U.S. 440 (1969), and *Serbian Eastern Orthodox Diocese v. Milivojevich,* 426 U.S. 696 (1976) variously deferring to ecclesiastical authorities; and *Jones v. Wolf,* 443 U.S. 595 (1979) allowing application by states of "neutral" principles of law.

11. Justice Anthony Kennedy presents the accommodationist view in his dissent in *County of Allegheny v. ACLU,* 492 U.S. 573 (1989). See also Justice William Rehnquist's dissent in *Wallace v. Jaffree,* 472 U.S. 38 (1985).

The Right to Protect Your Rights: Justice and the Right to Counsel

Kenneth L. Manning

The concept of limited government contends that there are, and should be, limits to government power. Without restrictions on what the state can and cannot do, unlimited government would quickly lead to oppression and the denial of liberty. In the article that follows, Kenneth Manning suggests that the right to have an attorney is one of the most fundamental rights we enjoy in a democracy because it limits the government's ability to keep it's citizens in the dark about their rights under the law. History provides stark examples in which citizens were put at an enormous disadvantage because, as non-attorneys, they were not schooled in the ways of the law. Having a lawyer, Manning argues, is critical to our ability to protect our rights against a potentially abusive government.

"In all criminal prosecutions the accused shall enjoy the right to a speedy and public trial, by an impartial jury of the State and district wherein the crime shall have been committed, which district shall have been previously ascertained by law, and to be informed of the nature and cause of the accusation; to be confronted with the witnesses against him; to have compulsory process for obtaining witnesses in his favor, and to have the Assistance of Counsel for his defense."

Amendment VI
Constitution of the United States

One of the more contradictory aspects of American life that those from outside the United States find remarkable is the fact that people accused of crimes in the United States have the right to a lawyer, but not a constitutional right to see a doctor.

If you ask the typical person in the United States to name one of the constitutional rights he or she enjoys, most would probably identify "freedom of speech" or "freedom of religion." Though most are probably familiar with the fact that they have the right to have a lawyer (the widely known police warnings state that one "has the right to an attorney"), we often overlook this legal protection. We shouldn't. The right to legal counsel is one of the very most important constitutional protections that we have, and in this essay I will lay out some of the background and theory underlying the right to counsel and why it is such an important right.

History of the Right to Counsel: Is Your Uncle a Lawyer?

When the American founders established a new government in America, they drew upon their experience as subjects to the English monarch and as bold explorers. This experience guided their understanding of government and its proper role in people's lives, and it influenced the political composition of colonial America. Following the failure of the Articles of Confederation, the colonists and founders once again relied upon their experience to guide their views and actions in forming a new federal constitution.[1] The Sixth Amendment to the Constitution, and especially the right to counsel, is a prime example of experience-guided pragmatism.

The founders sought to guarantee individuals accused of federal criminal acts generous means with which they could prove, to a jury of their peers, their innocence. This included the right to counsel. In doing so, the founders relied upon the virtue of members of the community to insure their security in life, liberty, and property. Experience had shown that the right to counsel, along with other rights of the accused, served to increase citizen's security and freedom.

In twentieth century America, we assume counsel to mean legal assistance in the form of an attorney. However, defining counsel as an attorney is a relatively new understanding.[2]

By 1300, there was already an established legal profession in England of people who were paid to represent litigants and defendants (Rackow, 1954).[3] These people, of course, served only those with the money to retain their services. In practice, few defendants were ever represented by professional legal counsel in early English courts. Counsel, for most defendants, meant a family friend or elder (in those days, almost invariably a man) to support the defendant and speak before a court upon their behalf. Imagine turning to your Uncle Joe, the shoe salesman, for help if you were in trouble with the law! Because formal education was rare in those times, many accused of crimes were illiterate and entirely ignorant of judicial proceedings. In fact, most counsel probably was as well. However, counsel provided an opportunity for defendants to establish some credibility before a court and to provide some assistance, however uneducated and unprofessional, to the accused. Though he may not have been very useful in terms of navigating the law, Uncle Joe was at least there to speak on your behalf and provide some level of comfort and support. It was something, but not much.

The American colonial definition of counsel mirrored that of England. Counsel in the colonies, as in England, did not imply or demand a person educated and trained in the law. This was certainly due in part to practical reasons—there were few trained lawyers in early colonial America. There was a very minimal system of established higher education in those early days, and most successful lawyers in England weren't prone to pack their bags and board a ship to go to an undeveloped new world. Indeed, the first law school in the United States was established in 1774, just before the signing of the Declaration of Independence.[4] There were so few lawyers that many judges themselves had minimal legal training—it was not until 1754 that a trained attorney was appointed to the Supreme Court of New Hampshire (Rackow, 1954).

However, as the colonies matured and the number of attorneys increased, counsel still did not necessarily mean a lawyer. In time, as United States' legal experience grew, counsel became recognized as meaning a professionally educated attorney. But it is worth noting that this acceptance of counsel as an attorney was not widely accepted until well into the nineteenth century. For the English and American legal experience prior to and including the time of the ratification of the U.S. Constitution, counsel did not require an attorney. For much of early U.S. history, counsel simply meant a person who would assist someone arguing their case in court.

The English practice of counsel rights prior to 1836 was extremely conservative by modern standards. Counsel was historically allowed in all English civil cases. In criminal cases, English law recognized a right to counsel in minor misdemeanor cases such as libel or perjury. In fact, in important misdemeanor cases tried before the Star Chamber (an important and high-ranking court of the time), counsel was necessary since the defendant's answers to the court were required to be signed by his counsel. However, there was no right to counsel in treason or felony trials, charges that were the most serious and often carried a death penalty upon conviction. English law allowed for counsel in all cases in which a legal question (not merely guilt or innocence) arose, and also allowed the accused counsel in appealed cases. However, English law did not allow for a defendant to obtain counsel in cases that were the most important to himself—cases in which his life may be at stake, original criminal trials involving felonies, and other serious crimes.

It may seem that allowing counsel in relatively minor offenses, but denying it in serious cases, was illogical. However, this attitude reflects assumptions about the law that are pillars of the American legal experience but were not accepted in early England.

The early English law on counsel rights is generally thought to be illogical today because we assume the existence of a legal and criminal justice system that begins with the belief that defendants should be allowed the proper means to assert their innocence in an unbiased court of law, and that the responsibility rests with the state to prove its case. We might consider the English rule of counsel rights to be irrational, but this is because we approach this issue from our modern perspective on American legal theory. It is difficult to comprehend the different legal system and tradition in past centuries.

The reality of English law and legal practice in the sixteenth and seventeenth centuries was quite different from contemporary American standards, standards largely instituted by the American founders. English courts did not claim nor seek to begin from an impartial position. The courts were a representation of the monarch and government, and these same courts were in place to guard and insure the king's authority. The English courtroom zealously sought to uphold the law in favor of the king, and thus the main purpose of the court was to achieve conviction. As Sir James Stephen, an English legal historian wrote, a criminal trial was "a race between the King and the prisoner, in which the King has a long head start and the prisoner was heavily weighted" (Stephen [1883] 1976). Rights of the accused, such as the right to counsel, would only help defendants gain acquittal. This, of course, was in direct confrontation with the goals of a court, which sought conviction. In less important misdemeanor cases counsel was allowed because the state's interest was not considered vital. Misdemeanor conflicts usually involved disputes between two subjects of the king with the state usually having no vested interest in the outcome. However, in felony cases—those in which forfeiture of money or land to the king were involved—the Crown's interest was considered too great to automatically allow counsel to defendants.

As bizarre as this may seem to us today, this lack of counsel for felony defendants was defended by English legal thinkers of the time. They thought that guilt or innocence should be so obvious that a defense would not be necessary. They also argued that the court would act as counsel for the accused, thus eliminating the necessity for other counsel.[5] However, the American colonists didn't buy this argument; they had seen the problems of giving courts too much power and wanted to limit the power of government.

While no law guaranteed that defendants would be allowed counsel in felony trials, in practice it was somewhat common for English courts to allow counsel at their own discretion. However, courts were by no means required to do so. This meant that there was great inconsistency in the retention of counsel—some had it, some didn't. This random and uneven allowance of the right to counsel had a great influence upon the thinking of the American founders.

The right to counsel in England took a significant step forward with Parliament's passage of the *Treason Act of 1695*. This breakthrough law was an advancement of the overall rights of the accused, including the right to counsel. The Treason Act allowed the assistance of counsel in all felony cases. This expansion of rights meant that from that point forward all those who were accused of crimes were allowed counsel in virtually all misdemeanor and felony cases, both at trial and on appeal. The only exceptions were in cases in which defendants were accused of counterfeiting money, the king's seal (which was very important since it carried the weight of law), and other acts of treason (Rackow, 1954). While this was major progress in achieving a universal right to counsel, it still allowed the king an advantage in treason cases. And almost all treason cases carried the death penalty!

It was not until Parliament's passage of the Act of 1836 that counsel was allowed to defendants in all cases. By this time, however, the fledgling communities in the New World were no longer colonies, and the United States had a constitution that had guaranteed counsel rights for over 40 years. In practice, the colonies enjoyed universal counsel rights decades before the English.

Supreme Court interpretations of the right to counsel subsequently expanded the understanding of the right to have an attorney in the United States. Whereas original counsel rights allowed defendants to obtain counsel on their own if they so desired, the Court has now ruled that individuals are guaranteed counsel in both federal and state courts, at trial and on an initial appeal, in all cases in which the accused faces possible jail time.[6] The right to counsel has been expanded from a procedural right extended to those who could, at their own option, choose to be represented by someone, to a guaranteed constitutional right to be represented in court by a licensed attorney. Though this change came about over many decades, by any definition it has marked an extraordinary progress in citizen rights.

American Experience and the Right to Counsel

The establishment of the counsel right in England, and the ideas about the law upon which the right was based, had provided valuable experience for the constitutional framers in America. The colonists had known a history in which courtroom procedures worked to favor the government. They had read arguments that supported the English legal system, but experience had shown them that this theory was not supported in practice. They had read the history of cases similar to that of Sir William Parkyns in 1695, who was denied the right to counsel in an English court because his trial took place *one day* before the *Treason Act of 1695,* which would have allowed Parkyns the right to have a lawyer, took effect (Rackow, 1954). Legal history showed that counsel had been withheld from those who had needed it the most, those accused of capital offenses. Even when counsel was retained the courts had often extended the right at its own discretion, and thus inconsistently. Colonists had known a common law system, which allowed counsel in cases when it pleased the king, and had seen counsel denied when it was often needed the most. These experiences shaped the colonists' views about rights of the accused, the proper role of the courts, and they influence the very foundation upon which they would establish a nation. The founders wanted a system that would limit the power of government while also achieving justice.

Thus courts were established in the United States with the guiding principle that they exist to reach just decisions, not merely achieve conviction. The quest for fair decisions was based in the founders' emphasis upon liberty and equality. Without fair courts, there is little assurance of freedom. If a criminal justice system is overly biased to the government, people cannot be truly free from the tyranny of the state. All the government would have to do to deny someone's liberty is charge them with a crime. If the deck is stacked so heavily to the prosecution side that a defendant has no virtually no hope of winning, then the control of freedoms lies not in the hands of the people but in the hands of government and its agents. This, it is not too hard to see, can easily lead to abuse of power that denies freedom—or, in other words, tyranny. The founders believed that fair and just courts, along with procedures to ensure evenhandedness and impartiality, would be a safeguard against tyranny. Having legal counsel who is trained and knows the law is arguably the most effective way to assure that the judicial proceedings involving a defendant are fair and just.

That is not to say, however, that these exalted principles have always been lived up to in American life. Historical facts tell us that these ideals have not always been realized. Indeed, courtrooms have been the setting for a multitude of injustices in the United States, and the lack of effective counsel has contributed to such instances.

Perhaps the most famous instance of this involved the 1930s "Scottsboro Boys" case, which involved nine African American teenagers who were falsely accused of raping two white women on a train in rural Alabama.[7] After their arrest—and after a close brush with a lynch mob intent on killing the youths before a trail was even held—no attorney was appointed for the teens. The trial court ultimately selected two reluctant lawyers to represent the youth in the courtroom: One of the attorneys was drunk on the first day of trial and the other was an absent-minded real estate lawyer who had not tried a case in years. The lawyers met with the youths for less than an hour before going to court. Just fifteen days after their arrest and two quick days in court, eight of the nine were found guilty and sentenced to death.[8] Ultimately, the U.S. Supreme Court overturned the convictions[9] but the trial of the "Scottsboro Boys" remains one of the most notorious instances of American injustice. Only after national attention was drawn to the case and skilled lawyers agreed to vigorously defend the youths in the appellate process did the courts ultimately begin to address the Scottsboro travesty. Of course, given the deep racial divide in Alabama in the 1930s, it is quite doubtful whether any black person accused of raping a white woman could have received a truly fair trial. But there is no question that the absence of counsel contributed to the tragedy of Scottsboro and this historical instance provides a telling example of how important it is to have legal representation.

Ultimately, the right to counsel helps to bring about a greater level of equality in legal proceedings. Of course, equality to the founders did not have the same understanding as it does to us today. Their definition of *all* was very inconsistent and profoundly flawed since it did not include women, African Americans, and members of other disadvantaged groups, and it was the vestiges of this prejudice that was played out in Scottsboro and countless other places.

But the founders did consider that all free men were born with the equality of natural rights, and compared to the legal theory in England at the time, that was quite a progressive idea. These rights were to be enjoyed by everyone. Or, as one scholar put it, "upon entering the realm of liberty, one was considered equal to all others in that realm. . . ." (Lutz, 1988). By allowing counsel, both wealthy and poor, the famous and obscure, were given the equal opportunity to secure the services of one who would defend the accused.

There are, moreover, limits to the amount of equality achieved. While the Supreme Court has recognized the importance of legal counsel in bringing about fundamental fairness in the criminal justice system, this does not mean that everyone gets to have the same number or quality of lawyers. It is no secret that those who have the money can hire more skilled attorneys, which means that inequalities in wealth can yield unequal outcomes in the legal system. But the idea that everyone has the right to a lawyer is an egalitarian procedural right, which provides at least some protection to help level the legal playing field.

This leads to the point of why the right to counsel is such an important one in a democracy. Democratic political systems are based on the rule of law. Rather than having the whims of a dictator determine the formal rules of society, democracies are based upon a system of lawmaking by elected decision-makers and it is the law made by these decision-makers that dictates the acceptable bounds of behavior. Most people aren't lawyers and thus are not professionally trained and educated in the law. That's okay for most of our lives; between socialization, common sense, and everyday notices of what the law does and does not allow, we can spend much of our time focused upon work and play.

But there may be certain times in our lives that we need to know more about the law. It is in these times that we may need to know what all of our rights are and what is allowed under the law. And it is through legal representation that we can achieve this goal. In essence, the right to have a lawyer is the right to know and protect our rights, for it is through the right to counsel that we can fully enjoy all the protections the law allows. In this manner, having a lawyer is one of the most fundamental rights we have because it assures that we can have someone who will work to protect all of our constitutional rights. The right to have an attorney is, at its simplest form, the right to know and protect your rights. This is why some have noted that "probably no other right guaranteed to the criminally accused is more important than the right to counsel" (Epstein and Walker, 2001).

Equality and liberty are very important to the success of democratic government. The right to counsel and other procedural rights of the accused are part of the building blocks of self-government and popular sovereignty. In a system of self-government, people must be secure in their lives, liberty, and property in order to govern themselves. The right to counsel was extended to those accused of crimes to provide ample opportunity for the accused to prove his or her innocence. Courts were not established to achieve conviction, but to oversee the administration of fair justice by and for the people. In such a criminal justice system, people will be treated equitably and justice will be served. When justice is served, people can be secure from the potential abuse of power by the government. However, when courts are tyrannical and arbitrary, justice cannot be secured and security cannot be held. Without this security, government by the people is doomed. The right to counsel assists in protecting individuals from the tyranny of government, and helps to achieve justice and enhance the success of democracy.

References

Argersinger v. Hamlin, 407 U.S. 25 (1972).

Beaney, William M. 1955. *The Right to Counsel in American Courts.* Ann Arbor, MI: University of Michigan Press.

Carter, Dan T. 1969. *Scottsboro—A Tragedy of the American South.* New York: Oxford University Press.

Coker v. Georgia, 433 U.S. 583 (1977).

Douglas v. California, 372 U.S. 353 (1963).

Epstein, Lee, and Thomas Walker. 2001. *Constitutional Law for a Changing America: Rights, Liberties, and Justice,* 4th ed. Washington, DC: CQ Press.

Gideon v. Wainwright, 372 U.S. 335 (1963).

Johnson v. Zerbst, 304 U.S. 458 (1938).

Lutz, Donald S. 1988. *The Origins of American Constitutionalism.* Baton Rouge, LA: Louisiana State University Press.

McDonald, Forrest. 1986. *Novus Ordo Seclorum: The Intellectual Origins of the Constitution.* Lawrence, KS: University of Kansas Press.

Powell v. Alabama, 287 U.S. 45 (1932).

Rackow, Felix. 1954. "The Right to Counsel: English and American Precedents," *William and Mary Quarterly* 11:3–27.

Scott v. Illinois, 440 U.S. 367 (1979).

Stephen, Sir James. [1883] 1976. *A History of the Criminal Law of England.* Reprint. Buffalo, NY: W.S. Hein.

Wood, Gordon S. 1993. *The Creation of the American Republic, 1776–1787.* New York: W.W. Norton.

Endnotes

1. The Bill of Rights was not part of the original constitution, of course, but due to its essential role in assuring ratification, I herein include the first ten amendments when referring to the constitution. For more on the theoretical underpinnings of the constitutional founding, see McDonald 1986 and Wood 1993.

2. For more on the early history of the right to counsel, see Beaney 1955.

3. This section on the English history of counsel rights draws heavily from Rackow 1954.

4. Though there is some debate about which school was truly first. The Litchfield Law School in Connecticut was established in 1774. However, the University of Pennsylvania also lays claim to the "first law school" moniker. Penn's law school opened its doors in 1791, but unlike Litchfield, which closed in 1833, the University of Pennsylvania's law school is still operating.

5. See Rackow 1954, who references Sir Edward Coke's classic *Third Part of the Institutes of the Laws of England, 1628–1644* (1628).

6. See *Johnson v. Zerbst,* 304 U.S. 458 (1938); *Gideon v. Wainwright,* 372 U.S. 335 (1963); *Douglas v. California,* 372 U.S. 353 (1963); *Argersinger v. Hamlin,* 407 U.S. 25 (1972); *Scott v. Illinois,* 440 U.S. 367 (1979).

7. For more on the "Scottsboro Boys," see Carter 1969. The law school at the University of Missouri at Kansas City has an informative web page on the case at http://www.law.umkc.edu/faculty/projects/FTrials/scottsboro/scottsb.htm.

8. The initial trial of the ninth youth ended in a mistrial after the jury could not agree on sentencing him to life in prison or death, even though the prosecution only sought life imprisonment. See Carter 1969. The Supreme Court later disallowed the death penalty in rape cases in its decision in *Coker v. Georgia,* 433 U.S. 583 (1977).

9. See *Powell v. Alabama,* 287 U.S. 45 (1932).

The Perennial Quest for Equality: The Controversy over Affirmative Action

JOHN FOBANJONG

The extent to which opportunity in America is shared equitably is the fundamental issue that underlies the policy of affirmative action. The nation's long history of discrimination toward women and minorities led to the establishment of affirmative action policies. Initially conceived as a remedy against past and continuing gender and race discrimination in employment, government contracting, and university admissions, the policy soon appeared to run against important principles of equality of opportunity. However, John Fobanjong explains that properly applied affirmative action programs can further the goal of expanding opportunity while also protecting individual equality.

Equality is one of the fundamental values of the American political creed. At the birth of the nation in 1776, this ideal was emphatically stated in the Declaration of Independence. Yet, as American democracy evolved, it soon became evident that this founding principle did not extend to all groups in society. In an effort to correct this, American political leaders developed a policy known as "affirmative action" to enable groups that were previously denied equality gain access to equal opportunity. As in most policies that govern the distribution of public goods, affirmative action soon became controversial. Indeed, it remains one of the most controversial issues in American politics today—contributing more to social disharmony than to the social harmony it was intended to promote. While proponents see it as a necessary means of addressing past and contemporary discrimination, opponents see it as synonymous with "quotas," "reverse discrimination," and "preferential treatment." Today, the country remains divided over this policy. But before we look at the reasons behind this polarizing controversy, we have to begin first by defining the concept of affirmative action, understanding how it was conceived, and examining why it has caused such an invidious backlash.

Defining Affirmative Action

Affirmative action is a set of public policy initiatives that are designed to help eliminate past and present discriminatory practices that are based on race, gender, religion, or national origin. Developed in the early 1960s, it encourages the recruitment, hiring, and promotion of qualified women and minorities by private and public employers. The policy requires that special consideration be given to minorities and women in employment, education, and pubic contracts.

When it was first conceived, employers were required to set goals and timetables for achieving diversity, and take appropriate measures to meet these goals. To enforce the policy, the federal government rewards companies and institutions that comply with the policy by doing business with them, and penalizes companies and institutions that do not comply with the policy by refusing to do business with them. The rewards could be in the form of grants in federal contracts or increased federal funding. The penalties could come in the form of lawsuits or denial of government funding and contracts.

In their efforts to eliminate discrimination, policymakers were faced, at conception, with the dilemma of whether to simply provide guarantees for "equality of opportunity" and adopt color-blind policies, or take affirmative steps by guaranteeing preferences to victims of past discrimination. In other words, the dilemma was over whether to provide guarantees for equality opportunity or equality of results. Sidney Verba and Gary Owen (1995) believe that where affirmative action provides guarantees for equality of opportunity—guarantees that provide a level playing field for everyone, irrespective of race or gender—then it is likely to gain widespread support. But when affirmative action focuses on equality of results by adopting quotas and gender or racial preferences, then it draws widespread opposition from groups that do not fall within these targeted categories (Verba and Owen, 1995, pp. 369–387).

For policymakers, the initial goal appeared to have been the establishment of a level playing field, where everyone was guaranteed equality of opportunity. According to David Rosenbloom, "it was not a program to offer special privilege to any one group of persons because of their particular race, religion, sex, or national origin" (Rosenbloom, 1973, pp. 236–251). This appeared to conform with the fundamental principle of equality around which the nation was founded. This principle was later restated in the Fourteenth Amendment of the U.S. Constitution, and reiterated in Title VI and VII of the 1964 Civil Rights Act. Faced with reluctance from employers to voluntarily implement nondiscrimination and color blindness in their hiring practices, and impatient with the slow pace at which progress was being made toward equality of opportunity, policymakers decided to take affirmative steps to mandate the adoption of programs that would lead to equality of results. Accordingly, the goal of civil rights organizations shifted from the traditional goal of equality of opportunity through nondiscrimination to affirmative action policies that provided specific goals and timetables for the achievement of racial and gender equality.

The Development of Affirmative Action Policies

The formulation and implementation of affirmative action policies in the United States have been carried out largely through the president's constitutional powers to sign executive orders. In the 1960s, all three presidents—Kennedy, Johnson, and Nixon—who occupied the White House chose to exercise this constitutional prerogative. Political lessons from the two previous decades reminded them that Congress was a hostile forum on matters relating to any policies that were directed at promoting equality of opportunity between blacks and whites.

The first lesson was President Harry Truman's 1946 decision to integrate the United States Armed Forces. The decision provoked an angry reaction from southern members of Congress. It produced a near-replay of the angry fallout that divided the North and the South on the eve of the American Civil War. This time, however, the anger did not lead into a push for secession. It led instead into a push for party realignment. Prominent members of the southern congressional delegation abandoned the Democratic Party and joined the newly formed Dixiecrat party. Among them was South Carolina senator, Strom Thurmond, who won the 1948 nomination for president of the newly founded States Rights party. Campaigning on a platform that stressed states' rights, the party failed to win the White House, but succeeded however in setting the stage that would lead to the transformation of the South from a Democratic bulwark into the Republican stronghold that it is today.

The Democratic Party, under Truman, won the White House and in 1953, the Committee on Government Contract Compliance urged the Bureau of Employment Security "to act positively and affirmatively to implement the policy of nondiscrimination."

The second lesson was the 1954 *Brown v. Board of Education* Supreme Court ruling on school desegregation. Just as in Truman's decision to integrate the Armed Forces, the decision to integrate public schools also provoked a rancorous reaction from southern members of Congress. The rancor was manifested in a 1965 document known as *The Southern Manifesto,* harshly criticized the U.S. Supreme Court for usurping the powers of Congress and for unduly interfering with states' rights.

Reminded by these two lessons, the executive branch saw that the chances of getting an affirmative action bill passed in Congress were bleak. As a result, most presidents have, since the 1960s, increasingly resorted to the use of executive orders in formulating race and gender-sensitive policies such as affirmative action. Thus, in 1961, President John Kennedy signed Executive Order 10925, instructing federal contractors to take "affirmative action to ensure that applicants were treated equally without regard to race, color, religion, sex, or national origin." It was the first time the term *affirmative action* was officially used by the United States government. As an indication that the law was intended to provide for equality of opportunity rather than for equality of results, the order established a committee that was known as the "Committee on Equal Employment Opportunity."

Four years later, President Lyndon Johnson signed another executive order—Executive Order 11246—requiring all government contractors and subcontractors to take affirmative action to expand job opportunities for minorities. The Office of Federal Contract Compliance was established to administer the Order. In 1967, the Executive Order was amended and expanded to include affirmative action for women.

In 1971, President Richard Nixon signed yet another executive order—Executive Order 11625—requiring federal agencies to develop comprehensive plans and specific goals for a national Minority Business Enterprise contracting program. Following up two years later, the Nixon administration issued "Memorandum-Permissible Goals and Timetables in State and Local Government Employment Practices," mandating the establishment of goals and timetables for reporting purposes. That the push toward increased reliance on statistical evidence and mandatory goals and timetable came from a Republican president is worth noting. It defies the generally held perception that affirmative action is a liberal policy, formulated by liberal presidents for their liberal constituencies. Not only was Nixon a Republican, he was a right-wing conservative.

Until 1972, the enforcement of affirmative action was directed primarily to eliminating discrimination in organizations that conducted business with the federal government. With the passage of the 1972 Equal Employment Opportunity Act, an Equal Employment Opportunity Commission was established to ensure state and local government compliance with Title VII of the 1964 Civil Rights Act prohibiting discrimination against employment. The Commission was empowered by the 1978 Civil Service Reform Act to investigate and bring suit against private and public employers accused of violating Title VII prohibitions against discrimination.

Finally, in 1979, President Jimmy Carter signed Executive Order 12138, establishing a National Women's Business Enterprise Policy, and requiring each government agency to use affirmative action to support women's enterprises.

The tendency for presidents to formulate affirmative action policies through executive orders has led Thomas Dye (1998) to see affirmative action as an elite-driven policy. In what he describes as "elite-mass conflict," Dye argues that when elite preferences differ from those of the masses, the preferences of elites prevail. In spite of opposition from the masses, elites see affirmative action policies as a necessary tool in achieving equality of opportunity. To avoid having these laws legislated through Congress, the elite allows its will to prevail over the will of the masses. This is why despite opposition from a majority of the white male population, the policy remains in force (Dye, 1998, pp. 40–69).

It is important to note that throughout their struggle for civil rights, blacks never campaigned for special privileges or preferential treatment. What Martin Luther King and the rest of the civil rights leadership ardently campaigned for was the right to vote. Blacks were convinced that to have equality with whites, all they needed was the right to vote. To deny them that right was to deny them equality. In 1965, the right to vote was granted in the Voting Rights Act. Along with the civil rights protections provided in the Civil Rights Act the year before, blacks felt that barriers against equality had been sufficiently eliminated to allow them to compete evenly with whites for political representation and economic opportunities. Two years later, in an unprecedented show of contrition, President Johnson delivered a national speech justifying the establishment of an affirmative action policy. In the speech he argued that you cannot take a man whose hands and feet were tied up for three hundred years, bring him to the starting line of a race, and tell him that he is now free to compete equally with others. The speech marked the Johnson administration's launch of affirmative action programs. For blacks, it was an unanticipated bonus. Aware that sooner or later the policy was going to draw partisan attacks, blacks, women, and other beneficiaries of the policy began mobilizing to defend it.

Backlash Against Affirmative Programs

In the face of elite intransigence, the masses in a democratic society often turn to other decision-making institutions for remedy. Thus, in *Understanding the Backlash Against Affirmative Action,* John Fobanjong argues that all three branches of our national government have at one time or another been turned to address the affirmative action controversy (Fobanjong, 2001, pp. 16–29). Here, we are going to begin by examining the role that the judicial branch of our government, the ultimate arbiter of social controversies in our society, has played in addressing the controversy over affirmative action. The social philosopher Alexis de Tocqueville has identified the judiciary as the one institution that Americans, like no other people, love to turn to when faced with a political or social controversy. In his classic, *Democracy in America,* de Tocqueville observes that in the United States, scarcely any political question arises that is not resolved sooner or later into a judicial question. It is thus that the largely white male population, which felt excluded from the benefits of affirmative action, was forced to seek remedy from the institutions of the judiciary.

The first affirmative action case that was brought before the United States Supreme Court was a controversy over a University of California's admissions policy that gave special considerations to minority medical school applicants. The policy reserved 18 seats for disadvantaged minority students in each entering class of 100. When Alan Bakke, a white male applicant, was denied admission, he sued claiming that the admission of applicants with less qualification constituted reverse discrimination and therefore a violation of his equal protection rights. The phrase *reverse discrimination* entered the American vocabulary for the first time. In *Regents of the University of California v. Bakke* (1978), the Supreme Court ruled that the use of quotas or set-aside in university admissions was unconstitutional, but that the University was welcomed to see race as a "plus" in the admissions process. Bakke was ordered admitted, and the University was invited to develop an admissions policy that did not discriminate against anyone on the basis of race, color, religion, or national origin.

The ruling failed to resolve the controversy over affirmative action. Supporters of affirmative action believed that the ruling was in their favor, because it allowed for the use of race as a positive factor in university admissions. On the other hand, opponents of the program also believed that the ruling was in their favor because it ordered the admission of Bakke, and outlawed for the consideration of race in university admissions.

One year later, in 1979, the Supreme Court ruled in *United Steel Workers of America, AFL-CIO v. Weber* that affirmative action programs designed to correct for past discrimination in the workplace were constitutional. The ruling gave a green light to an affirmative action plan that was developed by Kaiser Aluminum Corporation and United Steel Workers of America to reserve 50 percent of higher-paying skilled jobs to minorities. In a community where 39 percent of the workforce was black, only 2 percent of skilled jobs in the company were black. To correct for this imbalance, blacks with less seniority were selected for training in higher-paying jobs. Brian Weber, a white employee who was not selected, sued claiming that he had been discriminated against in violation of his equal protection rights. The Supreme Court held that Title VII of the Civil Rights Act "left employers and unions in the private sector free to take such race-conscious steps to eliminate manifest racial imbalances in traditionally segregated job categories. We hold that Title VII does not prohibit such . . . affirmative action plans." In the opinion of the Court, it would be "ironic indeed," if the Civil Rights Act were used to deny voluntary, private race-conscious efforts that are taken to eliminate the lingering effects of past discrimination.

Meanwhile, in yet another case dealing with seniority, the Supreme Court ruled in *Firefighters Local Union v. Stotts* (1984) that a city could not lay off white firefighters in favor of black firefighters with less seniority.

In 1987, the Supreme Court made two important rulings upholding affirmative action protections for minorities. In *United States v. Paradise,* the Court ruled in favor of a 50 percent quota system for blacks in the Alabama Department of Safety, which had until 1972 excluded blacks from serving as state troopers, and had until 1984 not promoted any black beyond the rank of corporal. In *Johnson v. Transportation Agency,* Santa Clara, California, the Court upheld a court-ordered 29 percent minority "membership admission goal" for a union that had historically discriminated against minorities. The ruling proved that just as the Court can order that measures be taken to eliminate lingering effects of past discrimination, it can also order the implementation of affirmative action policies that correct and prevent against future discriminatory practices.

The affirmative action controversy remained unresolved as the decade gradually wound down. The Court's inability to rule decisively on the issue drove opponents of affirmative action to look for alternative decision-making avenues. In Ronald Reagan's campaign platform for the1980 presidential elections was an agenda to abolish affirmative action policy. He promised that if elected, he was going to use his "stroke of the pen" authority to revoke Executive Order 11246, which granted affirmative action benefits to minorities and women. Opponents of affirmative action—most of whom were white male—mobilized to support Reagan's bid for the White House. It would be the beginning of an organized opposition against affirmative action. Reagan's victory was attributed largely to a new political class known as "Reagan Democrats" that had emerged during the campaign. It was composed mainly of white male democrats who were disenchanted with the lack of a platform in the Democratic party that was opposed to affirmative action.

When Reagan got into the White House, his first order of business was to fulfill his campaign promise. Realizing that he could not count on the Democratic controlled Congress to work with him in ending affirmative action, Reagan considered revoking Executive Order 11246. Several members of his cabinet, including Secretary of State George Schultz, Labor Secretary William Brock, and Transportation Secretary Elizabeth Dole, advised against it, arguing that revoking it was going to cause unnecessary controversy.

Reacting against a decision by the University of Arizona's Fiesta Bowl to contribute $100,000 to each participating institution's minority scholarship fund, the first Bush administration, acting through the Assistant Secretary of Education in Charge of Civil Rights Michael Williams, an African American, stated that minority scholarships violated Title VII of the 1964 Civil Rights Act, which prohibits discrimination in programs that receive federal funds. The decision produced a public uproar, and the administration was forced to rescind it. However, four years later, the Supreme Court let stand a decision by the Fourth Circuit Court of Appeals ending a University of Maryland program that set aside an annual scholarship fund for African Americans. Once the Reagan-Bush administrations realized that they could not achieve their policy objectives through the institutions of Congress or through the bureaucracy, they turned their attention to the institution of the judiciary.

But in order to be able to work with the legal system, they first had to change its ideological makeup. With many federal judges coming up for retirement in the 1980s and early 1990s, this could be done through the president's powers to appoint federal judges. In exercising these powers, the Reagan-Bush administrations made sure that their appointees were all conservatives with a known record of overt opposition to affirmative action programs. By the end of the 1980s, much of the federal bench had gone from liberal to conservative. The liberal decade of the sixties, according to Professor Fobanjong, was now replaced by the conservative decade of the eighties—giving anti-affirmative action forces a good chance in getting their suits addressed favorably by the federal bench.

The first test of the new Court would come in 1989, when it was asked to rule on two affirmative action cases. In the first case, *City of Richmond v. Croson,* the Court ruled against a Richmond, Virginia, affirmative action program that set aside 30 percent of the city's construction contracts for minorities. Unless it is justified by a "compelling interest," and narrowly tailored to ensure that the program furthers that interest, such set-asides violate of the Equal Protection Clause of the Fourteenth Amendment. In the second case, the Supreme Court ruled in *Wards Cove Packing Co., Inc. v. Atonio* that statistical imbalances in race or gender in the workplace were not sufficient evidence by themselves to prove discrimination. In cases where an employment evaluation process was found to be biased against any group, the Court further stated that it was the responsibility of the plaintiffs to prove that the employer had no obvious business reason to administer such an evaluation. It was a ruling that made it difficult for plaintiffs to prove job discrimination.

The ruling overturned a 1971 Supreme Court ruling in *Griggs v. Duke Power Co.*, in which the Court unanimously ruled that if a test or qualification requirement disproportionately disqualified minorities, the burden of proof was on the employer to defend it as a bona fide occupational qualification. The ruling resulted from a suit that was filed by black employees against Duke Power challenging the company's use of tests that disproportionately screened out blacks from hiring and promotion, but had no demonstrable relationship to job performance. In placing the burden of proof on the employer in this earlier case, the Court made it easier for plaintiffs to prevail in discrimination cases.

Outraged by the Supreme Court's reinterpretation of affirmative action in the *Wards Cove* case, affirmative action supporters mobilized and turned to Congress to have the law rewritten to correct for this new interpretation. In 1991, Congress passed the Civil Rights and Women's Equity Act to correct for the Supreme Court's 1989 decisions. The new law returned the burden of proof for any evaluation mechanisms that created "disparate impact" on certain groups to the employer.

In a 1994 ruling known as *Adarand Constructors, Inc. v. Pena,* the Supreme Court struck down a federal construction contract set-aside for minorities, arguing that affirmative action programs must be subject to "strict scrutiny" in order to accomplish a compelling government interest such as correcting for past discrimination, and narrowly tailored so as not to cause adverse impact on other groups. While the ruling narrowed the definition of current affirmative action policies, it did not strike down any specific federal program that currently executed such policies.

Despite their gains in the Supreme Court, the opposition against affirmative action did not relent. Responding to their plea, Senator Robert Dole and Rep. Charles Canady introduced a bill in Congress in 1995 that sought to ban all federal affirmative action programs. Using slogans that sought to portray the white male as an "endangered specie," they continued to mobilize against the continuous implementation of affirmative action programs. The unfair stigma that appears to link all African Americans with affirmative action benefits has pushed some members of the minority community to join hands with anti-affirmative action forces in campaigning for its ban. For those who admit that inequalities still exist in society, they suggest that such inequalities can be better corrected with class-based rather than with race- or gender-based policies.

Caving in to pressure from anti-affirmative action forces, and motivated by the need to bring the federal government in compliance with the Supreme Court's ruling in *Adarand v. Pena,* President Bill Clinton in 1995 ordered a review of all federal affirmative action programs. According to Clinton, "any program must be eliminated or reformed if it: creates quotas; creates preferences for unqualified individuals; creates reverse discrimination; continues even after its equal opportunity purposes have been achieved." At the conclusion of the review, President Clinton restated his administration's support for affirmative action in an encapsulating slogan that read, "Mend it, don't end it!" Clinton's position was concurred by a 1995 bipartisan Glass Ceiling Commission report, which found that there were existing barriers in society that continued to block the access of women and minorities to decision-making positions. The Commission invited corporate America to continue to use affirmative action as a tool to ensure that all qualified individuals have equal access and opportunity to compete on the basis of ability and merit.

Despite Clinton's support, and despite the findings of the Glass Ceiling Commission, the Regents of the University of California voted that same year to end affirmative action programs at all University of California campuses. The following year, in 1996, Californians voted in a statewide referendum to abolish all public-sector affirmative action programs, with the passage of Proposition 209. A ruling by the Fifth Circuit Court of Appeals, known as *Texas v. Hopewood* would in the same year, pass a ban on the use of affirmative action in university admissions in Texas. Still in Texas, voters in Houston voted in 1997 to reject a proposition that would have abolished affirmative action programs in city hiring and contracting. Experts believed that the phrasing of the ballot initiative had much to do with the outcome. When phrased in the form of "minority preferences," most people would vote against the program. But when phrased as "programs for equal opportunity," people would usually vote to support it. In 1998, voters in the state of Washington followed California's lead in voting in a referendum to pass Initiative 200 abolishing affirmative action in higher education, in hiring, and in public contracting. In 2000, the Florida legislature passed the "One Florida" plan, banning affirmative action.

In reaction to declining minority enrollment in state institutions of higher learning, the Texas legislature passed the Ten Percent Plan in 1997, guaranteeing university admission to the top 10 percent of all high school graduates in the state. The Florida legislature also adopted a bill that guaranteed admission for the top 20 percent of its high school graduates to the University of Florida system. California went beyond a new plan that guaranteed admission into the University of California System to the top 4 percent of its high school graduates, to repealing Proposition 209 in college admissions and completely banning the SAT as an admission requirement.

What started out as a tough and uncompromising stance against affirmative action in these various states was gradually watered down into a more moderate policy that promoted inclusiveness.

Twenty-five years after the *Bakke* ruling, the Supreme Court was brought once again to rule on affirmative action. In a twin decision issued on June 23, 2003, the Court found a point system that was used in undergraduate admissions at the University of Michigan unconstitutional, upholding the consideration of race in the University's Law School admission policy. In *Grutter v. Bollinger,* the justices ruled that "the Constitution does not prohibit the law school's narrowly tailored use of race in admissions decisions to further a compelling interest in obtaining the educational benefits that flow from a diverse student body." The Court recognized that there are advantages to be obtained in diversity, and that the state may have a very high interest ("compelling," in legal language) in making sure that diversity in the educational process is achieved. As a means of ensuring this diversity, the Court upheld the consideration of race as a factor in the admissions process.

However, in *Gratz v. Bollinger,* the justices struck down a point system used in the undergraduate admissions process at the University of Michigan. Under that system, applicants were assigned points for a variety of factors, including race, in order to reach a certain score that allowed admission to the school. This point system was considered too similar to a quota system, which the Court has long held to be unconstitutional.

Both rulings did not go as far as supporters and opponents of affirmative action wanted. The Court, for example, rejected *amicus curraie* arguments by the Bush administration that the University of Michigan affirmative action policies should be struck down. It also did not agree with arguments from supporters of affirmative action that the point system in the admissions policy be upheld. It would appear therefore that the controversy over affirmative action has not been definitively settled.

Types of Affirmative Action Programs

Although affirmative action may be controversial, it remains public policy that is still actively enforced by both public and private sector managers across the nation. It is important to distinguish among the various major categories of affirmative action that are currently in force in the United States, if we are to fully understand the nature of the policy. Jonathan Tompkins has distinguished between three types of affirmative action policies that are currently in force today. They include executive-ordered affirmative action, court-ordered affirmative action, and voluntary affirmative action (Tompkins, 1995, pp. 161–180).

Executive-Ordered Affirmative Action Programs

These are affirmative action programs that are decreed by the president, usually by executive order. Like all legislation, they do have the force of law. Almost all of the affirmative action laws that are in force today were executive ordered in the 1960s. Their enforcement is monitored by various government agencies, including among others, the Department of Labor, the Department of Justice, and the Equal Employment Opportunities Commission. Frequently, employers are required to submit a written affirmative action plan for approval, and to set goals and timetables that show progress toward compliance. Revised Order #4 of Executive Order 11246 requires government contractors to determine the underutilization of women and minorities in major job categories.

Court-Ordered Affirmative Action Programs

These are affirmative action programs that are established by court ruling to remedy proven discriminatory practices. Court involvement here usually comes about through a lawsuit filed by an aggrieved party, or by any of the government agencies that are charged with monitoring the implementation of the policy. Usually, the Court would mandate in its decision, a certain line of action that an employer must take. In *U.C. Davis v. Bakke,* for example, the University of California Davis was ordered to admit the plaintiff, Allan Bakke. While it instructed the University to use race as a "plus" in its admission process, it ordered the elimination of any practices that adversely impacted whites.

Another example of a court-ordered affirmative action program was the Supreme Court ruling in *U.S. v. Paradise,* in which the Court ordered the Alabama Department of Public Safety to hire one black for every one white until 25 percent of its state troopers were black. The order was passed after determining that the department had, over the years, systemically discriminated against the hiring and promotion of blacks.

Voluntary Affirmative Action Programs

Occasionally, employers do voluntarily establish affirmative action programs to avoid potential lawsuits from such government watchdog agencies as the Equal Employment Opportunity Commission or the U.S. Civil Rights Commission. Ironically, however, such voluntary actions do run the risk of exposing such employers to accusations of reverse discrimination by white plaintiffs. This was the case in *U.S. Steelworkers v. Kaiser Aluminum,* when the company reserved 50 percent of an on-the-job training program for its black employees, in a voluntary effort to increase their pay and job skill. A white male employee sued claiming reverse discrimination. In another voluntary effort to improve the status of its female employees, an employer, Transportation Agency of Santa Clara County, decided to promote women to positions where they were underrepresented. When Diane Joyce was promoted to the position of dispatcher over Paul Johnson, a white male, who had more years of experience, Johnson sued accusing the company of reverse discrimination. The Supreme Court ruled in *Transportation Agency of Santa Clara v. Johnson,* upholding the plan on the grounds that its purpose was to eliminate manifest gender and racial imbalances.

Finally, when the Jackson Board of Education voluntarily adopted plans to protect minorities with less seniority during layoffs, the company's white employees challenged the plan on the basis of reverse discrimination. Ruling in *Wygant v. Jackson Board of Education,* the Supreme Court argued that although affirmative action can be used to apportion hiring, it cannot be used to apportion layoffs.

Conclusion

Affirmative action, as implemented today, invites employers who are faced with two equally qualified candidates to employ the minority over the majority candidate or a qualified woman over a similarly qualified male. Unlike in the past, affirmative action policies are no longer based on quotas. No longer is the practice of reverse discrimination, or the hiring of unqualified or less-qualified candidates over more qualified candidates considered acceptable practice.

Despite this redefined approach, the controversy over affirmative action policies remains unresolved. The debate continues to heat up, and the pro- and anti-affirmative action forces are refusing to relent. While the increasingly assertive opposition argues that the battle to guarantee equal rights for all citizens has been fought and won, therefore affirmative action policies should be dismantled, supporters of the program argue that the program should be kept in place because the playing field is not yet level. In the view of most supporters, granting modest privileges to women and minorities is more than fair, given the hundreds of years of discrimination that benefited the majority white population as a whole. Efforts by all the major decision-making institutions in the country—from the presidency to Congress to the judiciary and the electorate—have all failed to produce a definitive resolution to this increasingly divided controversy. The inability of the present generation to resolve this controversy means that affirmative action is one of the social controversies that is going to be handed down to future generations.

APPENDIX 1

**Excerpts of President Johnson's Commencement Address Launching
Affirmative Action at Howard University
June 4, 1965**

. . . In far too many ways American Negroes have been another nation: deprived of freedom, crippled by hatred, the doors of opportunity closed to hope.

In our time change has come to this nation too. Heroically, the American Negro—acting with im pressive restraint—has peacefully protested and marched, entered the court-rooms and the seats of government, demanding a justice long denied. The voice of the Negro was the call to action. But it is a tribute to America that, once aroused, the courts and the Congress, the President and most of the people, have been the allies of progress . . .

Freedom is the right to share, fully and equally, in the American society—to vote, to hold a job, to enter a public place, to go to school. It is the right to be treated, in every part of our national life, as a man equal in dignity and promise to all others.

But freedom is not enough. You do not wipe away the scars of centuries by say: Now, you are free to go where you want, do as you desire, and choose the leaders you please.

You do not take a man who, for years, has been hobbled by chains, liberate him, bring him to the starting line of a race, saying "you are free to compete with all of the others," and still justly believe you have been completely fair.

This it is not enough to open the gates of opportunity. All our citizens must have the ability to walk through those gates.

This is the next and the more profound stage of our battle for civil rights. We seek not just freedom but opportunity—and not just legal equity but human ability—not just equality as a right and a theory, but equality as a fact and a result.

For the task is to give twenty million Negroes the same chance as every other American to learn and grow—to work mental and spiritual and to pursue their individual happiness.

To this end equal opportunity is essential, but not enough. Men and women of all races are born with the same range of abilities. But ability is not just the product of birth. It is stretched or stunted by the family you live with, and the neighborhood you live in—by the school you go to, and the poverty or richness of your surroundings. It is the product of hundred unseen forces playing upon the infant, the child, and the man . . .

. . . Here are some of the facts of this American failure.

Source: Albert P. Blaustein and Robert L. Zangrando, *Civil Rights and the Black American* (Simon and Schuster, 1968), 559–566.

Thirty-five years ago the rate of unemployment for Negroes and whites was about the same. Today the Negro rate is twice as high. In 1948 the percent unemployment rate for Negro teenage boys was actually less than of whites. By last year it had grown to 23 percent, against 13 percent for whites.

Between 1949 and 1959, the income of Negro men relative to white men declined in every section of the country. From 1952 to 1963 the median income of Negro families compared to white actually dropped from 57 percent to 53 percent.

In the years 1955–57, 22 percent of experienced Negro workers were out of work at some time during the year. In 1961–63 that proportion had soared to 29 percent.

Since 1947 the number of white families living in poverty has decreased 27 percent while the number of poor nonwhite families went down only by 3 percent.

The infant mortality on nonwhites in 1940 was 70 percent greater than whites. Twenty-two years later it was 90 percent greater.

Moreover, the isolation of Negro from white communities is increasing, rather than diminishing as Negroes crowd into the central cities—becoming a city within a city . . .

. . . First, Negroes are trapped—as many whites are trapped—in inherited, gate-less, poverty. They lack training and skills. They are shut in slums, without decent medical care. Private and public poverty combine to cripple their capacities.

We are attacking these evils through our poverty program, our education program, our health program and a dozen more—aimed at the root causes of poverty.

We will increase, and accelerate, and broaden this attack in years to come, until this most enduring foes yield to our unyielding will.

But there is a second cause—more difficult to explain, more deeply grounded, more desperate in its force. It is the devastating heritage of long years of slaver; and a century of oppression, hatred and injustice.

For Negro poverty is not white poverty. Many of its causes and many of its cures are the same. But there are many differences—deep, corrosive, obstinate differences—radiating painful roots into the community, the family, and the nature of the individual.

These differences are not racial differences. They are solely and simply the consequence of ancient brutality, past injustice, and present prejudice. They are anguishing to observe. For the Negro they are a reminder of oppression. For the white they are a reminder of guilt. But they must be faced, and dealt with, and overcome; if we are to reach the time when the only difference between Negroes and whites is the color of their skin.

Nor can we find a complete answer in the experience of other American minorities. They made a valiant, and largely successful effort to emerge from poverty and prejudice. The Negro, like these others, will have to rely mostly on his own efforts. But he cannot do it alone. For they did not have the heritage of centuries to overcome. They did not have a cultural tradition which had been twisted and bartered by endless years of hatred and hopelessness. Nor were they excluded because of race or color—a feeling whose dark intensity is matched by no other prejudice in our society.

Nor can these differences be understood as isolated infirmities. They are a seamless web. They cause each other. They result from each other. They reinforce each other. Much of the Negro community is buried under a blanket of history and circumstance. It is not a lasting solution to lift just one corner. We must stand on all sides and raise the entire cover if we are to liberate our fellow citizens.

There is also the burden a dark skin can add to the search for a productive place in society. Unemployment strikes most swiftly and broadly at the Negro. This burden erodes hope. Blighted hope breeds despair. Despair brings indifference to the learning which offers a way out. And despair coupled with indifference is often the source of destructive rebellion against the fabric of society.

There is also the lacerating hurt of early collision with white hatred or prejudice, distaste or condescension. Other groups have felt similar intolerance. But success and achievement could wipe it away. They do not change the color of a man's skin. I have seen this uncomprehending pain in the eyes of young Mexican-American school children. It can be overcome. But for many, the wounds are always open.

Perhaps most important—its influence radiating to every part of life—is the breakdown of the Negro family structure. For this, most of all, white America must accept responsibility. It flows from centuries of oppression and persecution of the Negro man. It flows from the long years of degradation and discrimination which have attacked his dignity and assaulted his ability to provide for his family . . .

. . . There is no single easy answer to all these problems.

Jobs are part of the answer. They bring the income which permits a man to provide for his family.

Decent homes in decent surroundings and a chance to learn is part of the answer.

Welfare and social programs better designed to hold families together are part of the answer.

An understanding heart by all Americans is also part of the answer.

—to move beyond opportunity to achievement.

—to shatter forever, not only the barriers of law and public practice, but the walls which bound the condition of man by the color of his skin.

—to dissolve, as best we can, the antique enmities of the heart which diminish the holder, divide the great democracy, and do wrong to the children of God.

I pledge this will be a chief goal of my Administration, and of my program next year, and in the years to come . . .

. . . The scripture promises: "I shall light a candle of understanding in thine heart, which shall not be put out."

Together, and with millions more, we can light that candle of understanding in the heart of America.

And, once lit, it will never go out.

APPENDIX 2

Excerpts of Executive Order 11246: Equal Employment Opportunity
SOURCE: The provisions of Executive Order 11246 of Sept. 24, 1965, appear at 30 FR 12319, 12935, 3 CFR, 1964–1965 Comp., p.339, unless otherwise noted.

Under and by virtue of the authority vested in me as President of the United States by the Constitution and statutes of the United States, it is ordered as follows:

Part I—Nondiscrimination in Government Employment

[Part I superseded by EO 11478 of Aug. 8, 1969, 34 FR 12985, 3 CFR, 1966–1970 Comp., p. 803]

Part II—Nondiscrimination in Employment by Government Contractors and Subcontractors

Subpart A—Duties of the Secretary of Labor
SEC. 201. The Secretary of Labor shall be responsible for the administration and enforcement of Parts II and III of this Order. The Secretary shall adopt such rules and regulations and issue such orders as are deemed necessary and appropriate to achieve the purposes of Parts II and III of this Order.

[Sec. 201 amended by EO 12086 of Oct. 5, 1978, 43 FR 46501, 3 CFR, 1978 Comp., p. 230]

Subpart B—Contractors' Agreements
SEC. 202. Except in contracts exempted in accordance with Section 204 of this Order, all Government contracting agencies shall include in every Government contract hereafter entered into the following provisions:

During the performance of this contract, the contractor agrees as follows:

(1) The contractor will not discriminate against any employee or applicant for employment because of race, color, religion, sex, or national origin. The contractor will take affirmative action to ensure that applicants are employed, and that employees are treated during employment, without regard to their race, color, religion, sex or national origin. Such action shall include, but not be limited to the following: employment, upgrading, demotion, or transfer; recruitment or recruitment advertising; layoff or termination; rates of pay or other forms of compensation; and selection for training, including apprenticeship. The contractor agrees to post in conspicuous places, available to employees and applicants for employment, notices to be provided by the contracting officer setting forth the provisions of this nondiscrimination clause.

(2) The contractor will, in all solicitations or advancements for employees placed by or on behalf of the contractor, state that all qualified applicants will

receive consideration for employment without regard to race, color, religion, sex or national origin.

(3) The contractor will send to each labor union or representative of workers with which he has a collective bargaining agreement or other contract or understanding, a notice, to be provided by the agency contracting officer, advising the labor union or workers' representative of the contractor's commitments under Section 202 of Executive Order No. 11246 of September 24, 1965, and shall post copies of the notice in conspicuous places available to employees and applicants for employment.

(4) The contractor will comply with all provisions of Executive Order No. 11246 of Sept. 24, 1965, and of the rules, regulations, and relevant orders of the Secretary of Labor.

(5) The contractor will furnish all information and reports required by Executive Order No. 11246 of September 24, 1965, and by the rules, regulations, and orders of the Secretary of Labor, or pursuant thereto, and will permit access to his books, records, and accounts by the contracting agency and the Secretary of Labor for purposes of investigation to ascertain compliance with such rules, regulations, and orders.

(6) In the event of the contractor's noncompliance with the nondiscrimination clauses of this contract or with any of such rules, regulations, or orders, this contract may be cancelled, terminated, or suspended in whole or in part and the contractor may be declared ineligible for further Government contracts in accordance with procedures authorized in Executive Order No. 11246 of Sept. 24, 1965, and such other sanctions may be imposed and remedies invoked as provided in Executive Order No. 11246 of September 24, 1965, or by rule, regulation, or order of the Secretary of Labor, or as otherwise provided by law.

(7) The contractor will include the provisions of paragraphs (1) through (7) in every subcontract or purchase order unless exempted by rules, regulations, or orders of the Secretary of Labor issued pursuant to Section 204 of Executive Order No. 11246 of September 24, 1965, so that such provisions will be binding upon each subcontractor or vendor . . .

REFERENCES

Bacchi, Carol Lee. 1996. *The Politics of Affirmative Action: 'Women', Equality and Category Politics.* London: Sage.

Bob Jones University v. U.S., 103 Sup.Ct. 2017 (1983).

Bolick, Clint. 1996. *The Affirmative Action Fraud: Can We Restore the American Civil Rights Vision?* Washington, DC: Cato Institute.

Cannon, Lou. 1982. *President Reagan: The Role of a Lifetime.* New York: G.P. Putnam.

Curry, George E., ed. 1996. *The Affirmative Action Debate.* Reading, MA: Addison-Wesley.

Delgado, Richard. 1996. *The Coming Race War?: And Other Apocalyptic Tales of America After Affirmative Action and Welfare.* New York: New York University Press.

Dowd, M. 1990. "President Orders Aides to Review New Minority Scholarship Policy," *New York Times,* December 15.

Drake, W. Avon, and Robert D. Holsworth. 1996. *Affirmative Action and the Stalled Quest for Black Progress.* Urbana, IL: University of Illinois Press.

Dye. Thomas. 1995. *Understanding Pubic Policy,* 9th Ed. New York: Prentice Hall.

Eastland, Terry. 1996. *Ending Affirmative Action: The Case for Colorblind Justice*. New York: Basic Books.

Edley, Christopher, Jr. 1996. *Not All Black and White: Affirmative Action, Race, and American Values*, 1st ed. New York : Hill and Wang.

Fobanjong, John. 2001. *Understanding the Backlash Against Affirmative Action*. New York: Nova Science Publishers.

Holmes, Steven. 1995. "Minority Scholarship Loans Are Dealt Setback by Court," *New York Times*, May 23.

Kahlenberg, Richard D. 1996. *The Remedy: Class, Race, and Affirmative Action*. New York: Basic Books.

Kurtz, Howard. 1985. "Affirmative Action Policy Gains a Reprieve," *Washington Post*, October 25.

McWhirter, Darien A. 1996. *The End of Affirmative Action: Where Do We Go from Here?* New York: Carol Pub. Group.

Mills, Nicolaus, ed. 1994. *Debating Affirmative Action: Race, Gender, Ethnicity and the Politics of Inclusion*. New York: Delta Trade.

Mosley, Albert G., and Nicholas Capaldi. 1996. *Affirmative Action: Social Justice or Unfair Preference?* Lanham, MD: Rowman & Littlefield.

Murray, J. Haberman. 1996. *Affirmative Action and the Courts*. Sacramento, CA: California Research Bureau, California State Library.

Nordquist, Joan, ed. 1996. *Affirmative Action: A Bibliography*. Santa Cruz, CA: Reference and Research Services.

Nye, Robert. 1998. *Understanding Public Policy*, 9th ed. Upper Saddle River, NJ: Prentice Hall.

One Hundred Fourth Congress. An Overview of Affirmative Action: Hearing Before the Subcommittee on the Constitution, Federalism, and Property Rights of the Committee on the Judiciary, United States Senate, Washington: U.S. G.P.O. : For sale by the U.S. G.P.O., Supt. of Docs., Congressional Sales Office, 1996.

Ong, Paul, ed. 1997. *The Impact of Affirmative Action on Public-Sector Employment and Contracting in California*. California Policy Center, UCB.

Rosenbloom, David. 1973. "The Civil Service Commission's Decision to Authorize the Use of Goals and Timetables in Federal Equal Employment Opportunity Programs," *Western Political Quarterly* 26: 236–251.

Skrentny, John David. 1996. *The Ironies of Affirmative Action: Politics, Culture, and Justice in America*. Chicago: University of Chicago Press.

Tomasson, Richard F., Faye J. Crosby, and Sharon D. Herzberger. 1996. *Affirmative Action: The Pros and Cons of Policy and Practice*. Washington, DC: American University Press.

Tompkins, Jonathan. 1995. *Human Resources Management in Government: Hitting the Ground Running*. New York: Addison Wesley.

Verba, Sidney, and Owen, Gary. 1995. "The Meaning of Equality in America," *Political Science Quarterly* 100: 369–387.

Williams, Patricia. 1991. *The Alchemy of Race and Rights*. Cambridge, MA: Harvard University Press.

Governmental Institutions:

Policies and Politics

Unilateralism and Idealism: U.S. Foreign Policy in the Bush Administration

KEVIN M. CUROW

Each new presidential administration brings changes in foreign policy. These changes emerge as a result of differing goals, agendas, interests, and personalities. As Kevin Curow points out, George W. Bush set about to remake foreign policy in a fashion that is consistent with his vision of the United States acting alone in leading the world, while adhering to a core set of values and beliefs. This foreign policy—like any policy—is the subject of much debate. The consequences of Bush's foreign policy may fray relations with some key U.S. allies, but supporters contend that this new foreign policy will bring peace and security in the post–Cold War world.

George W. Bush's administration[1] has often been criticized for its approach to foreign policy. In particular, it has come under fire for its unilateralist approach to almost any issue or crisis. While the most recent and extreme example has been the handling of the Iraq crisis, it is clear that this tendency to act unilaterally is not an entirely new phenomenon, either in respect to the Bush administration or to American post–Cold War foreign policy in general. While the last three administrations have all, to some extent, responded to the status of the United States as the world's sole superpower by pursuing American interests, the current administration's aggressive and strident use of unilateralism is a departure from the tendency of previous administrations to favor multilateralism.

What perplexes many observers about the Bush administration is that despite this strong unilateralist streak, there is an equally apparent streak of idealism. The Bush administration clearly advocates the spreading of democracy and the free market system as the primary means for achieving the long-term foreign policy objectives of the United States. Bush's idealism perplexes mainly because unilateralism is generally seen as the outgrowth of the pessimistic viewpoint of the realist and the idealist is, if anything, an eternal optimist. Idealism and realism are historically the two dominant approaches to foreign policy and are always contrasted with one another for holding opposing viewpoints in terms of causes, consequences and policy approaches to international relations. The faith placed in democracy and the market system, however, is not at all new to the Bush administration and is better seen as an intensification of this idealist goal by means normally associated with realism.

The foreign policy of the Bush administration can be simplified by dividing it into its two key components: unilateralism and idealism.

Unilateralism

What is meant by the label *unilateralism?* In terms of foreign policy, it is casually used to refer to a state's willingness to act alone, without the approval or consent of other actors in the international system, to secure its own interests. A hallmark of the international system, however, is that states generally act in their own interest to ensure their own survival by safeguarding their prosperity and security. In this sense, even states that normally act through international organizations, such as the United Nations (UN), generally do so because it is in their best interests to seek their security and prosperity through multilateral institutions. Likewise, states that oppose multilateral approaches to specific foreign policy issues generally do so because they perceive their interests as better served by a unilateral or bilateral approach. A glance at any state's foreign policy decisions will reveal a mix of both approaches. For example, the United States has oftentimes relied on the United Nations as a means to achieve its own ends and yet rejected UN involvement at other times.

The controversial aspect of unilateralism is inherent in the implications of acting alone. A bilateral or multilateral approach implies reliance upon cooperation and compromise in international relations. A unilateral approach does not necessarily imply reliance upon conflict but it does imply placing less emphasis and importance on cooperation and compromise. Under the Bush Sr. (1989–1993) and Clinton (1993–2001) administrations, the emphasis clearly leaned to the side of cooperation and compromise with multilateral and bilateral solutions sought for nearly all international problems. As one scholar has remarked, the new Bush administration "emphatically rejected the Clintonian premise that geoeconomics were now more important than geopolitics" and instead "sees foreign policy as the management of threats to U.S. national security."[2] The Clinton approach called for multilateral action to manage the system as a whole, while the Bush approach is more likely to call for unilateral action. The change in approaches, however, has jarred both the American public and European diplomats who were accustomed to the "Clintonian premise." Even more jarring is the rhetoric of the Bush administration, which implied that the United States was always right, characterized most famously by the president's own words: "You're either with us or against us in the fight against terror."

For the purposes of this article, unilateralism is defined as an approach to foreign policy characterized by policy changes after little or no consultation with allies, by an effort to impose solutions rather than seek consensus and compromise, and by a willingness to ignore international norms and institutions as perceived necessary due to national interests.[3] Naturally, states oftentimes rely on multilateral approaches to their foreign policy because it is in their interests, as well. In fact, the unilateral approach is nearly only possible for extremely powerful states that are capable of imposing their will on others. Nonetheless, because multilateralism implies that the solutions are arrived at jointly by a group of states, it tends to dampen the role national interest plays in determining outcomes. Multilateralism also implies a certain level of respect for and adherence to international treaties, laws, and norms, which are generally lacking when a state ignores these conventions. In this light, calling for "coalitions of the willing" is another way of seeking to impose solutions, by preselecting solutions and calling for supporters, and is not an example of multilateralism.

The Bush administration's foreign policy displayed a strong tendency toward unilateralism from the beginning, although the tendency grew stronger after 9/11, and there is some evidence that the administration was not unified in this approach. In fact, the tendency of U.S. administrations to have competing internal approaches to foreign policy—namely, the differing approaches of the Department of State and the Department of Defense—has long been evident.[4] In peacetime, however, the Defense Department generally has less influence on foreign policy. The changed circumstances after 9/11, however, led to an increased role for Secretary of Defense Rumsfeld as the administration approached combating international terrorism as a "War on Terror." As a result, what was already a unilateralist foreign policy became, if not more unilateralist, at least more strident in its unilateralism as the United States became actively engaged throughout the world, often relying on military force to achieve its goals.

Examples of U.S. unilateralism under the Bush administration are easy to come by. The administration set the tone early in 2001 by pulling back from treaties and other agreements that had been negotiated by the Clinton administration. The decision to move ahead with a National Missile Defense system, although it threatened to weaken defense ties to our traditional allies in Europe while also threatening Russian and Chinese nuclear arsenals with irrelevance, is a perfect example of a foreign policy change announced by the administration with apparently no consultation with its allies. In early 2002, the United States cancelled the Anti-Ballistic Missile Treaty over Russian objections, after threatening to do so for more than a year. The decision to reject the Kyoto Protocol on global warming in early 2001 is illustrative not only of the unilateral nature of the administration but also the "in-your-face" approach, which called for the public rejection of a treaty that was for all intents and purposes already a dead issue.[5] Opposition to the International Criminal Court (ICC), which was opposed on the grounds that U.S. peacekeepers could theoretically find themselves tried for war crimes in another country, is just one case of the United States pulling out of an internationally negotiated treaty or institution. Whatever the merits of the ICC, the decision was once again an example of the United States taking a separate path, despite a great deal of international support for the multilateral approach.

The so-called "Bush Doctrine," outlined in Section V of the National Security Strategy released by the White House in September 2002, is easy to single out as the most blatant declaration of a unilateralist approach to foreign policy. Positing a fundamental change in the nature of the threat faced by the United States, the Bush Doctrine calls for preemptive strikes against "rogue states" and terrorist networks to forestall anticipated attacks by these groups against the

United States. While the document is correct in pointing out that every state has the right under international law to self-defense, it is mostly controversial because it legitimizes preemptive strikes, or first-strikes, by arguing that the existence of "rogue states" like Iraq make an attack upon the United States by these states or terrorists imminent. In the past, imminence in preemptive wars was always defined as an immediate threat of attack to occur within days. The Bush Doctrine redefines imminence by arguing that states like Iraq under Saddam Hussein are an imminent threat because one cannot foresee the attacks of terrorists. The logic of the war in Iraq, according to the Bush Doctrine, was that Iraq's attempt to acquire WMDs meant it would use them against the United States once acquired or it would pass them on to terrorists who would use them against the United States. These leaps in logic, disputed by many inside and outside of the administration, suggested to critics that the Bush Doctrine was a justification for unilateral military action.

The war against Iraq is another example of unilateralism. As far as the Bush administration is concerned, the efforts of the United Nations to resolve the Iraq issue, particularly as it pertained to weapons of mass destruction (WMDs), were not only an utter failure but ultimately futile. Likewise, sanctions were never going to succeed in forcing Saddam Hussein to give up whatever WMDs Iraq may have possessed. As a result, the United States resolved to force a regime change through military force. The administration's notable lack of patience in dealing with the UN probably undermined the potential for international consensus. For a variety of reasons, including domestic political considerations, most of the European states in particular were unwilling to support a war against Iraq without at least a *pro forma* attempt to resolve the issue through multilateral mechanisms. Repeated assertions by administration officials and their supporters indicated that the United States was willing and capable of dealing with Iraq alone, regardless of the outcome in the UN. This suggested that the administration defined multilateralism as other countries' unqualified support for unilateral decisions by the United States.

The Bush administration sees a unilateralist approach to foreign policy as necessary to "negotiate from a position of strength, break out of treaty obligations that shackle its ability to defend itself" and to reestablish U.S. credibility by ending engagement with competitors.[6] Even if it were necessary to strengthen the already strong U.S. position, to break international treaties for national security reasons, or to abandon engagement—and all of these are in dispute—there are serious consequences to a unilateralist foreign policy. The Bush Doctrine, for example, risks encouraging other states such as China and Russia to adopt similarly loose restrictions for their own use of force, which could destabilize not only their neighbors but also threaten American interests. It could also encourage states like Iran and North Korea to more actively seek to acquire WMDs to avoid becoming the "next Iraq." The unilateralist approach can also be counterproductive by weakening multilateral institutions that favor the strength of U.S. influence, by encouraging allies to cooperate to limit U.S. activities, by encouraging "rogue states" to form anti-American coalitions, by weakening international treaties that are supported by the United States, such as the Nuclear Non-Proliferation Treaty,[7] and by discouraging others from cooperating with an "untrustworthy" United States. Unilateral action is not always the wrong choice but it might be better to "make a clear presumption, as the elder Bush did, in favour of multilateralism."[8]

Idealism

The long-term objective of any state's foreign policy is to acquire friends and allies by promoting one's own ideology or worldview. Not surprisingly, then, the idealist program of American foreign policy calls for active engagement with the rest of the world for the purposes of spreading democracy and free markets. Two assumptions inform this idealist agenda. The first assumption is that democratic states and international free trade are likely to lead to more cooperation and less conflict in the world, which is a way of saying that capitalist democracies are stable and peaceful. The second assumption is that capitalist democracies share the same worldview and are thus natural allies against nondemocratic states and forces. Both free market forces and democracy, in this view, can solve international political problems for the United States. By promoting democracy and free trade around the world, the United States is engaging in the long-term objective of securing a stable political order, which suits its needs as the lone superpower, while at the same time increasing the pool of likely allies. As one observer put it, the "spread of liberty and democracy around the world is a U.S. national security interest."[9]

Idealism in American foreign policy, however, is nothing new.[10] From almost the very beginning, the United States strived to set itself apart from the states of Europe by adopting a moral tone in its foreign policy. Woodrow Wilson has become the historical icon of idealism in international relations, having promoted liberal values and cooperative solutions to world problems in the face of skeptical European diplomats and a reluctant American Congress. As early as the Carter administration, promoting democracy became a hallmark of U.S. foreign policy. Under Reagan, it reached its rhetorical zenith and the importance of spreading free trade became more pronounced than it had been during the Cold War. Of course, the promotion of international free trade and free market systems was the basis for the entire post-war international economic system developed at the Bretton Woods meetings during World War II and led by the United States.

This does not mean, of course, that any of these administrations, including the current Bush administration, is purely devoted to the spread of democracy and the free market to the exclusion of all other concerns. During the Cold War, various administrations calculated the importance of promoting either based on the perceived risks regarding the Soviet threat, leading to U.S. support for various dictators around the world and efforts to restrict trade with those states failing to adopt capitalist economic principles. Indeed, critics of the Bush administration's foreign policy have been quick to condemn its support for dictatorships around the world in return for support in the War on Terrorism.[11] Likewise, the decision to impose steel tariffs in 2002 was clearly a step back for the United States as the champion of international free trade. Nonetheless, the Bush administration clearly promotes strains of American idealism in its approach to foreign policy. The National Security Strategy, for example, begins by pointing out that there is only one "model for national success—freedom, democracy, and free enterprise."[12]

Francis Fukuyama has identified the idealist strain in the administration's Middle East policy by pointing out that a "variety of administration spokesmen and advisers have suggested that a different government in Iraq will change the political dynamics of the entire region, making the Israeli-Palestinian conflict more tractable, putting pressure on authoritarian regimes in Egypt, Syria, Iran and Saudi Arabia, and broadly promoting the cause of democracy in a hostile part of the world that has proven stubbornly resistant to all democratic trends."[13] The belief behind these suggestions is that promoting democracy in the Middle East will eventually lead to a region of stable, pliant, and friendly states. The faith in this approach extends, therefore, to the heart of the war against terrorism. In the short term, the United States is doing all it can to hinder the activities of al-Qaeda and other terrorist networks through a wide range of active and passive counterterrorism techniques. In the long term, some in the Bush administration believe that the root causes of terrorism are best removed by spreading democracy and capitalism.[14]

One of the key differences from earlier approaches to this strain of idealism is the means by which the Bush administration is seeking to spread both democracy and free markets. In the past, administrations have relied for the most part on U.S. influence and multilateral institutions, such as the United Nations, the World Trade Organization, and the World Bank, for promoting democracy and capitalism. The new administration has, not surprisingly, resorted to unilateral approaches. The prominence of regime change through force in administration thinking is a case in point. On only rare occasions since World War II has the United States directly involved its military forces to overthrow the government of another country and neither has it been attempted with a country the size of Iraq until now. In addition, an example was made of Iraq, which is now being used to implicitly threaten other authoritarian governments to reform or face a similar U.S. action. This approach is somewhat reminiscent of the Reagan administration's support for anti-Communist guerrillas, who were not always democratic. The Clinton administration relied on linking American aid to reform or used engagement to encourage reform without actually punishing authoritarian governments such as China.

While few Americans would argue the desirability of the outcomes suggested by an idealist foreign policy, there are some concerns that should be highlighted. A prominent criticism is that there seems to be more rhetoric than policy to American ideals about democracy. In addition to supporting various dictators who aid the United States in its fight against terrorism, the American track record regarding its promises to spread democracy is not good. In places like Haiti and Bosnia, successes have been marginal. In Afghanistan, some see evidence that the United States has neither the will nor the capability to bring democracy and prosperity—as promised at the time of the invasion.[15] The argument that the United States should spread democracy and can succeed in a project to recast the world in its own image is not unique to the Bush administration.[16] Not everyone, however, is convinced that achieving democracy in Afghanistan or Iraq is likely to be achieved. While some might argue that culture or religion in the region prevents the adoption of democratic principles and institutions, it is far more persuasive to make the argument that the practical obstacles to achieving democracy are so great as to make the project's success unlikely. Neither Afghanistan nor Iraq has a history of liberal constitutionalism, especially as characterized by a rule of law, or the large entrepreneurial middle class normally associated with democratic development, or even a recent experience with pseudo-democratic parliamentary institutions that would suggest they are as prepared for democratic institutions as even Japan and Germany were after World War II. Furthermore, it is at best unclear as to whether or not capitalism actually brings with it prosperity. In other words, as laudable as idealist foreign policy goals are, there are many reasons to doubt their success.

Looking Ahead: A New Era of Cooperation?

Has Bush's unilateralism ruined America's relations with the rest of the world? Is the Transatlantic Partnership formed between the United States and Europe after World War II permanently on the rocks? While some on both sides of the Atlantic argue that the partnership is ended, and even that it is good for both sides, this seems very unlikely. Not only do the United States and Europe share a great deal in common in terms of values, goals, and national interests but the importance of trade between the two will almost certainly always bring them back together again.[17] Indeed, within weeks of the end of the war in Iraq, there were already signs that both sides wanted to heal the wounds and carry on, through compromise if necessary. Signs of cooperation, and even hints of multilateralism, are already emerging in discussions for the reconstruction of Iraq and the handling of the Israeli-Palestinian peace process.

Europe and the rest of the world will remain suspicious, however, and there is no sign that the Bush administration has abandoned its preference for the unilateral approach, so the relationship will likely remain rocky, and the disadvantages of that approach will continue to complicate U.S. foreign policy. Likewise, the administration is certain to continue its policy of promoting democracy and free markets around the world as a long-term means to securing American national security. Their success in the latter will likely be determined by how determined and successful they are in achieving the former.

REFERENCES

Bergsten, C. Fred. November/December 2002. "A Renaissance for U.S. Trade Policy?" *Foreign Affairs* 81(6).

Busby, Joshua W. March 2003. "Climate Change Blues: Why the United States and Europe Just Can't Get Along," *Current History* 102(662).

Carothers, Thomas. January/February 2003. "Promoting Democracy and Fighting Terror," *Foreign Affairs* 82(1).

Clarke, Michael, and Brian White, eds. 1990. *Understanding Foreign Policy: The Foreign Policy Systems Approach.* Brookfield: Gower Publishing Company.

Diamond, Larry. June/July 2003. "Universal Democracy?" *Policy Review* (119).

Dumbrell, John. July 2002. "Unilateralism and 'America First'? President George W. Bush's Foreign Policy," *The Political Quarterly* 73(3).

Dunn, David Hastings. March 2003. "Myths, Motivations, and 'Misunderestimations': The Bush Administration and Iraq," *International Affairs* 79(2).

Gordon, Philip. January/February 2003. "Bridging the Atlantic Divide," *Foreign Affairs* 82(1).

Hirsh, Michael. September/October 2002. "Bush and the World," *Foreign Affairs* 81(5).

McFaul, Michael. April/May 2002. "The Liberty Doctrine," *Policy Review* (112).

National Security Strategy of the United States of America (White House document). September 2002.

Perkovich, George. March/April 2003. "Bush's Nuclear Revolution," *Foreign Affairs* 82(2).

Record, Jeffrey. Spring 2003. "The Bush Doctrine and War with Iraq," *Parameters* XXXIII(1).

Serfaty, Simon. March 2003. "Europe Enlarged, American Detached?" *Current History* 102(662).

Van Oudenaren, John. February/March 2003. "What Is 'Multilateral'?" *Policy Review* (117).

Walker, Martin. Summer 2001. "Bush's Choice: Athens or Sparta," *World Policy Journal* XVIII(2).

Zakaria, Fareed. November/December 1997. "The Rise of Illiberal Democracy," *Foreign Affairs* 76(6).

Endnotes

1. Throughout this chapter, references to the Bush administration should be read as referring to George W. Bush's administration, which began in early 2001. Any references to the earlier administration of George H.W. Bush (1989–1993) will be clearly identified as such.

2. David Hastings Dunn, "Myths, Motivations, and 'Misunderestimations': The Bush Administration and Iraq," *International Affairs* 79(2) (March 2003): 283.

3. A similar but shorter definition is given in John Dumbrell, "Unilateralism and 'America First'? President George W. Bush's Foreign Policy," *The Political Quarterly* 73(3) (July 2002): 284.

4. Walker has referred to the differing traditions of State and Defense as Athenian and Spartan, respectively, arguing that the State Department traditionally seeks cooperation and compromise through multilateral institutions and bilateral talks, while the Defense Department prefers unilateral solutions, which do not undermine U.S. sovereignty. Martin Walker, "Bush's Choice: Athens or Sparta," *World Policy Journal* XVIII(2) (Summer 2001).

5. The U.S. Congress had declined to ratify it and there was only lukewarm support for it among European governments, many of which had also not ratified the Protocol. On the other hand, European voters were more supportive, which may indicate why the decisions aroused so much resentment in Europe.

6. Dunn, 286.

7. George Perkovich, "Bush's Nuclear Revolution," *Foreign Affairs* 82(2) (March/April 2003).

8. Dumbrell, 284.

9. Michael McFaul, "The Liberty Doctrine," *Policy Review* (112) (April/May 2002): 5.

10. McFaul has termed America's ideological approach the "liberty doctrine" and has developed a thorough definition of it in urging the Bush administration to embrace idealism more fully. See Michael McFaul, "The Liberty Doctrine," *Policy Review* (112) (April/May 2002).

11. Though not especially critical, Thomas Carothers has thoroughly covered the Bush administration's record in this regard. Thomas Carothers, "Promoting Democracy and Fighting Terror," *Foreign Affairs* 82(1) (January/February 2003).

12. National Security Strategy, 1.

13. He originally made this argument in an editorial that appeared in the *Wall Street Journal* in December 2002. Francis Fukuyama, "Beyond Our Shores," http://www.opinionjournal. com/ac/?id=110002988. A similar point is made by Dunn, 290.

14. Obviously, the administration places a great deal of faith in the capacity for free market reform to promote prosperity. Free markets, however, have not proven a guarantee for success.

15. Carothers, 87–88.

16. Indeed, theorists also argue that liberal democracy can be and is spread by the actions of the United States, Europe, the United Nations, and other key actors in the international system. Even scholars such as Diamond and Zakaria, who disagree somewhat on what should be emphasized, fundamentally agree that the United States should encourage the spread of liberal democracy. (See "Universal Democracy?" by Diamond and "The Rise of Illiberal Democracy" by Zakaria.)

17. See Serfaty and Gordon.

Security and Terrorism
in the Twenty-First Century

LEENA THACKER–KUMAR AND JOEL R. CAMPBELL

Few, if any, issues in recent years have received as much attention as the threat of terrorism and weapons of mass destruction. Leena Thacker-Kumar and Joel Campbell put these terms in perspective and teach us that many of the dangers these threats pose have been part of human history for a very long time. However, the face of terrorism, like technology and political issues, has changed over time. The authors provide an overview of the origins of terrorism and the threats of weapons of mass destruction. Ultimately, they tell us, the war on terrorism may be a struggle that is here to stay.

The September 11, 2001, attacks by terrorists against the very icons of American economic and political power was viewed as an unprecedented event in U.S. history.* In subsequent months, many observers felt that 9/11 was a watershed event. As CNN put it, on September 11, "the world changed." Previously, America had seen only isolated instances of terrorism on its soil, most notably the 1995 bombing of the Federal Building in Oklahoma City by Timothy McVeigh, and a previous World Trade Center bombing in 1993. At the time, these acts seemed to be solitary acts of either psychologically disturbed individuals or fringe political groups, and had only limited political consequences. The September 11 Incident was for America and the world an act of previously unseen scale and audacity.

After the shock of the attacks, with strong congressional support President George W. Bush declared "War on Terrorism" and war against the countries that harbored terrorists. The U.S. government quickly blamed the attack on the al-Qaeda network of anti-American Muslim extremists loosely led by Osama Bin Laden, a Saudi citizen who had fought against the Soviet occupation of Afghanistan in the 1980s, and then worked closely with the country's ultra-conservative Muslim government in the 1990s known as the Taliban. Bin Laden saw America as the enemy of Islam due to its unstinting support for Israel, its organization of sanctions against Iraq following the First Gulf War (1991), and its basing of military personnel in Saudi Arabia, site of Islam's holiest shrines. He intended al-Qaeda (meaning "the base" in Arabic) as an umbrella organization for various Muslim struggles around the world. Al-Qaeda blew up a U.S. housing facility in Saudi Arabia in 1996 and two U.S. embassies in East Africa in

---

*The 24,000 gallons of aviation fuel in planes that were scheduled for transcontinental flights turned the aircraft into powerful missiles.

1998, and severely damaged the U.S. Navy destroyer *Cole* in Yemen in 2000. Within six weeks of the 9/11 incident, the United States and the United Kingdom attacked Afghanistan to destroy both al-Qaeda bases and the Taliban government, and the country was declared secure by the end of 2001.

Afghanistan may have been purged of Bin Laden's forces, but the al-Qaeda was not finished. Bin Laden was not captured or killed, and appeared in several clandestine videos. A spectacular bombing of two nightclubs crowded with Western tourists on the resort island of Bali in October, 2002, was quickly linked to Jama'ah Islamiyah, a band of Indonesian Muslim radicals connected with al-Qaeda. Meanwhile, Bush shifted from pursuit of the War on Terrorism to "regime change" in Iraq, following his suggestion that Saddam Hussein's government was both a source of weapons of mass destruction and a supporter of al-Qaeda. In March, 2003, the United States and the United Kingdom invaded Iraq, and declared the Hussein regime destroyed the next month. Like Bin Laden, Hussein was not found and apparently escaped. Just three weeks after the United States claimed victory in Iraq, al-Qaeda struck with major bombings in Riyadh, Saudi Arabia, and Casablanca, Morocco. The War on Terrorism continued, and no one knew when it would end.

What Is Terrorism?

The root of the term *terrorism* lies in the Latin word *terrere,* meaning "to frighten." Inducing fear is the clear intent of all those who commit acts of terror, yet the word *terrorism* has been used very loosely. Casual review of newspaper or television news coverage indicates that terrorism can refer to diverse acts, including the car bombings of buildings, the massacre of civilians by rogue military units, or the poisoning of medicine on supermarket shelves. Thus, it is very difficult to define terrorism, and there is no universally accepted definition of it. Alex Schmidt made a list of 100 definitions of terrorism and felt none of them were all inclusive.

The Oxford dictionary defines terrorism as "a policy intended to strike with terror those against whom it is adopted; the employment of methods of intimidation; the fact of terrorizing or being terrorized." While this definition accurately points out the fear-inducing quality of terrorism, it is too sweeping to merely apply the term to almost any action that scares us. The United Nations has tried hard to define terrorism, most notably after the 1972 Olympic massacre in Munich.* Neither developed nor developing nations can agree on which groups should be labeled as terrorists. Governments routinely brand antigovernmental guerrilla groups as terrorists. Some experts from developing countries point out that groups opposed to regimes holding power, which may be perceived as

---

*Terrorists claiming to be from Black September, a Palestinian guerrilla group, killed two Israelis and took nine hostage. The terrorists demanded the release of 200 Arab guerrillas jailed in Israel and safe passage for themselves and the hostages.

oppressive, should not necessarily be categorized as terrorist. They feel that people who struggle to liberate themselves from domestic or foreign oppression and exploitation have the right to use all methods at their disposal.

Even within the U.S. government, there are at least three definitions of terrorism. The Department of State, the Federal Bureau of Investigation (FBI), and the Department of Defense (DOD) each has a different take on terrorism. The State Department defines terrorism as premeditated, politically motivated violence perpetrated against noncombatant targets by subnational groups or clandestine agents, usually intended to influence an audience. The FBI, on the other hand, classifies terrorism as an unlawful use of force of violence against persons or property to intimidate a course of government, the civilian population, or any segment thereof in furtherance of political and social objectives. Finally, the DOD defines terrorism as the unlawful use of, or threatened use of, force of violence against individuals or property to intimidate governments or societies, often to achieve political, religious, or ideological objectives. Ultimately, definitions of terrorism most commonly center on four basic elements: (i) an act of violence, (ii) driven by a political goal or motive, (iii) perpetrated against innocent people, and (iv) staged or played out before an audience whose reaction of fear and terror is the desired result.

It should be noted that the labeling of a person or group as terrorist is in the eye of the beholder. It is often said that "one person's terrorist is another's freedom fighter." Many governments have been formed by revolutionary or nationalist groups that used extreme violence in their struggles against the regimes that they replaced. Once in office, the former "terrorists" were elevated to the status of national heroes. Twentieth century statesmen once branded as terrorists include Cuba's Fidel Castro, Vietnam's Ho Chi Minh, China's Mao Zedong, Israel's Menachem Begin, and South Africa's Nelson Mandela.

Causes of Terrorism

Why do some people become terrorists? Are they crazy? Are they fanatics, ideologues, or thrill seekers? Can one delineate a terrorist personality type? Political scientists and psychologists who have studied personality traits of known terrorists failed to find a clear terrorist type. Scholars of terrorism most commonly list as motivators a strong sense of grievance, perceived inequality and unfairness within a society, and general conditions of poverty in a country. However, many noted terrorists have come from middle-class and privileged backgrounds. In fact, there are no clear personality types who are more likely to turn to terrorism.

Hacker (1976) suggests three categories of persons who resort to terrorism: crazies, criminals, and crusaders. He notes that these are not exclusive or "pure," but each category provides some insight into why individuals resort to terrorism. Understanding these categories allows for more effective counterterrorist policies and tactics. "Crazies," or emotionally disturbed individuals, commit acts for "reasons of their own that often make no sense to anybody else" (Hacker, 1976: 8). Examples include assassins without political affiliations or mass killers claiming political justification for their crimes. Conversely, criminals engage in terrorist acts for personal gain. They often use tactics centering on personal gain, such as kidnapping for ransom. This type has been common in Latin America and more recently in the Philippines. The "narco-terrorists" of Colombia use terror and guerrilla tactics to protect their illegal drug businesses, and sometimes ally with antigovernmental guerrilla groups. Crusaders, Hacker contends, do not seek personal gain, but work to attain a collective end, and so commit terrorist acts for a "higher cause." These are the well-known terrorists active in postwar Western Europe or the Middle East. Knowing the type of terrorist with whom they are dealing can help law enforcement to determine appropriate tactics. A criminal is much more likely to talk to police or private negotiators and could be more easily induced to release hostages than either a "crazy" or a crusader.

Some scholars have tried to create a profile of a terrorist. O'Balance (1979) offers several essential characteristics of "successful" terrorists. These include dedication to a cause, seeking to become *fedayeen* (men of sacrifice), personal bravery because of the possibility of death or injury, and lack of pity or remorse because most victims are innocent men, women, and children. The terrorist belief system often centers on a few essential elements: (1) dehumanization of an enemy, (2) responsibility for bringing about major change because the masses do not understand important political or social issues, that is, terrorists believe in their own righteousness, and therefore, (3) the terrorist struggle is not a choice but a duty, and use of violent means implies not murder of innocents, but execution of traitors.

In order to craft effective counterterrorist measures, one must understand the reasons that lead people to take radical actions. Combs (2003) suggests a variety of factors that may lead a person toward terrorism:

Religious fanaticism. The increased popularity of religious fundamentalism around the world has been accompanied by the rise of violent organizations with politico-religious agendas. While most fundamentalists eschew violence, fringe groups with fundamentalist religious beliefs go further. Prominent examples are the Muslim al-Qaeda network operating in the Middle East, Africa, and South and Southeast Asia, Christian abortion clinic bombers and snipers in the United States, and Jewish terrorists in Israel and the West Bank.

Anarchism. This began in nineteenth century Europe, when groups perpetrated acts of violence to destroy all government. They were most active in Russia and Spain, but a few groups today follow this violent ideology. Nihilism, which seeks to destroy all social structures, is the most extreme form of anarchism and finds some adherents among Western European nationalists.

Neo-fascism, Neo-Nazism, and militia and survivalist movement. Various groups in Western Europe and the United States embrace Neo-Nazi or far right-wing ideas. In the United States, the Aryan Nations and several of its splinter groups, including the Christian Identity Movement and Christian Patriots, have been involved in violent activities. Some of these groups overlap the antigovernmental, millenarian militia and survivalist groups of the 1990s.

Separatist movement. Such groups seek to form a nation based on shared ethnicity, culture, or religion in an area controlled by a larger nation-state. These include the ETA, a Basque separatist movement; the FLQ, a French-Canadian separatist organization; the Abu-Sayaf Group in the Philippines, which seeks a separate Muslim nation on the island of Mindanao.

Nationalism. These are groups fighting for the rights of a particular nationality or ethnic group, or to form a new government within a nation. The Irish Republican Army (IRA), the Tupamoros of Uruguay, and Sendero Luminoso (or Shining Path) in Peru are examples of nationalist groups. However, it is sometimes difficult to distinguish separatism, nationalism, and leftist ideology as motivators of such groups. Sendero Luminoso, for instance, is often described as a Maoist group that seeks to establish a hard-line agrarian-based society in Peru.

Issue-oriented terrorism. During the latter part of the twentieth century, various forms of issue orientation have aroused militant violent sentiments that have led to terrorist violence in service of strongly held beliefs, for example, the environmentalist Earth Liberation Front and the anti-abortion Operation Rescue.

Ideological mercenaries. This refers to terrorists-for-hire. The legendary Ilyich Ramirez Sanchez, popularly known as "Carlos the Jackal," and Sabri al-Banna (Abu Nidal) are the most famous examples of ideological mercenaries.

Pathological terrorists. Some people kill and terrorize for the apparent enjoyment of violence, or for a muddled cause or belief. Charles Manson, leader of a "family" of young followers, supposedly believed that his murderous spree in 1969 would lead to an American racial civil war, from which he would emerge leader of a new nation (Combs, 2003).

Psycho-group dynamism. By being a member of a group, one may feel psychological pressure to accept or indulge in violent group behavior. People who otherwise would not consider violent means to achieve their goals may participate in it due to group dynamics (Rubenstein, 2003).

Whatever the motivations, two key facts dominate the thinking of most terrorists. First, terrorists use violence because they feel it is the only way to gain attention, to put their concerns on the national or international agenda, in order to attain their objectives. Some people call terrorism "the poor man's atomic bomb." Second, people use terrorism because, unfortunately, *it works*. Small acts of violence can have far-reaching effects, and they often induce exactly the sort of terror or paralysis intended. For example, in 1983, a truck bomb killed over 230 U.S. Marines at a barracks outside Beirut, Lebanon. A few weeks later, U.S. President Reagan withdrew the Marines from Lebanon—exactly the intended goal of the terrorists.

Terrorism Through History

Terrorism is not a new phenomenon. It can be traced back to the ancient world, and the label *terrorism* has been applied to various kinds of acts. Incidents of political terror can be seen in ancient Greece and the Roman Republic. The assassinations of Julius Caesar in 44 B.C., Caligula in A.D. 41, and Claudius in A.D. 54 were acts of terror carried out by, respectively, politicians, military officers, and family members of an emperor. Modern use of the term *terrorism* emerged from an act committed by the state, the execution of Queen Marie Antoinette on October 16, 1793. The Jacobian regime under Maximilien Robespierre who governed France in 1793–1794 was called the "Reign of Terror." Nonetheless, there are two striking similarities between Jacobian and modern terrorism. In both cases, terrorism is organized, deliberate, and systematic, and its goal and its very justification is to create a "new and better society" in place of a perceived corrupt political system.

Much of early post–World War II terrorism was related to the process of decolonization. Terrorism found its first postwar battleground in the British-controlled territory of Palestine. Jewish extremists, such as Irgun and the Stern Gang, attacked British facilities and killed soldiers to try to force the United Kingdom to give up control and allow the creation of a Jewish state. After the declaration of the state of Israel in 1947, neighboring Arab countries invaded, and both Jewish and Arab groups used widespread terror killings to force the other side to vacate land. By the 1960s, Palestinian activists had formed the Palestinian Liberation Organization (PLO), an umbrella organization for various groups fighting against Israel, including several that used terrorist methods. Another early terrorist struggle gripped the French colony of Algeria, where both pro- and anti-independence groups used widespread terror, until the frustrated French left following an independence plebiscite in 1962.

Terrorism first emerged as a major international concern in the 1960s, but during the 1970s and 1980s, it became associated with a series of spectacular incidents intended to awe the world with daring tactics. Most of these were connected with the Arab-Israeli struggle in the Middle East or extreme leftist politics in Western Europe, which in turn were shaped by the background of the ongoing Cold War between the United States and the Soviet Union. The Popular Front for the Liberation of Palestine (PFLP) hijacking and blowing up of jetliners in the Jordanian desert in 1970 was the first of these incidents, followed by the Black September kidnapping and killing of Israeli athletes at the 1972 Olympics, Carlos the Jackal's kidnapping of representatives of the Organization of Petroleum Exporting Countries (OPEC) in Vienna in 1975, and the Palestinian Liberation Front seizure of the *Achille Lauro* cruise ship in 1985. Lebanon's civil war of the 1980s saw the kidnapping by Muslim groups of several Westerners who were working in the country. In some cases, these captives were held for several years. Meanwhile, European nationalist or separatist groups such as the Irish Republican Army (IRA) and the Basque ETA organization carried on long-term bombing and assassination campaigns against European governments. Leftist organizations such as Italy's Red Brigades and Germany's Baader-Meinhof Gang organized spectacular kidnappings, assassinations, and robberies.

So far, the twenty-first century has witnessed two emerging trends. First, there has been a dramatic decline in formation of terrorist groups, but this is unrelated to the level of terrorist activity. Second, the causes of terrorism are narrowing. A heterogeneous collection of groups advocating social revolutionary, secular nationalist, and radical right-wing causes in the 1970s has largely given way to a collection of groups with religiously inspired agendas. There are a number of differences between religious and secular terrorism, but perhaps the most significant distinction is that while secular terrorists are often constrained by political, moral, or practical considerations, religious terrorists tend to view violence as a sacramental act or divine duty, and consequently see few constraints on their actions.

Modern Challenges in Confronting Terrorism

Weapons of Mass Destruction

Today there are a variety of daunting challenges for those confronting terrorism in the twenty-first century. Foremost among these challenges is the threat of weapons of mass destruction (WMD). The term *WMD* usually refers to biological, chemical, and nuclear weapons. Concern over Saddam Hussein's supposed WMD programs and alleged links to terrorist organizations served as the *casus belli* when the United States and the United Kingdom invaded Iraq in 2003. Once thought impossible, the notion that terrorists could obtain weapons of mass destruction now must be taken seriously.

Somewhere between thirty and forty countries have the capacity to manufacture biological weapons, many of which are incredibly lethal and difficult to trace. This makes such weapons very dangerous in the hands of terrorists. Biological weapons can cause a variety of sickness, ranging from relatively mild ailments like exhaustion, stomach pain, and diarrhea, to excruciating death by asphyxiation or massive internal hemorrhaging (Combs, 2003).

Biological warfare has been used by many countries since ancient times. In the sixth century B.C., the Assyrians poisoned enemy wells with rye ergot, a biological agent. In the fourteenth century, the Mongols were pioneers of biological warfare. They spread the bubonic plague by catapulting infected corpses over castle or city walls, causing the disease to spread, sow panic, and kill thousands. North America saw use of biological warfare as early as the 1760s, when infected blankets with smallpox were given as "peace offerings" to Native Americans in Pennsylvania.

Bio-war became more frequent in the twentieth century. During World War I, Germany was accused of spreading cholera in Italy, plague in St. Petersburg, and anthrax in Mesopotamia and Romania. During the Japanese invasion of China in 1937, fleas infected with the plague, smallpox, typhus, and gas gangrene were added to wheat distributed in China. The Japanese Army Unit 731 in Manchuria also conducted hideous bio-war experiments on live subjects. In December 1990, the Iraqis filled bombs with botulinal toxin, anthrax, and aflatoxin and deployed them at four locations. Anthrax remains a salient threat since it was sent through the mail shortly after the 9/11 Incident, mostly in the United States, by a yet unknown perpetrator (Schmid, 2000).

Chemical weapons also pose a grave threat. One of the greatest dangers of chemical weapons is that most materials needed to make them have legitimate uses and can be easily obtained. Chemical agents are classified according to the symptoms they cause, and the main types are blistering, nerve, blood, choking, and harassing agents. Blistering agents include mustard gas and lewisite, which cause chemical burns and destroy lung tissue. Nerve agents such as sarin gas, soman, and VX cause paralysis of the neuromuscular system and can result in death. Blood agents block the blood supply to the brain, causing cardiac arrest, and include arsine, cyanogens chloride, and hydrogen chloride. Choking agents, which cause the lungs to close and induce pulmonary edema, include phosphene and chlorine gas.

Chemical weapons are greater in number, relatively easy to acquire, and are inexpensive to manufacture. Nonetheless, they are not easily manufactured in the quantities needed for large-scale attacks, nor are they easy to disperse. Major symptoms caused by chemical attacks vary from blistering skin or burning eyes, coughing, respiratory difficulties, dizziness, nausea, drowsiness, headache, convulsions, involuntary defecation and urination, twitching, jerking, and miosis (Combs, 2003).

The first use of chemical weapons by a terrorist group was by Aum Shinri Kyo, a Japanese religious cult, which released sarin nerve gas into the Tokyo subway system during morning rush hour in 1995. The attack killed eleven and injured over 5,500 people. Although chemical weapons are extremely lethal and easily accessible, they are not easy to disperse and might not cause large-scale casualties. If terrorists want to send a psychological message and induce terror, chemical weapons can be quite effective. If they want to create a lot of damage, they would have to choose another weapon.

Nuclear weapons rely on elemental chain reactions to create huge blast, heat, and radiation effects, destroying vast areas and killing thousands of people. They have only been used twice; in 1945, the United States dropped two nuclear bombs (then called "atomic bombs") on the Japanese cities of

Hiroshima and Nagasaki. The shock effect of the bombings, along with Soviet entry into the war in East Asia, brought World War II to an end. Nuclear devices are the most difficult weapons of mass destruction to manufacture because of the expensive and hard-to-acquire materials that are needed for production. Either plutonium or enriched uranium is required to produce a nuclear bomb, but currently only seven countries are known to have this technology: the United States, Russia, the United Kingdom, France, China, India, and Pakistan.* In 2002–2003, North Korea admitted it has been working on both plutonium and uranium-based weapons, while Iran and Iraq, until the fall of Saddam Hussein, have apparently had nuclear weapons development programs. Due to the fall of the Soviet Union in 1991 and limited resources of the post–Soviet Russian Federation, nuclear technology and materials may have become more accessible to terrorist groups.

If a nuclear device were used by a terrorist organization, the casualties and consequences could be mind-boggling. Terrorists might use a stolen or purchased nuclear missile or bomb to blackmail a government. Rather than risk the destruction of a city, the government may feel it has no choice but to negotiate terrorist demands. However, neither acquisition nor handling of a nuclear weapon would be easy for poorly organized political groups lacking technical expertise. More likely to be used could be a "dirty bomb," that is, a conventional bomb (or car bomb) that would spread radiation or radioactive particles over a large area. It might be possible to make such a weapon by collecting radioactive waste from hospitals or medical research facilities. Exploded in a densely crowded urban area, a dirty bomb would be an ideal terror weapon.

Strategic Intelligence

The lack of intelligence may be the most serious shortcoming in efforts to defeat terrorism. Acquiring intelligence is vital to acting decisively to disarm or destroy terrorists and terror organizations. It involves several phases, from planning, collection, and processing to analysis and dissemination. Intelligence professionals call this the "intelligence cycle." Central to discussion of the intelligence cycle is the need to change from the Cold War confrontation with communist countries to dealing with terrorist organizations.

During the Cold War, human spy networks were gradually neglected and the intelligence community became overly impressed with satellite surveillance and other "machinery" that cannot look into caves, through tent roofs, or into mud huts. HUMNIT (human intelligence), or use of secret agents, is the only way to get deep into a terrorist organization and find out what it may be

---

*Israel also is widely believed to possess several nuclear weapons, mainly as a deterrent against invasion by the armies of neighboring Arab nations. For various political and strategic reasons, the Israeli government refuses to confirm or deny the existence of these weapons. Other nations, especially South Africa, Argentina, Brazil, Taiwan, and South Korea, have given up development of nuclear weapons.

planning. Another concern is the conversion of information from original non-English sources or visual materials into easily interpreted data. The cacophony of telephone intercepts and satellite photographs available to Western governments is useless unless the state can actually move fast and with sufficient skill. Information collected must be studied for insights in an attempt to predict future events. In order for the intelligence reports to be useful, accurate analysis must be distributed to the decision-makers in a timely fashion, that is, in time to act and prevent so that they are not "overtaken by events" (Johnson, 2003).

Any attempt to deal with effectively with terrorism would require a multi-layered approach. It takes more than military strength to control terrorism. A lasting Middle East peace and the construction of effective alliances between nations are key to dealing with contemporary terrorism. Al-Qaeda would find far fewer recruits if Muslim grievances against the West were adequately addressed. Immediately after the 9/11 Incident, while the international community sympathized with U.S. suffering, Bush emphasized the creation of an international coalition to fight terrorism. Many Europeans and Asians resented Bush's us vs. them rhetoric, but were willing to cooperate with the United States. That coalition largely fell apart when in 2002 Bush shifted his focus to the removal of Saddam Hussein. Any future counterterrorist attempt will require effective partnerships among nations.

Threats to Civil Liberties and Civil Rights

One of the most worrisome aspects of any counterterrorism campaign is the curtailment of citizens' normal activities that governments feel is necessary to stop terrorists. The tough measures necessitated by antiterror campaigns may make democratic governments less willing to protect civil liberties and civil rights, and force citizens to accept such changes. For instance, as a result of the IRA campaign against British rule of Northern Ireland from the 1970s to 1990s, British citizens have become used to tight security checks and more vigorous antisubversive activities of MI5, Britain's domestic intelligence organization, and other government organizations. As a result of the 9/11 Incident, U.S. airline passengers willingly put up with intrusive airport personal and luggage searches, as well as the presence of armed soldiers in most major airports.

After the attack on Afghanistan in 2001, various alleged Taliban and al-Qaeda figures were detained by U.S. forces, and shipped to the U.S. military base in Guantanamo, Cuba. These prisoners were denied the rights of prisoners of war under the Geneva Convention, and were not allowed basic due process of law granted to those accused of crimes in the United States. Some of them were forced to wear face masks and sit in animal cages. Despite widespread protests from various countries, the DOD continued to hold these people as prisoners without due process for many months. The U.S. government justified such treatment as necessary to obtain information about al-Qaeda's operations.

After the 9/11 Incident, the U.S. Congress passed the Patriot Act, which gave the government more power to fight terrorist organizations that might be operating in the United States. This includes increased ability to examine personal records, including library checkout records, of those who may be investigated for terrorist links. These changes trouble many Americans, and some local city councils have passed ordinances mandating noncompliance with the Patriot Act. Also, some observers have criticized U.S. government harassment and detention of foreigners in the wake of September 11. Many people wonder if fighting the war on terrorism means using methods that are as bad as those of terrorists, and if winning that war means sacrificing democratic freedoms. And if antiterrorism results in the destruction of democracy, have the terrorists won the ultimate victory?

Conclusion: A War without End?

Troubling to many observers is the diversion of societal resources that a war on terrorism entails. The Bush administration's response to the 9/11 Incident required allocations of between $100 and $200 billion, in order to aid struggling airlines, partially fund the reconstruction of the Manhattan business district in New York, assist the families of victims, create a new Department of Homeland Security, and prosecute wars in Afghanistan and Iraq. Even more was spent on tax cuts to help stimulate an economy that was still suffering from the effects of September 11. Huge budget surpluses projected by the Clinton administration in 2000, necessary to deal with looming deficits in the Social Security and Medicare funds, were replaced by massive deficits. These deficits are likely to continue for several years.

A "War on Terrorism" is not easy, and the struggle is likely to be a long one. Any "victory" over a terrorist organization comes only after intense intelligence gathering, criminal investigations, and perhaps military operations. The IRA campaign against British rule in Northern Ireland went on for over 25 years. Israel and its Palestinian opponents have been battling for over 50 years, and there is no end in sight. Will America's war against al-Qaeda continue for decades? *Time* magazine suggests as much. Since losing their training camps and several key leaders in Afghanistan, al-Qaeda has changed tactics. Its operatives dispersed to hideouts in Chechnya in southern Russia, Yemen, Georgia, and East Africa. Bin Laden is still at large, but the decentralized network apparently depends less on his leadership. Attacks remain sophisticated and well planned. Post-Iraq actions focused on Western targets within the Muslim world, which are cheaper to attack and more resented by local people. Al-Qaeda, like a virus or a mold, spreads opportunistically and without much central direction.* And like any virus or mold that invades the body (or country), it will only be defeated as each patient builds up sufficient defenses to overwhelm it.

---

*Michael Elliott, "Why the War on Terror Will Never End," *Time* (Asian edition), May 26, 2003, pp. 18–25.

References

Combs, Cindy. 2003. *Terrorism in the Twenty-First Century,* 3rd ed. Englewood Cliffs, NJ: Prentice Hall.

Elliott, Michael. 2003. "Why the War on Terror Will Never End." *Time* (Asian edition): 18–25.

Hacker, Frederick. 1976. *Crusaders, Criminals, Crazies: Terror and Terrorism in Our Time.* New York: W.W. Norton.

Henderson, Harry. 2001. *Terrorism,* Facts on File Inc.

Hoffman, Bruce. 1998. *Inside Terrorism.* New York: Columbia University Press.

Johnson, Loch. 2003. "Strategic Intelligence: The Weakest Link in the War against World Terrorism." In Charles W. Kegley Jr., ed., *The New Global Terrorism; Characteristics, Causes, Controls,* Englewood Cliffs, NJ: Prentice Hall.

O'Balance, Edgar. 1979. *The Language of Violence: The Blood Politics of Terrorism.* San Rafael, CA: Presidio.

Pedahzur, A., William Eubank, and Leonard Weinberg. 2002. "The War on Terrorism and the Decline of Terrorist Group Formation: A Research Note," *Terrorism and Violence* 14: 141–147.

Rubenstein, Richard. 2003. "The Psycho-Political Sources of Terrorism." in Charles W. Kegley Jr., ed., *The New Global Terrorism; Characteristics, Causes, Controls,* Englewood Cliffs, NJ: Prentice Hall.

Schmidt, Alex. 2000. "Terrorism and the Weapons of Mass Destruction: From Where the Risk." In M. Taylor and J. Horgan, eds., *The Future of Terrorism,* London: Frank Cass Publishers.

Combat Operations in Iraq Have Ended
PRESIDENT GEORGE W. BUSH

The following text is a speech delivered by President George W. Bush on May 1, 2003, while aboard the USS Abraham Lincoln, *off the coast of San Diego, California. The setting was meticulously planned by the White House to maximize the political advantage for Bush: The president flew onto the aircraft carrier aboard a fighter jet and delivered the speech while surrounded by cheering military personnel against the backdrop of a large sign emblazoned "Mission Accomplished."*

My fellow Americans: major combat operations in Iraq have ended. In the battle of Iraq, the United States and our allies have prevailed. And now our coalition is engaged in securing and reconstructing that country.

In this battle, we have fought for the cause of liberty, and for the peace of the world. Our nation and our coalition are proud of this accomplishment—yet, it is you, the members of the United States military, who achieved it. Your courage, your willingness to face danger for your country and for each other, made this day possible. Because of you, our nation is more secure. Because of you, the tyrant has fallen, and Iraq is free.

Operation Iraqi Freedom was carried out with a combination of precision and speed and boldness the enemy did not expect, and the world had not seen before. From distant bases or ships at sea, we sent planes and missiles that could destroy an enemy division, or strike a single bunker. Marines and soldiers charged to Baghdad across 350 miles of hostile ground, in one of the swiftest advances of heavy arms in history. You have shown the world the skill and the might of the American Armed Forces.

This nation thanks all the members of our coalition who joined in a noble cause. We thank the Armed Forces of the United Kingdom, Australia, and Poland, who shared in the hardships of war. We thank all the citizens of Iraq who welcomed our troops and joined in the liberation of their own country. And tonight, I have a special word for Secretary Rumsfeld, for General Franks, and for all the men and women who wear the uniform of the United States: America is grateful for a job well done.

The character of our military through history—the daring of Normandy, the fierce courage of Iwo Jima, the decency and idealism that turned enemies into allies—is fully present in this generation. When Iraqi civilians looked into the faces of our servicemen and women, they saw strength and kindness and goodwill. When I look at the members of the United States military, I see the best of our country, and I'm honored to be your Commander-in-Chief.

In the images of falling statues, we have witnessed the arrival of a new era. For a hundred of years of war, culminating in the nuclear age, military technology was designed and deployed to inflict casualties on an ever-growing scale. In defeating Nazi Germany and Imperial Japan, Allied forces destroyed entire cities, while enemy leaders who started the conflict were safe until the final days. Military power was used to end a regime by breaking a nation.

Today, we have the greater power to free a nation by breaking a dangerous and aggressive regime. With new tactics and precision weapons, we can achieve military objectives without directing violence against civilians. No device of man can remove the tragedy from war; yet it is a great moral advance when the guilty have far more to fear from war than the innocent.

In the images of celebrating Iraqis, we have also seen the ageless appeal of human freedom. Decades of lies and intimidation could not make the Iraqi people love their oppressors or desire their own enslavement. Men and women in every culture need liberty like they need food and water and air. Everywhere that freedom arrives, humanity rejoices; and everywhere that freedom stirs, let tyrants fear.

We have difficult work to do in Iraq. We're bringing order to parts of that country that remain dangerous. We're pursuing and finding leaders of the old regime, who will be held to account for their crimes. We've begun the search for hidden chemical and biological weapons and already know of hundreds of sites that will be investigated. We're helping to rebuild Iraq, where the dictator built palaces for himself, instead of hospitals and schools. And we will stand with the new leaders of Iraq as they establish a government of, by, and for the Iraqi people.

The transition from dictatorship to democracy will take time, but it is worth every effort. Our coalition will stay until our work is done. Then we will leave, and we will leave behind a free Iraq.

The battle of Iraq is one victory in a war on terror that began on September the 11, 2001—and still goes on. That terrible morning, 19 evil men—the shock troops of a hateful ideology—gave America and the civilized world a glimpse of their ambitions. They imagined, in the words of one terrorist, that September the 11th would be the "beginning of the end of America." By seeking to turn our cities into killing fields, terrorists and their allies believed that they could destroy this nation's resolve, and force our retreat from the world. They have failed.

In the battle of Afghanistan, we destroyed the Taliban, many terrorists, and the camps where they trained. We continue to help the Afghan people lay roads, restore hospitals, and educate all of their children. Yet we also have dangerous work to complete. As I speak, a Special Operations task force, led by the 82nd Airborne, is on the trail of the terrorists and those who seek to undermine the free government of Afghanistan. America and our coalition will finish what we have begun.

From Pakistan to the Philippines to the Horn of Africa, we are hunting down al-Qaeda killers. Nineteen months ago, I pledged that the terrorists would not escape the patient justice of the United States. And as of tonight, nearly one-half of al-Qaeda's senior operatives have been captured or killed.

The liberation of Iraq is a crucial advance in the campaign against terror. We've removed an ally of al-Qaeda, and cut off a source of terrorist funding. And this much is certain: No terrorist network will gain weapons of mass destruction from the Iraqi regime, because the regime is no more.

In these 19 months that changed the world, our actions have been focused and deliberate and proportionate to the offense. We have not forgotten the victims of September the 11th—the last phone calls, the cold murder of children, the searches in the rubble. With those attacks, the terrorists and their supporters declared war on the United States. And war is what they got.

Our war against terror is proceeding according to principles that I have made clear to all: Any person involved in committing or planning terrorist attacks against the American people becomes an enemy of this country, and a target of American justice.

Any person, organization, or government that supports, protects, or harbors terrorists is complicit in the murder of the innocent, and equally guilty of terrorist crimes.

Any outlaw regime that has ties to terrorist groups and seeks or possesses weapons of mass destruction is a grave danger to the civilized world—and will be confronted.

And anyone in the world, including the Arab world, who works and sacrifices for freedom has a loyal friend in the United States of America.

Our commitment to liberty is America's tradition—declared at our founding; affirmed in Franklin Roosevelt's Four Freedoms; asserted in the Truman Doctrine and in Ronald Reagan's challenge to an evil empire. We are committed to freedom in Afghanistan, in Iraq, and in a peaceful Palestine. The advance of freedom is the surest strategy to undermine the appeal of terror in the world. Where freedom takes hold, hatred gives way to hope. When freedom takes hold, men and women turn to the peaceful pursuit of a better life. American values and American interests lead in the same direction: We stand for human liberty.

The United States upholds these principles of security and freedom in many ways—with all the tools of diplomacy, law enforcement, intelligence, and finance. We're working with a broad coalition of nations that understand the threat and our shared responsibility to meet it. The use of force has been—and remains— our last resort. Yet all can know, friend and foe alike, that our nation has a mission: We will answer threats to our security, and we will defend the peace.

Our mission continues. Al Qaeda is wounded, not destroyed. The scattered cells of the terrorist network still operate in many nations, and we know from daily intelligence that they continue to plot against free people. The proliferation of deadly weapons remains a serious danger. The enemies of freedom are not idle, and neither are we. Our government has taken unprecedented measures to defend the homeland. And we will continue to hunt down the enemy before he can strike.

The war on terror is not over; yet it is not endless. We do not know the day of final victory, but we have seen the turning of the tide. No act of the terrorists will change our purpose, or weaken our resolve, or alter their fate. Their cause is lost. Free nations will press on to victory.

Other nations in history have fought in foreign lands and remained to occupy and exploit. Americans, following a battle, want nothing more than to return home. And that is your direction tonight. After service in the Afghan—and Iraqi theaters of war—after 100,000 miles, on the longest carrier deployment in recent history, you are homeward bound. Some of you will see new family members for the first time—150 babies were born while their fathers were on the Lincoln. Your families are proud of you, and your nation will welcome you.

We are mindful, as well, that some good men and women are not making the journey home. One of those who fell, Corporal Jason Mileo, spoke to his parents five days before his death. Jason's father said, "He called us from the center of Baghdad, not to brag, but to tell us he loved us. Our son was a soldier."

Every name, every life is a loss to our military, to our nation, and to the loved ones who grieve. There's no homecoming for these families. Yet we pray, in God's time, their reunion will come.

Those we lost were last seen on duty. Their final act on this Earth was to fight a great evil and bring liberty to others. All of you—all in this generation of our military—have taken up the highest calling of history. You're defending your country, and protecting the innocent from harm. And wherever you go, you carry a message of hope—a message that is ancient and ever new. In the words of the prophet Isaiah, "To the captives, 'come out,'—and to those in darkness, 'be free.'"

Iraq War Was Unprovoked Invasion of a Sovereign Nation

SENATOR ROBERT BYRD

The following text is a speech delivered by United States Senator Robert Byrd (Democrat-West Virginia) on the floor of the Senate on May 21, 2003. Sen. Byrd is considered the Dean of the Senate Democrats, an honorary title granted to one of the most senior and leading members. A frequent critic of the Bush administration, Sen. Byrd is known as a skilled orator and passionate champion of the Senate's rules, traditions, and history.

Truth has a way of asserting itself despite all attempts to obscure it.

Distortion only serves to derail it for a time. No matter to what lengths we humans may go to obfuscate facts or delude our fellows, truth has a way of squeezing out through the cracks, eventually.

But the danger is that at some point it may no longer matter. The danger is that damage is done before the truth is widely realized. The reality is that, sometimes, it is easier to ignore uncomfortable facts and go along with whatever distortion is currently in vogue. We see a lot of this today in politics. I see a lot of it—more than I would ever have believed—right on this Senate Floor.

Regarding the situation in Iraq, it appears to this senator that the American people may have been lured into accepting the unprovoked invasion of a sovereign nation, in violation of long-standing international law, under false premises.

There is ample evidence that the horrific events of September 11 have been carefully manipulated to switch public focus from Osama bin Laden and al-Qaida who masterminded the September 11th attacks, to Saddam Hussein, who did not.

The run-up to our invasion of Iraq featured the president and members of his cabinet invoking every frightening image they could conjure, from mushroom clouds, to buried caches of germ warfare, to drones poised to deliver germ laden death in our major cities. We were treated to a heavy dose of overstatement concerning Saddam Hussein and his direct threat to our freedoms. The tactic was guaranteed to provoke a sure reaction from a nation still suffering from a combination of post traumatic stress and justifiable anger after the attacks of 9/11. It was the exploitation of fear. It was a placebo for the anger.

Since the war's end, every subsequent revelation which has seemed to refute the previous dire claims of the Bush administration has been brushed aside.

Instead of addressing the contradictory evidence, the White House deftly changes the subject. No weapons of mass destruction have yet turned up, but we are told that they will in time. Perhaps they yet will. But, our costly and destructive bunker busting attack on Iraq seems to have proven, in the main, precisely the opposite of what we were told was the urgent reason to go in. It seems also to have, for the present, verified the assertions of Hans Blix and the inspection team he led, which President Bush and company so derided. As Blix always said, a lot of time will be needed to find such weapons, if they do, indeed, exist. Meanwhile bin Laden is still on the loose and Saddam Hussein has come up missing.

The administration assured the U.S. public and the world, over and over again, that an attack was necessary to protect our people and the world from terrorism. It assiduously worked to alarm the public and blur the faces of Saddam Hussein and Osama bin Laden until they virtually became one.

What has become painfully clear in the aftermath of war is that Iraq was no immediate threat to the U.S. Ravaged by years of sanctions, Iraq did not even lift an airplane against us. Iraq's threatening death-dealing fleet of unmanned drones about which we heard so much morphed into one prototype made of plywood and string. Their missiles proved to be outdated and of limited range. Their army was quickly overwhelmed by our technology and our well-trained troops.

Presently, our loyal military personnel continue their mission of diligently searching for weapons of mass destruction. They have so far turned up only fertilizer, vacuum cleaners, conventional weapons, and the occasional buried swimming pool. They are misused on such a mission and they continue to be at grave risk. But, the Bush team's extensive hype of WMD in Iraq as justification for a pre-emptive invasion has become more than embarrassing. It has raised serious questions about prevarication and the reckless use of power. Were our troops needlessly put at risk? Were countless Iraqi civilians killed and maimed when war was not really necessary? Was the American public deliberately misled? Was the world?

What makes me cringe even more is the continued claim that we are "liberators." The facts don't seem to support the label we have so euphemistically attached to ourselves. True, we have unseated a brutal, despicable despot, but "liberation" implies the follow up of freedom, self-determination and a better life for the common people. In fact, if the situation in Iraq is the result of "liberation," we may have set the cause of freedom back 200 years.

Despite our high-blown claims of a better life for the Iraqi people, water is scarce, and often foul, electricity is a sometime thing, food is in short supply, hospitals are stacked with the wounded and maimed, historic treasures of the region and of the Iraqi people have been looted, and nuclear material may have been disseminated to heaven knows where, while U.S. troops, on orders, looked on and meanwhile, lucrative contracts to rebuild Iraq's infrastructure and refurbish its oil industry are awarded to administration cronies, without benefit of competitive bidding, and the U.S. steadfastly resists offers of U.N. assistance to participate.

Is there any wonder that the real motives of the U.S. government are the subject of worldwide speculation and mistrust? And in what may be the most damaging development, the U.S. appears to be pushing off Iraq's clamor for self-government. Jay Garner has been summarily replaced, and it is becoming all too clear that the smiling face of the U.S. as liberator is quickly assuming the scowl of an occupier. The image of the boot on the throat has replaced the beckoning hand of freedom. Chaos and rioting only exacerbate that image, as U.S. soldiers try to sustain order in a land ravaged by poverty and disease. "Regime change" in Iraq has so far meant anarchy, curbed only by an occupying military force and a U.S. administrative presence that is evasive about if and when it intends to depart.

Democracy and freedom cannot be force fed at the point of an occupier's gun. To think otherwise is folly. One has to stop and ponder. How could we have been so impossibly naive? How could we expect to easily plant a clone of U.S. culture, values, and government in a country so riven with religious, territorial, and tribal rivalries, so suspicious of U.S. motives, and so at odds with the galloping materialism which drives the western-style economies? As so many warned this administration before it launched its misguided war on Iraq, there is evidence that our crack-down in Iraq is likely to convince 1,000 new bin Ladens to plan other horrors of the type we have seen in the past several days. Instead of damaging the terrorists, we have given them new fuel for their fury. We did not complete our mission in Afghanistan because we were so eager to attack Iraq. Now it appears that al-Qaida is back with a vengeance. We have returned to orange alert in the U.S., and we may well have destabilized the Mideast region, a region we have never fully understood. We have alienated friends around the globe with our dissembling and our haughty insistence on punishing former friends who may not see things quite our way. The path of diplomacy and reason have gone out the window to be replaced by force, unilateralism, and punishment for transgressions. I read most recently with amazement our harsh castigation of Turkey, our longtime friend and strategic ally. It is astonishing that our government is berating the new Turkish government for conducting its affairs in accordance with its own Constitution and its democratic institutions.

Indeed, we may have sparked a new international arms race as countries move ahead to develop WMD as a last-ditch attempt to ward off a possible preemptive strike from a newly belligerent U.S. which claims the right to hit where it wants. In fact, there is little to constrain this president. This Congress, in what will go down in history as its most unfortunate act, gave away its power to declare war for the foreseeable future and empowered this president to wage war at will.

As if that were not bad enough, members of Congress are reluctant to ask questions which are begging to be asked. How long will we occupy Iraq? We have already heard disputes on the numbers of troops which will be needed to retain order. What is the truth? How costly will the occupation and rebuilding be? No one has given a straight answer. How will we afford this long-term massive commitment, fight terrorism at home, address a serious crisis in domestic healthcare, afford behemoth military spending and give away billions in tax cuts amidst a deficit which has climbed to over $340 billion for this year alone?

If the president's tax cut passes, it will be $400 billion. We cower in the shadows while false statements proliferate. We accept soft answers and shaky explanations because to demand the truth is hard, or unpopular, or may be politically costly.

But, I contend that, through it all, the people know. The American people unfortunately are used to political shading, spin, and the usual chicanery they hear from public officials. They patiently tolerate it up to a point. But there is a line. It may seem to be drawn in invisible ink for a time, but eventually it will appear in dark colors, tinged with anger. When it comes to shedding American blood—when it comes to wrecking havoc on civilians, on innocent men, women and children, callous dissembling is not acceptable. Nothing is worth that kind of lie—not oil, not revenge, not re-election, not somebody's grand pipe dream of a democratic domino theory.

And mark my words, the calculated intimidation which we see so often of late by the "powers that be" will only keep the loyal opposition quiet for just so long. Because eventually, like it always does, the truth will emerge. And when it does, this house of cards, built of deceit, will fall.

Polarization and Partisanship
in the Modern Congress

CRAIG GOODMAN

If you think politicians increasingly ignore the views of the "average" person, Craig Goodman might tell you that you may be right. Using sophisticated statistical techniques that have analyzed thousands of Congressional votes over time, scholars have found that members of Congress are ever more partisan and, consequently, Capitol Hill is a deeply polarized institution. These profound political differences have made governing more difficult and increased the importance of money in the political process. Sharp differences between the parties continue, and despite his pledge to work in a bipartisan fashion, George W. Bush has proven to be a deeply polarizing figure. Goodman suggests that intense political divisions are here to stay.

Traditional explanations for how the United States Congress operates presented in most basic American government textbooks are no longer accurate. The descriptions of the "textbook" Congress (Shepsle, 1989) where members of Congress introduce legislation and the proposed bills work their way through the legislative process until they reach a vote on final passage no longer exists. Instead, the textbook process of government has been replaced with resurgent levels of polarization and partisanship in Congress, which have resulted in fewer compromises as both parties attempt to pursue their political agenda. The consequences of polarization and partisanship are profound because the differences between Democrats and Republicans have widened to such levels that finding accommodation between the two parties has become nearly impossible.

While it has become more difficult to craft policies that can command agreement from all actors, the increased levels of partisanship have also resulted in a number of organizational changes in Congress as both sides pursue their legislative agenda. Most of these organizational changes have occurred in the House of Representatives, which is a majoritarian institution, but Senate rules, which protect the rights of individual senators, are threatened as well because of increased partisanship in that chamber. These changes in the United States Congress are representative of broader changes that have occurred in American politics and the consequences of higher levels of polarization go beyond affecting legislation alone. Heightened partisanship and polarization has resulted in a greater emphasis on campaign fundraising because there are fewer congressional districts that are legitimately considered competitive. Much has changed in the United States Congress during the last ten years and the Republican successes in the 1994 election helped propel forward many of the existing trends. In 2003, the United States Congress can best be understood as an institution that is very polarized and partisan.

Moving Toward the Extremes

The increased levels of polarization that we have observed during the last two decades are not a new phenomenon. Despite the relatively recent focus on polarization, some scholars have argued that polarization has been increasing in the United States since the 1970s. Examining the roll call behavior of United States senators, Poole and Rosenthal (1984) suggest that senators representing the same state, but from different parties, voted very differently in an effort to appeal to certain constituencies. The basic logic behind the study of polarization is that the preferences of members of Congress have become more homogenous over time. By examining roll call votes across American political history, Poole and Rosenthal (1997) developed a scale that allows us to classify members of Congress as liberal or conservative. The scores these researchers developed range from −1.0 (very liberal) to +1.0 (very conservative) and effectively reflect the partisan divide in the United States, since these scores are closely correlated with party loyalty. Republicans generally have ideological scores on the positive side of zero while Democrats tend to have scores on the negative side of zero. By computing these scores across time, scholars can examine the degree of political polarization in the United States Congress. Recent figures indicate that the gap between the two parties has continued to increase and there are few members clustered near the midpoint (zero), who might be considered moderates. Over the last two decades, Democrats have become more liberal and Republicans have become more conservative (Barone, Cohen, and Ujifusa, 2001). In short, both parties are tilting more to their extremes.

The increased levels of polarization in the United States are reflective of other broad changes that have occurred in the United States during the last fifty years. One of the most important trends has been the increasing competitiveness, if not dominance, of the Republican Party in the South. The former states of the Confederacy had almost always been a solid bloc that the Democratic Party could count on in Congress. As a result of the Civil Rights Movement and eventually the passage of the 1965 Voting Rights Act, the composition of the Southern electorate changed dramatically. The increased number of African Americans drove many conservative, white southerners from the Democratic Party to the Republican Party (Black and Black, 2002). In 1948, Democrats held more than 98 percent of Southern congressional seats, but by 2000 that number had fallen to less than 45 percent (Black and Black, 2002).

In addition to the changes in the South, there is also evidence that voters in the electorate have become more conservative as well. Using the National Election Study, Jacobson (2000) argues that voters have also become more ideologically distinct particularly the most partisan supporters in each party. This trend toward the growing polarization of voters can be confirmed by looking at the number of congressional districts with split results. In the 2000 election, only 19.8 percent of districts were carried by presidential candidate of one party and a House candidate of another party. This represents a dramatic decline from the early 1970s (Ornstein, Mann, and Malbin, 2002).

A final issue to consider as a source of growing polarization is the lack of competitive districts in congressional elections. Redistricting has tended to create districts that are drawn to protect one party or the other and limits the ability of quality challengers to face incumbents (Cox and Katz, 2002) and have placed the courts in position as key arbiters of congressional redistricting when state legislatures are not successful in redrawing district boundaries.

The increased polarization has had an important impact on congressional parties, especially in the House of Representatives. By any number of measures, the differences between the parties have grown dramatically. As mentioned previously, the Poole and Rosenthal ideological scores provide evidence that the two parties in Congress have become more distinct. Additionally, party unity scores, which represent the percentage of votes in which an individual supports his/her party on party votes, has increased dramatically. In 2000, House Democrats on average supported their party 86 percent of the time and House Republicans supported their party 90 percent of the time. The patterns are similar in the Senate where Democrats supported their party 90 percent of the time and Republicans supported their party 91 percent of the time (Ornstein, Mann, and Malbin, 2002). These scores represent dramatic increases since the 1970s.

By either measure, the differences between Democrats and Republicans in Congress have increased and this has resulted in important changes within the legislative process. While the parties have become more alike internally, it does not mean that all members vote automatically along party lines. There are a few members in the House of Representatives from districts that would seem to favor the other party, but representatives from these districts typically take positions that are consistent with the preferences of their constituents. For example, Representative Tim Holden (D) represents a central Pennsylvania district (the 17th) that is quite conservative and on core social issues Holden often votes against his party (Harwood, 2002b) if he wants to remain a member of the House of Representatives. The electoral connection has not disappeared; however, these kinds of members who have defied the growing polarization of American political politics are rare (Mayhew, 1974).

Perhaps the most significant change that has occurred in Congress is that power within each of the parties has become increasingly centralized and the party leadership plays a more active role in the lawmaking process and in making organizational decisions. The willingness of party members to delegate greater powers to its leadership is conditional, which means that as the parties become more homogenous, this increases the likelihood that party members will grant more powers to the leadership and other party organizations in an effort to achieve outcomes favored by the majority party (Rohde, 1991). Additionally, there are benefits for members to delegate responsibility to their leaders because it allows members of the party to run on a party label that enhances their probability of winning reelection (Cox and McCubbins, 1993). In order for party leaders to successfully guide their parties and prevent members from working at cross-purposes with the party goals, they need increased control over resources that members desire, such as prized committee assignments as well as control of the legislative agenda. While the party leadership may have more power now than they did twenty years ago, party leaders must also be successful if they are to maintain their positions.

The typical flow diagram in American Government textbooks that illustrates how a bill becomes a law is not completely accurate. Legislation no longer travels in a direct line from introduction to committee consideration to final passage (Sinclair, 2000). Instead, there are a wide variety of tools available for congressional leaders to use in order to pass legislation and successful leaders are increasingly relying on these unorthodox tactics, such as restrictive rules and multiple referral, to accomplish their legislative goals. Following passage of the Legislative Reorganization Act in 1946, congressional committees and their chairmen played important roles in the legislative process by controlling the flow of legislation to the floor. However, reforms in the 1970s increased the number of subcommittees and allowed more members to play an active role in the legislative process. In the 1980s and early 1990s, the growing homogeneity within the parties resulted in an increase in powers granted to the leadership. While seniority continues to be an important factor in committee assignments, it no longer is a guarantee. It has become increasingly common for parties to violate seniority in appointing committee chairs and the leadership has taken a much more active role in approving committee and subcommittee chairs (Koszczuk, 1996). While committee chairs have lost ground in the legislative process under the new lawmaking procedures, such tactics as multiple referral and post-committee adjustments have weakened the power of committees to shape legislation.

The Rise of the Republican Majority

These trends toward polarization and partisanship and increased use of unorthodox tactics of lawmaking were occurring simultaneously with other developments in Washington. Perhaps the most prominent development was Representative Newt Gingrich's (R-GA) efforts to build a conservative Republican Party by opposing congressional Democrats at every turn. Gingrich's strategy was to weaken Democratic incumbents by forcing them to vote on amendments that involved divisive political issues, such as school prayer and abortion rights. Gingrich's plans were well-received by Republicans who had been frustrated by their minority status in the House of Representatives. In addition to challenging Democrats on legislative issues, Gingrich also engaged in activities to build the conservative wing of the Republican Party. After becoming the head of GOPAC, which was a Republican political action committee, Gingrich began recruiting conservative Republicans to run for state and local offices and develop a "farm system" of experienced Republican challengers, who would be supportive of the party's cause in future elections (Dodd and Oppenheimer, 2001).

Gingrich's efforts culminated in 1994 when Republicans regained control of the House of Representatives for the first time since 1952 by gaining 52 seats. The first order of business for Speaker Gingrich and the Republican majority was passing the Contract with America, which was a list of ten Republican legislative priorities that the party hoped to pass during the first 100 days of the new Congress. While the House passed many elements of the Contract with America, most stalled in the Senate. Eventually, Republican plans for reducing the size of the federal government by reducing the federal budget ran into problems. By the fall and winter of 1995, the Republican Congress and President Clinton were engaged in a showdown over the size of the budget that eventually resulted in the federal government shutting down. While the budget dispute was eventually resolved, by all accounts President Clinton saved his presidency and the momentum that House Republicans had was broken (Dodd and Oppenheimer, 2001).

In addition to pursuing a more conservative legislative agenda, the Republican victory in 1994 also resulted in major organizational changes as well. On the first day of the 104th Congress, congressional Republicans enacted rules changes that reduced the number of congressional committees, placed term limits on committee chairs, and term limits for the Speaker of the House (Cloud, 1995). One of the other major changes Speaker Gingrich pushed for was using the Appropriations Committee and its subcommittees to enact major policy changes since they controlled funding for many programs Republicans wanted to reduce (Aldrich and Rohde, 2000). While the use of the Appropriations Committee for policy changes decreased after the failed budget strategy in 1995, the House leadership in the 108th Congress has again focused on the Appropriations Committee as the vehicle to enact major changes in public policy. The most notable change is that the GOP Steering Committee, consisting of leading Republicans, must now approve all Appropriations subcommittee chairs, which the Appropriations Committee chair traditionally appointed (Cohen, Victor, and Baumann, 2003). Since becoming Speaker of the House in the 106th Congress, Dennis Hastert (R-IL) has continued to amass power in the Speaker's office by having the ability to control the flow of legislation as well as no longer having to deal with the term limits imposed in 1994 (Cohen, 2003; Billings and Crabtree, 2003). Hastert's power is often understated compared to House Majority Leader, Tom DeLay (R-TX), but Hastert has accumulated a great deal of support among Republicans by managing the agenda to their benefit (Broder, 2003b).

Many of the changes that have occurred during the past decade have had a more dramatic impact on the House of Representatives. As the more majoritarian institution, the House of Representatives has generally been more successful in passing the president's legislative agenda in the 107th Congress and in the early days of the 108th Congress. Much of the reason that the House has been more successful is that more power is concentrated within the majority party leadership and they have been able to use the tools at their disposal to pass legislation relatively quickly. The House has been successful in passing tax cuts, legislation creating a Department of Homeland Security, a budget for 2003, and legislation that would allow drilling for oil in the Arctic National Wildlife Refuge. The same cannot be said for the Senate.

The ability of the majority party to completely control the agenda in the Senate is much more limited. While there are advantages to being in the majority, the Senate is characterized by greater concerns for individual members' rights, which place important constraints on the lawmaking process (Binder, 1997). When the 108th Congress convened, despite having a majority, Republicans have found it very difficult to govern for a number of reasons and it will not be an easy task for the Senate Majority Leader, Bill Frist (R-TN), to find common ground and consensus with Senate Democrats (Hunt, 2003; Ornstein, 2003). One reason for this is recent history; Republicans want to avoid having members switch parties like Senator James Jeffords (I-VT) did in May 2001 and giving Democrats control of the Senate. The early debate over tax cuts in 2003 highlighted some of the tensions among Senate Republicans as a number of moderates forced a compromise on the size of the bill. A second reason is the Senate's long history of minority rights, which makes it more difficult for the majority party to pass legislation because of individual prerogatives like the filibuster and the need for unanimous consent to move legislation to the floor. Passage of legislation generally requires greater levels of bipartisanship in the Senate.

The Polarization Continues

As Republicans pursued their agenda in the 108th Congress, it became clear that the Democrats were committed to using their procedural rights to oppose the GOP. One prominent example is of this is the Democratic efforts to filibuster contentious judicial nominees like Miguel Estrada and Priscilla Owens. As a consequence of these rules, the Senate has been transformed into a supermajority institution that requires 60 votes to pass controversial legislation and confirm nominees, with the exception of budget bills, because of the threat of filibusters and this makes the legislative process increasingly difficult (Dewar, 2003).

While the Congress remains highly partisan and very polarized, it has increased the importance of campaign contributions and congressional elections. The amount of money it costs to win elections to the House and Senate has greatly increased. In 2000, it cost nearly $850,000 to win a seat in the House of Representatives and nearly $7.4 million to win a U.S. Senate seat (Ornstein, Mann, and Malbin, 2002).

As a result of the increased need for money, many members of Congress are engaged permanently in campaign mode. In addition to their lawmaking responsibilities, many lawmakers from the time they are elected begin the process of fundraising for their next election (Corrado, 2000). While candidates are constantly engaged in chasing campaign contributions, very few congressional districts are legitimately in play. Most districts are safely Republican or Democratic, leaving the battle for majority control in a small number of districts (Harwood, 2002a). In these so-called "toss-up" districts, large amounts of money are being spent not only by the candidates themselves, but by each party's congressional campaign committee, and various interest groups (Harwood, 2002c). Besides the large amounts of money being spent in competitive districts, President George W. Bush and his advisors played an important role in recruiting Republican candidates in 2002 for those races, helping them raise money, and campaigning with them during the latter days of the campaign (Cummings and Hamburger, 2002).

While President Bush was very successful in helping his party gain seats in the 2002 midterm election, it has also had an important impact on legislative-executive relations. In 2001, President Bush reached out to key Democrats in order to win support for his package of tax cuts, but later campaigned against some of those Democrats in 2002 creating ill will among Democrats (Weisman and Milbank, 2003). In 2003, President Bush has been very active in using his political capital to "go public" and attempt to pressure members of Congress to support his legislative agenda (Kernell, 1997). The president's insistence on such strategies will make it increasingly difficult for Republicans to pass legislation because many Democrats are looking for confrontations with the Bush administration in anticipation of the 2004 presidential campaign.

At the start of the 108th Congress, respected *Washington Post* columnist David Broder (2003a) predicted that despite the pledges of bipartisanship from both sides, it would not happen. The increased levels of polarization and partisanship have had a significant impact on governance in the United States as both parties become tilted toward their extremes, it becomes much more difficult to find any middle ground and produce public policies. In many respects, politics in the United States has become a contact sport as both parties try to raise as much money as possible and do everything in their efforts to defeat the other side.

When President Bush was elected, one of his goals was to change the tone of politics in Washington, but it has not happened. In fact, politics has become even more partisan than it was before. Therefore, what happens in Washington is likely to be less compromise and more obstruction, and polarization and partisanship are an important fact of life in modern congressional politics. Political parties tend to exert the most influence over procedural issues (rules for debate) and issues that define the two parties, such as the size of government (Cox and Poole, 2002; Ansolabehere, Snyder, and Stewart, 2001). But on other issues, such as gun control, members are often free to vote their conscience. While party pressures are not constant, the race to raise campaign funds and planning for future elections will continue to complicate life for members of Congress.

References

Aldrich, John H. 1995. Why Parties? *The Origin and Transformation of Political Parties in America.* Chicago: University of Chicago Press.

Aldrich, John H., and David W. Rohde. 2000. "The Republican Revolution and the House Appropriations Committee," *Journal of Politics* 62(2): 1–33.

———. 2001. "The Consequences of Party Organization in the House: The Role of Majority and Minority Parties in Conditional Party Government." In Jon R. Bond and Richard Fleisher (eds.), *Polarized Politics: Congress and the President in a Partisan Era.* Washington, DC: Congressional Quarterly Press.

Ansolabehere, Stephen, James M. Snyder, Jr., and Charles Stewart, III. 2001. "The Effects of Party and Preferences on Congressional Roll Call Voting," *Legislative Studies Quarterly* 26(4): 533–572.

Barone, Michael, Richard E. Cohen, and Grant Ujifusa. 2001. *The Almanac of American Politics.* Washington, DC: National Journal.

Billings, Erin P., and Susan Crabtree. 2003. "House Rules Spark Fight," *Roll Call,* January 8.

Binder, Sarah. 1997. *Minority Rights, Majority Rule: Partisanship and the Development of Congress.* New York: Cambridge University Press.

Black, Earl, and Merle Black. 2002. *The Rise of Southern Republicans.* Cambridge, MA: Harvard University Press.

Broder, David S. 2003a. "Don't Bet on Bipartisan Niceties," *Washington Post,* January 1.

———. 2003b. "'Accidental Speaker' Hidden in Sight." *Washington Post,* January 17.

Cloud, David. 1995. "GOP, to its Own Great Delight, Enacts House Rules Changes," *Congressional Quarterly Weekly Report,* January 7.

Cohen, Richard E. 2003. "Remember Denny?" *National Journal,* January 11.

Cohen, Richard E., Kirk Victor, and David Baumann. 2003. "Republicans to Watch," *National Journal,* January 18.

Corrado, Anthony. 2000. "Running Backward: The Congressional Money Chase." In Norman Ornstein and Thomas Mann (eds.), *The Permanent Campaign and Its Future.* Washington, DC: American Enterprise Institute and The Brookings Institution.

Cox, Gary W., and Jonathan N. Katz. 2002. *Elbridge Gerry's Salamander: The Electoral Consequences of the Reapportionment Revolution.* New York: Cambridge University Press.

Cox, Gary W., and Keith T. Poole. 2002. "On Measuring Partisanship in Roll-Call Voting: The U.S. House of Representatives, 1877–1999." *American Journal of Political Science,* 46(3): 477–489.

Cox, Gary W., and Mathew D. McCubbins. 1993. *Legislative Leviathan: Party Government in the House.* Berkeley, CA: University of California Press.

Cummings, Jeanne, and Tom Hamburger. 2002. "How White House Crafted Win," *Wall Street Journal,* November 7.

Dewar, Helen. 2003. "Polarized Politics: A Senate Game of Tit for Tat," *Washington Post National Weekly Edition,* May 19–25.

Dodd, Lawrence C., and Bruce I. Oppenheimer. 2001. "The Struggle for Partisan Control, 1994–2000." In Dodd and Oppenheimer (eds.), *Congress Reconsidered* (7th ed). Washington, DC: Congressional Quarterly Press.

Harwood, John. 2002a. "Control of Congress Lies in a Few Races in Smaller Locales," *Wall Street Journal,* October 14.

———. 2002b. "Control of Congress May be Determined by Party Moderates," *Wall Street Journal,* October 23.

———. 2002c. "Money is Raining in Strange Places in Midterm Polls," *Wall Street Journal,* November 1.

Hunt, Albert R. 2003. "This Senate Won't be Any 'Saucer' in 2003," *Wall Street Journal,* January 9.

Jacobson, Gary C. 2000. "Party Polarization in National Politics: The Electoral Connection." In Jon R. Bond and Richard Fleisher (eds.), *Polarized Politics: Congress and the President in a Partisan Era.* Washington, DC: Congressional Quarterly Press.

Kernell, Samuel. 1997. *Going Public: New Strategies of Presidential Leadership,* 3rd ed. Washington, DC: Congressional Quarterly Press.

Koszczuk, Jackie. 1996. "Regained Footing," *Congressional Quarterly Weekly Report,* March 23.

Mayhew, David R. 1974. *Congress: The Electoral Connection.* New Haven, CT: Yale University Press.

Ornstein, Norman. 2003. "Margins Pose Big Challenges for Frist, Daschle," *Roll Call,* January 8.

Ornstein, Norman J., Thomas E. Mann, and Michael J. Malbin. 2002. *Vital Statistics on Congress, 2001–2002.* Washington, DC: AEI Press.

Poole, Keith T., and Howard Rosenthal. 1984. "The Polarization of American Politics," *Journal of Politics* 46(4): 1061–1079.

————. 1997. *Congress: A Political-Economic History of Roll Call Voting.* New York: Oxford University Press.

Rohde, David W. 1991. *Parties and Leaders in the Post-Reform House.* Chicago: University of Chicago Press.

Shepsle, Kenneth A. 1989. "The Changing Textbook Congress." In John E. Chubb and Paul Peterson (eds.), *Can the Government Govern?* Washington, DC: Brookings Institution Press.

Sinclair, Barbara. 2000. *Unorthodox Lawmaking: New Legislative Processes in the U.S. Congress,* 2nd ed. Washington, DC: Congressional Quarterly Press.

Victor, Kirk. 2003. "Challenges for Bill Frist," *National Journal,* January 11.

Weisman, Jonathan, and Dana Milbank. 2003. "Bush Tax Cut Drive: Heat Replaces Sweet," *Washington Post,* May 5.

The Impact of Term Limits in State Politics: A Case Study

ART ENGLISH

"What do you think of term limits?" To find answers to this question, Art English has participated in a research project that has gone directly to people inside the political process to find out their opinions. In doing so, we are provided a discussion of the potential merits and faults of term limits. Though limited at the national level by the Supreme Court's ruling in U.S. Term Limits v. Thornton, *the term limit movement has seen quite a bit of success at the state level throughout the United States. Though term limits have generally enjoyed a significant level of popular support, questions remain about the value of these electoral constraints and effects that they may have upon the democratic process once they are implemented.*

Introduction

The issue of term limits in American politics is extraordinarily controversial. Debated by the framers in our founding constitutional convention, enshrined in our Constitution by the Twenty-second Amendment, embedded in several state constitutions, the issue of term limits raises fundamental questions about political power, fundamental electoral fairness, and democratic theory. Term limits have always had implications for our political system and the large number of states that have adopted term limits in the past decade has made this even more dramatic. This article, which is part of a larger study being conducted by the National Conference of State Legislatures of both term limited and non-term limited states, takes a preliminary look at the origin, arguments for and against, and implications of term limits in a nonprofessional legislature state. Arkansas may not be representative of all of the states in which term limits has been introduced, but it does provide an interesting test case because of the citizen character of its legislature and the strictness of its term limits.

It is fair to say that the term limits movement surprised the Arkansas General Assembly before they could develop a strategy to oppose it. For years the Arkansas General Assembly had not enjoyed great confidence with the people of Arkansas despite its part-time citizen character. Public opinion polls have long indicated citizens, for numerous reasons, do not view legislatures favorably. The collective nature of legislatures, their complex agendas and rules, perceived as well as some actual corruption and scandal, have outweighed their few redeeming qualities in the eyes of the mass public. In short, legislatures have been easy to dislike and even hate. Indeed when a long dormant amendment that required an intervening election before a congressional pay raise could take effect was brought before the people, it was quickly ratified as the Twenty-seventh Amendment to our Constitution in 1992.

Ironically, the long sessions of the Arkansas General Assembly in the early portion of the twentieth century were partly responsible for term limits, as citizens dissatisfied with their legislature adopted the initiative and referendum process that eventually led to the adoption of the term limits amendment in 1992 (Ledbetter, 1993). Amendment 73 of the Arkansas Constitution, the term limits amendment, was part of movement—really a national movement on behalf of term limits in state legislatures throughout the nation: California, Michigan, Arkansas, Florida, and Maine to name just some of the states where term limit initiatives were introduced and adopted.

This national movement, U.S. Term Limits, Inc., was bipartisan in part with a Republican leadership core. Its major aim was to impose term limits on Congress with the state legislatures a satisfyingly secondary target. As the primary target, Congress has long been an unpopular institution with the mass public and political activists who believe it to be worse than just a necessary evil of government. As the argument goes, members of Congress make too much money while spending too much of the taxpayers' money. Members of Congress don't provide a tangible product. Congressional members often have a hard time proving their worth, especially when citizens viewing Congress in "action" on television see a handful of members debating arcane subjects. Legislatures are collective bodies and it is hard for legislators to get noticed or get credit in them. Most of their esteem comes from their frequent visits back to the home district where they meet and greet constituents. Polls have long shown that while many constituents believe their own member of Congress is doing a good job, they do not believe the institution as a whole merits approval.

Collectively legislative bodies have always had an uphill battle to win favor with the public (Rosenthal et al., 2003). Throw in the occasional legislative scandal and the seemingly never-ending attacks by the media and it is easy to understand an environment in which term limit initiatives could prevail. In fact, looking back to the late eighties and early nineties when the forces for term limits started their push, perhaps the most debilitating congressional scandal of the last 50 years—the check bouncing scandal—had recently been in the news, and two members of the Arkansas congressional delegation—Tommy Robinson (1984–1990) and Bill Alexander (1968–1992)—were two of the most flagrant offenders. Their preferred treatment (the House bank covered checks before their monthly salary was actually deposited) did not go unnoticed and it certainly contributed to the adoption of the term limits amendment in Arkansas by 60 percent of the voters.

Amendment 73 subjected Arkansas legislators to some of the most rigorous term limits in the nation: three two-year terms for members of the Arkansas House of Representatives and two four-year terms for members of the 35-person Arkansas Senate. Constitutional officers were limited two four-year terms. The length of the terms was further exacerbated by the fact that the biennial 60-day sessions of the Arkansas General Assembly theoretically limited house and senate members to only 180 and 240 session days, respectively, for their entire career if no special sessions were called or the existing legislative session was not extended by a two-thirds vote of the Assembly.

The limits on members of Congress were subtler but just as devastating to incumbents. Members of the House and Senate would not be able to have their names placed on the ballot after three and two terms, respectively. These ballot access limitations, generally upheld under state power by federal courts in the past, made it possible for incumbent members to be elected only by a write-in vote, a very improbable task for even a very popular incumbent. However, in *U.S. Term Limits, Inc., v. Thornton,*[1] which was an Arkansas case, the Supreme Court held in a 5–4 decision that the states lacked the reserved power to set qualifications for the national legislature, which were fixed in the Constitution. However, the power of the state to set term limits on their state elective office-holders was perfectly within the power of the people by constitutional amendment and never was really subjected to severe judicial scrutiny.

When Amendment 73 was adopted, its future impact on the Arkansas General Assembly was likely unclear to many of its members. Part of the reason was that its major effect would not be felt until the very late nineties. It is probably fair to say that some of the veteran legislators simply did not believe their legislative life would be over in the next six or eight years given the environment in which they had long worked. How could legislators, some of whom had been in office for over 20 years, believe that under term limits they would no longer be legislative players in just a bit over 180 days excluding special sessions and extensions? Perhaps a comparison might be similar to a person who despite serious illness does not believe it is his or her time to die.

Term Limits: Pros and Cons

The length of time before term limits was to take effect in Arkansas and in the rest of the states allowed the debate about the plusses and minuses of term limits to continue. Many arguments both for and against were made.

Those in favor of term limits suggested that term limits would allow for more competitive elections because they limit long-term incumbents. In Arkansas this was a particularly compelling argument for the Republican Party, which has long had difficulty in winning seats in the Arkansas General Assembly.

Term limits supporters also noted that term limits have been used for executive officials in other states. Why shouldn't then legislators be term-limited also? Of course, Amendment 73 did term-limit executive branch members in Arkansas also. However, in Arkansas this argument did not seem to carry a lot of currency. Constitutional officers in Arkansas had not been previously term-limited and with the notable recent exceptions of Orval Faubus, Bill Clinton, and Mike Huckabee, governors in Arkansas usually followed a two-term tradition.

U.S. Term Limits, Inc. v. Thorton, 514 U.S. 779 (1995).

On the other hand, Arkansas constitutional officers, almost always Democratic, often served for well over a decade, especially at the lower constitutional office end: land commissioner, state auditor, and treasurer.

Another argument in favor of term limits was that term limits would inject new blood and ideas into the legislature. Perhaps the most compelling of the arguments advanced by the proponents, this argument suggested that there were many talented people in the state who would now consider running for the legislature making the state the winner because of the new ideas and enthusiasm these talented people would bring to the legislative process.

It was also suggested that term limits would level the campaign playing field. This argument appealed to those who wished to limit the power of incumbency in elections and to an overall sense of fairness in the electoral process. This argument may have had more currency in Arkansas, which despite its citizen nature of its legislature has had a large number of veteran legislators over the years. For example, in 1981 over half the senate had served at least two terms and almost one third of the house had served over four terms (Paschall, 2001).

Term limit supporters also argued that limits would place merit over seniority. This was a very appealing argument to many citizens that focused on an important American cultural norm—that a person should advance in the legislature because of their merit not because of their longevity.

Backers of limits also contended that term limits would change the focus of legislators from lawmaking to reelection. This argument suggested that legislators who were not term-limited were more likely make reelection their main focus. As a consequence they would either spend too much time on electoral concerns or push policy that was election driven ignoring the real and important policy issues.

Yet another point made by term limit supporters was that limits would remove the cozy ties that legislators have with interest groups. This argument carried currency with attentive citizens and went to heart of a democratic political system. How could the people rule in Arkansas (the motto of the state is "The People Rule") if their interests are frequently subjected to those with the resources to lobby the legislators daily on-site, in the capitol corridors, in the restaurants, and through their campaign committees?

Furthermore, it was alleged that term limits would restore legislatures as citizen institutions. In Arkansas this argument had clout. The Arkansas General Assembly is often rightly described as a part-time citizens' legislature that meets only for 60 to 80 days biennially in the odd year. As legendary Director of the Bureaus of Legislative Research for the Assembly Marcus Holbrook once said: "The Arkansas General Assembly is a citizens' legislature. It is not and was not supposed to be a professional legislature" (English and Carroll, 1983).

Finally, backers of term limits suggested that term limits would result in more women, African Americans, and other minorities in the legislature, a goal that fits with the pluralistic promises of America.

While there were numerous arguments leveled in support of limiting terms of office, there were also many points made in opposition to term limits.

Opponents of limits contended that term limits are contrary to democratic theory. This argument says that the people are the ultimate judges of whether their representative ought to continue or not—not a mechanism in the state constitution that terminates a member's career in office simply because he or she has served six or eight years. One facet of this argument was not quite accurate however. Voters would still have the power to vote for or against a legislator Arkansas running for reelection. It is just that they would not have the power to vote for or against that legislator again once he or she completed their last term.

Those opposed to limiting terms also suggested that term limits are not needed because state legislative turnover is already high. In many states legislative turnover approaches if not exceeds 30 percent. While turnover in the Arkansas General Assembly has rarely if ever been that high, it has often exceeded 15 percent especially during elections after reapportionment. One of our respondents, a leader in the senate, ironically made this argument to illustrate in his case that incumbents do get beat so why are term limits needed?

Term limit foes argued that limits will strip the legislature of its institutional memory. Perhaps the most frequent and most compelling of the pro arguments, the essence of this argument is that new legislators simply don't have the experience, the time on the learning curve, and the senior members to rely on when they enter the complex world of state legislative budgets, education, and revenue issues. Legislators need experience to make good decisions. With term limits those who have grappled with the procedure, with the rules, and with the issues are suddenly gone, usually not to return unless it is to the other chamber.

Additionally, it was contended that term limits cede power to the executive branch. This argument posits that the legislative branch—especially if it is term-limited and the executive branch is not—loses its co-equal branch status. Again the argument is that a collective body without institutional memory and experience becomes a much weaker body when confronting an executive branch focused around the energies and direction of one person leading a unified administration. Proponents of this argument, usually legislators, argue that even if the governor is term-limited, he or she still has greater relative political advantage under these conditions than members of the legislature.

Opponents also claimed that term limits increase the power of interest groups. This argument takes the view that newly elected legislators are more likely to be taken advantage of by special interest groups, which now fill the vacuum created by the loss of senior legislators. This occurs because the new legislators do not know what the rules of the game are in dealing with lobbyists and interest groups. This may actually cut two ways. On the one hand, new legislators may be inordinately distrustful of lobbyists, thereby losing valuable information on issues they might garner. On the other hand, they might commit too soon on an issue or perhaps be overly impressed with the position of an interest group without seeking out additional information from other sources.

Furthermore, term limit opponents stated that limits lead to a loss of legislator accountability to his or her district. What happens to a constituent's issue when a new legislator comes in? Although this is perhaps much more of a citizens' issue rather than a term limits one, the argument is that constituents, many of whom don't even know who their legislator is, will be even more confused with the frequent turnover of legislators under term limits. Also, will term-limited legislators be as responsive to their constituency as they once were? Without the electoral connection present, some legislators may simply write off constituency service during their last term.

Finally, it was argued that term limits will unduly focus a legislator's energies on reelection and job hunting. Put simply the argument is that legislators early in their term-limited career focus too much on reelection rather than policy. As they approach their last term, say in the house, they shift their focus to running for the senate or members of the senate might be thinking about resigning early to seek out a lobbyist or staff-related job before their last term ends. Whatever the reason, the view is that public policy suffers when this happens (Chi and Leatherby, 1998).

Some Legislative Observations

I had the opportunity to interview 23 legislators and staff of the Arkansas General Assembly as part of a National Conference of Legislatures Terms Limits Study.[2] These interviews were with some of the key legislators and personnel associated with the Arkansas General Assembly and form the basis for the discussion in this article. What, then, were some of the key points about the impact of term limits that seemed to be common to these legislators and staffers?

One theme that frequently came up was the inexperience of the new legislators. Several legislators said "that the new legislators would be blown away by the complexity of the budget process." Inexperienced legislators, they said, would be unable to ask the right questions and would be easily led off the proper mark by cagey agency heads. Considering that budgetary oversight is one of the Assembly's key powers, this would indeed be a downside of term limits. During the fall this writer attended several rounds of budget hearings. What I observed was that the questions that were being asked—tough questions asked in a "tough tone"—were all coming from the veteran term-limited legislators.

During our interviews several legislators expressed dismay over the loss of institutional spokespersons in the legislature. The concern was that with the loss of senior legislators, some of whom had been members for over 15 years, there would be a lack of legislative stature in standing up to the executive branch in particular. As long-time observers of the Arkansas General Assembly know, there have been dominant personalities in the assembly over the years that have been emblematic of the institution. In this regard several legislators made the point—especially in reference to the senate—that institutional speakers who

*Brian Weberg, National Conference of State Legislatures, and Art English, University of Arkansas at Little Rock, conducted the interviews during November of 2001 and May of 2002. While this study is still underway and none of the quantitative data are yet ready for analysis, it is nevertheless interesting to obtain the views of those who have been directly impacted by term limits. And while the interviews will be coded for communality in the larger study, the findings presented herein only represent a wide-ranging review of the interviews.

knew the institution, had solid policy knowledge, and the communication skills to get ideas across to the executive branch and the public—would be fewer and fewer under term limits.

On the other hand, a number of legislators made the point that with term limits leaders had to step up. There was no time to sit on the sidelines and learn. When leaders in the house were put in a disadvantaged position in terms of the more institutionalized leadership in the senate, several of the house respondents said it was their signal to step up and lead, to make sure their chamber would not be disadvantaged in negotiations with the senate. Other legislators made similar points. Term limits provided opportunities for members to develop their leadership skills and have them tested almost immediately. Under term limits legislators could quickly move into leadership positions. Second-term legislators could become committee chairs, first-term legislators received important committee assignments, and two of the last three incoming Speakers of the House were elected to their positions at the incredibly youthful age of 33 and 26, respectively, less than half the age of some of the former speakers of that body.

But how could leaders develop quickly enough to be effective. Former Arkansas Speaker Bob Johnson brought in new legislators in groups in 1999 to provide training and orientation well before the session, a practice that was continued by the next Speaker of the House, then 26-year-old Shane Broadway. In California "The Capitol Institute" was established in 1998 with former members of that body as faculty who offer "hands-on" training for new legislators. New members are instructed in topics that cover legislative life, ethics, organizing district offices, committee procedure, getting staff on board, and learning budget procedures. The institute develops training and instructional curriculum for the legislators, gets feedback on its methods, and reloads after feedback to provide more effective training. Training is mandatory for all staff but voluntary for the legislators, although most legislators have opted for it. The institute faculty does not try to smother the members in information. Care is taken to give them practical information, technical information that can be adjusted in terms of knowledge backgrounds, and time for them to get to know each other (Feustel and Jones, 2001). This latter technique is considered very important in getting new legislators comfortable with each other so that disagreements in the future won't be divisive and that legislators understand one of the key norms of legislative life: that it is all right to disagree as long as it is not personalized.

Another common theme evident in the staff interviews in particular was the view that term limits had substantially enhanced the civility of legislators in relation to the staff. The majority of the staff respondents talked about how much more courteous the new legislators were as compared to the veteran legislators who had left because of term limits—those gone and happily forgotten for some of these staff respondents. Staff respondents went on to say the new members sought their help more frequently than many former veteran legislators who often impersonally asked for a report or information to be provided right on the spot. Some staff members did report, however, that some of the newcomers didn't know what questions to ask or did not know whom to approach on the staff, certainly a down side of term limits. But staff members did not say, as is commonly assumed, that they assumed more power with the loss of institutional memory. The sense that I got from the staff interviews was that the staff knew its place in an elected institution and would not take advantage of power leverages because of term limits. That norm was in the culture.

One theme that was mentioned by several legislators was that term limits would hinder the ability of the legislature to follow through with programs because those instrumental to the passage and oversight of programs would no longer be around to see them implemented. While no specific examples emerged from the comments mentioned, the writer did see an example while observing a session of the Legislative Black Caucus during the fourth week of the 84th Assembly. In response to a presentation by several minority business-people about the lack of economic development programs for minority legislators, one member of the caucus said, "that we will support these programs for you as hard as we can, but if we don't get rid of term limits, none of us will be here to push these programs to fruition."

Finally a common point articulated by both legislators and staff members alike was that term limits had resulted in more power for the speaker and the standing committees. Their argument centered on the importance of the speaker in appointing chairs and vice chairs and as a focal point for the house with so many new members each cycle. In terms of committees, the common appraisal was that without the long-term veteran legislator who used to chair the committees, power in committees was now much more decentralized and "that just about every bill got a fair hearing." With the big bull legislators now gone, new members also get a much better shot at a good committee. Two examples of this in the 84th Assembly—besides the numerous committees that are chaired by second-term members—were the large number of house Republicans who bid to be on the House Judiciary Committee as a means to have a strong say in tort reform legislation. In addition, a current rule in the senate is that every A or B committee is required to have at least one Republican on it.

Discussion—The 84th Arkansas General Assembly as a Test Case

Other trends, of course, came up in the interviews. The movement of house members to the senate has given the senate a distinctly house look. The absence of lawyers in the senate and on the judiciary committee in particular has concerned legal staff and legislators alike. Still the effect of term limits in removing the occasional out and out complacent or corrupt member came up in several interviews as a positive of term limits (English, 1991). However, some of the most interesting evidence about the status of term limits in Arkansas developed during this past legislative session. During this session Arkansas legislators confronted as did many of their peers in other states difficult revenue and budget problems. Arkansas legislators also faced a school consolidation issue that proved to be highly divisive between urban and rural legislators. And if this was not enough, the governor, who was providing the leadership for school consolidation (Arkansas has 310 school districts and generally mediocre to poor public schools by many measures), also was trying to ram through an executive branch reorganization plan that would have merged over 50 executive branch agencies into 10 super-departments headed by a cabinet secretary.

While the jury on term limits is still out, some of the evidence from the 84th Arkansas General Assembly does not appear to be supportive of the concept of term limits. More bills than ever before were introduced in the Assembly (over 2,700) and the session dragged on for 94 days without agreement on a revenue package and school consolidation. Legislators seemed more interested in getting special projects for their districts than addressing the state's major problems. Leadership, especially core leadership in the senate, did not seem to be present, although a more consensual-bargaining style type of leadership emerged both within and without the senate with virtually all of the senior legislators gone. Lobbyists, many of the legislators themselves, and the print and broadcast media uniformly criticized the session as rudderless and unproductive. Many legislators believed the lack of experience in the body was a major liability, hence the submission of a constitutional amendment by the Arkansas General Assembly that would lengthen term limits to 12 years in both the house and the senate with the aim of institutionalizing higher levels of experience in the Assembly while still providing opportunities for the infusion of new blood and ideas.

Whether all or even some of these "legislative problems" can be blamed on term limits is not clear. Virtually every state legislature in the nation is facing revenue and budget problems, which makes legislating even more difficult than it already is. With more evidence from the states with and without term limits coming from the National Conference of State Legislatures 2001–2004 study, the worth of term limits will be able to be more accurately assessed. What is clear though, at least in Arkansas and perhaps in other states, is that term limits still is a powerful force with many constituencies. Term limits will continue in Arkansas it appears for many more years—but perhaps in a more flexible context that will allow legislatures to combine both experience and opportunity in the legislative process.

References

Chi, Keon S., and Drew Leatherby. February 1998. "State Legislative Term Limits," *Solutions: Policy Options for State Decision Makers*, 6(1).

English, Art, and John J. Carroll. 1983. *A Citizen's Manual to the Arkansas General Assembly.* Institute of Politics and Government.

English, Art. 1991. "Work Styles in the Arkansas General Assembly." Paper presented at the annual meeting of the Arkansas Political Science Association.

Feustel, Bruce, and Rich Jones. September 2001. "Legislator Training 101," *State Legislatures Magazine* (National Conference of State Legislatures).

Ledbetter, Cal R., Jr. 1993. *Carpenter from Conway: George Washington Donaghey as Governor of Arkansas, 1909–1913.* University of Arkansas Press.

Paschall, Bill. 2001. *The Arkansas Legislature: A 20 Year Retrospective.* Little Rock: Paschall Associates.

Rosenthal, Alan, et al. 2003. *Representative Government on Trial: The Case for Representative Democracy.* Washington DC: Congressional Quarterly Press.

Ambition and Its Impact
on Representation

ADOLFO SANTOS

Politicians are not generally known for being modest or slothful. It takes quite a bit of nerve—and ambition—to work to gain office. The founders generally believed that ambition, properly channeled, could be used for the common good in society. Just as in a free market system where vendors vigorously compete to offer the best goods at the lowest possible price, politicians, in the view of the framers, would vie against one another to deliver the best policies to their constituents. However, Adolfo Santos broaches a related but difficult question: what if politicians' ambitions are channeled not to the public good but to the benefit of themselves or special interests? This, he suggests, raises the specter of distorting the representational process and thwarting democratic governance.

The eighteenth century British statesman Edmund Burke defended the notion that there was a natural aristocracy that was born to govern (Burke [1791] 1962). This natural elite represented the interest of the nation by discovering and enacting the common good (Pitkin, 1967: 169). It is the aristocracy that has the capacity to understand the public good. And it is found, not by querying the sum of the parts, but by discovering it through reason. The public good had to be reasoned out—not summed up. And to do this, the representative had to reason about what was in the nation's best interest. This required that the representatives put aside the interests of constituencies, and instead contemplate the interests of the nation as a whole. "This is the center of our unity," writes Burke, "This government of reference is a trustee for the whole, and not for the parts" ([1790] 1950: 207–208). It is a government that circumvents the concerns of individual interests, for the sake of the nation as a whole. Those chosen to represent are not to represent the concerns of individual districts, or simply those who elected the representatives. They are to represent the wishes of the commonwealth. In fact, much of the dispute over the extent to which the colonists were represented in the British parliament revolved around the two sides' understanding of the concept of representation. While the colonists insisted that they were not receiving representation in the House of Commons, the British response was that as members of the commonwealth, every member of Parliament represented the interests of the colonists. From the British perspective, the members of Parliament were serving as trustees chosen to serve the commonwealth.

But the cornerstone of the Burkean model of representation is the *quality* of the representatives. Burke writes, "There is no qualification for government but virtue and wisdom" (1790). The natural aristocracy is the one group that is in a position to make choices about what is right and wrong. But this does not mean that the aristocracy is one of intellectuals, rather, it is one of virtuous individuals (1790). They possess both a moral and intellectual ability that allows them to make practical decisions about the lives of individuals. But in order for the natural aristocracy to function properly, it must be able to divorce itself from those who elected them. And, the governing body must remain clean of those who do not belong to the natural aristocracy. Failure to keep the legislative body pure, he argues, will make the few who possess true virtue instruments of those with "sinister ambition and a lust of meretricious glory" (1790).

The American model of representation as presented by James Madison takes a different view of representation. The Burkean model relies heavily on the nature of those chosen to represent, and gives little regard to the structure of political institutions as instruments that ensure the public good. The American model, in contrast, focuses almost exclusively on the creation of political institutions that will provide political representation in spite of who is elected into office. "Enlightened statesmen will not always be at the helm," writes Madison in *The Federalist* No. 10 (1787). It is the structure of the institution that would ensure that the government represented the public good. The framers of the Constitution were keenly aware that in order for the political system to work, it should not have to depend on virtuous individuals disinterested in preserving or improving their personal lot. The political system that was created by the framers of the Constitution assumed human nature to be driven by *ambition*, and harnessing this ambition would ensure representation without undermining liberty. The framers attempted to control ambition by binding human nature to the institutional structure (Hamilton, Madison, and Jay, *The Federalist No. 10* and *No. 51* [1788] 1990: 267). The chief method of binding the individual's ambition would be through the use of elections (Hamilton, Madison, and Jay, *The Federalist No. 57* [1788] 1990: 296). Publius writes:

> As it is essential to liberty that the government in general, should have a common interest with the people; so it is particularly essential that the branch of it under consideration, should have as immediate dependence on, and an intimate sympathy with the people. Frequent elections are unquestionably the only policy by which this dependence and sympathy can be effectually secured (*The Federalist No. 52* [1788] 1990: 274).

Representatives interested in holding on to power would be compelled to represent the interest of the people. Ambition would be "made to counteract ambition" (*The Federalist No. 51* [1788] 1990: 267). Failure to represent the interest of the constituency would lead competitors to challenge the incumbent official, leading the electorate to vote those incumbents who were not representing adequately out of office. The result has been that the Constitution has created political institutions that simplify human motives, making the behavior of elected officials "understandable and predictable" (Schlesinger, 1966: 2).

The framers of the Constitution set out to create a republic in which individuals would represent the interests of their constituents. Representation would occur because those elected to public office would desire to hold those seats, and in order to hold on to those seats they would serve the interests of their constituents. However, it is important to note that the electoral process serves a meaningful role in controlling the ambitions of representatives only when the public official wishes to remain a *public* official. Madison warns that representatives "will be compelled to anticipate the moment when their power is to cease" (*The Federalist No. 57* [1788] 1990: 290). If representatives have ambitions that extend past their public lives, then those private ambitions may influence how the representatives behave in their public life. Elections only serve to control the ambitions of individuals who wish to remain in office. Once the public official no longer cares to remain in office, elections no longer constrain the ambitions of individuals.

Political Ambition in America

The ambition that Madison hopes to control can only be controlled in certain contexts, that is, when the official wishes to remain in public life. Those wishing to remain in public life, either in their present position or in a higher office would be expected to serve the public interest so as not to compromise their reputations. But the representative may hold other ambitions that are not so easily constrained by the electoral process. And while other ambitions may not be so easily constrained, the preservation of ambition is critical to the maintenance of the American political system. Without a good supply of ambitious individuals democracy in America would not be possible. Ambitious individuals will run for office and will be driven to continue to run. Because of their desire to win reelection, they will be compelled to represent their constituents' interests and it is their constituents who will control their ambitions. Ambition theory, therefore, adds to the theory of representation by presenting the idea that the future ambitions of a representative affect their behavior while in office (Prewitt and Nowlin, 1969: 299). The role of ambition in the American democratic process, therefore, is an important one, and one that requires a firm understanding.

Perhaps the best attempt to understand the concept of political ambition is presented by Joseph Schlesinger. He attempts to define the term by breaking it down into three categories—*progressive, static,* and *discrete ambitions.* The first of these—progressive ambition—refers to the politician's desire to move up to more powerful offices, while static ambition refers to a public official's desire to make a career out of a particular office. Discrete ambition refers to the desire to serve for a specific period of time and then withdraw from public life (Schlesinger, 1966: 10). It is the last of these that I believe presents the most serious threat to the Madisonian model. In the following sections, I will elaborate on the three concepts of ambition.

Progressive Ambition

Work on ambition theory in the political science literature has generally focused on "progressive ambition" rather than static or discrete ambition (Abramson, Aldrich, and Rohde, 1987; Brace, 1984; Prewitt and Nowlin, 1969; Rohde, 1979; Schlesinger, 1966). Much of this work attempts to describe and explain the behavior of members of legislative bodies who have goals for higher offices. Hain, for instance, has found a relationship between the progressive goals of state legislators and their age (1974). Rohde, also attempting to explain progressive ambition, has found that those hoping to advance to a higher office evaluate their chances of winning, as well as determine the costs and benefits of attempting to advance (1979). Others have found clear evidence that the behavior of those members of Congress who plan to seek a higher office tend to have broader policy goals than those who do not (Prewitt and Nowlin, 1969). And, their roll call votes tend to change depending on whether they are seeking a higher office or not (Hibbing, 1986).

Static Ambition

Members of Congress who have static ambitions arrive to their seats with the intention of holding on to them for as long as they can. While this type of ambition has been relatively ignored, it manifests itself in the declining turnover rates that Congress has experienced in modern times. Although rarely mentioned, static ambition has been assumed by political scientists like Anthony Downs (1957) and David Mayhew (1974) when they argue that elected officials have one central goal—winning reelection. And many members, at least during much of this century, have had good reason to remain in their seats. The seniority rule rewarded those who could hold on to their seats the longest with committee chair positions. And, with time, congressional service has become more prestigious and formal, leading to longer tenures (Polsby, 1968). The proactive nature of government during the periods of the New Deal and the Great Society also encouraged representatives to stay in office longer. But congressional change, brought on during the late 1960s and early 1970s, led to a sudden increase in the number of members of Congress who were voluntarily retiring from office (Hibbing, 1982b). Some claimed that serving in Congress was simply "no fun" anymore, with members increasingly becoming disaffected with service (Cooper and West, 1981a, 1981b; Theriault, 1998).

Discrete Ambition

Moore and Hibbing have questioned the extent to which credence can be given to the argument that members of Congress were leaving voluntarily because serving was no longer fun (1998). They argue that there are other contextual factors that drive the choice to leave office. Members of Congress have left office voluntarily because they have ulterior motives. Hall and Van Houweling, for instance, have found that recent increases in voluntary retirement have been due to members' desires to capitalize on lucrative pensions (1995). John Hibbing, similarly, finds that pension improvements affect the rate of voluntary retirement (1982a). Others have found that members left voluntarily in 1992 because this would be the last time that members would be allowed to keep unspent campaign contributions (Groseclose and Krehbiel, 1994; Borders and Dockery, 1995). These examples serve as evidence that personal avarice and ambition play a role in the calculus to leave office. And it would not be too far removed that other post-congressional ambitions might also prompt members to retire. Once the member of Congress no longer desires to be a member of Congress, then the capacity of the system to compel the representative to *represent* fails. Once a former member of Congress no longer has been reelected, creating public policy, or gaining influence in Congress as a goal, then the member of Congress is no longer constrained by the demands of his or her constituents. The use of elections to constrain ambition is a useful tool, but it is only useful at constraining progressive and static ambition.

Once the ambitions of a member of Congress change from being progressive or static to discrete, or if the ambitions were discrete all along, the Madisonian model comes under the very serious threat of being undermined. The potential problem posed by discrete ambition has, unfortunately, been virtually ignored in the political science literature. Rohde, for instance, has written:

> We say "almost all" (members of the House hold progressive ambition) because we believe that discrete ambition should be maintained as a separate category. There are some members of the House who begin service with the intent of simply filling out the present term. The most obvious case of this is the wife of a deceased member who agrees to run in a special election to fill the vacancy and serve only as a "care taker" until the next regular election. Such cases are, we believe, few and uninteresting (1979: 3).

The dismissal of cases of discrete ambition as being "few and uninteresting" is a serious mistake because such cases are neither few nor uninteresting. It is important that we recognize that discrete ambition is held by many more representatives than just those rare cases where widows fill a seat on a temporary basis. The error occurs because of our misunderstanding of the term. The thrust of discrete ambition is not a short tenure, or simply seeing one's term end. The thrust of discrete ambition refers to the goals and desires that a member of Congress have upon retiring from public life.

For some members of Congress, their discrete ambitions may simply be to retire to Florida, or to spend time with their family. But for others, their discrete ambitions may be to profit from their congressional career. Members of Congress may have the desire to become lobbyists or consultants upon the completion of their congressional career. Elected officials who are on the verge of leaving elected office may have post-congressional ambitions that conflict with their representative role while they remain in office. And, if their behavior

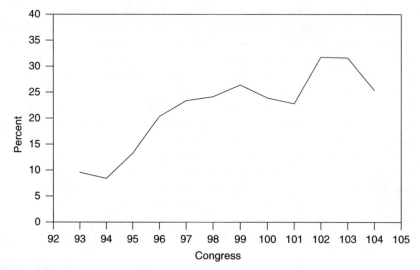

FIGURE 1   Percentage of Former Members Turned Lobbyists

changes to compensate for those ambitions, they may create public policy that runs counter to the interests of the representative's constituency. This possibility draws attention to the importance of understanding discrete ambition and the role of congressional retirement patterns. Where a member of Congress chooses to retire, and what function he or she chooses to perform upon leaving office, serve as manifestations of discrete ambition. Members of Congress who become lobbyists oftentimes have been driven by discrete ambitions during their last term of office.

Evidence is beginning to show that increasingly, more and more ex-lawmakers are becoming lobbyists. Figure 1 shows the percentage of the exiting class of members of Congress choosing a post-congressional lobbying career rather than returning home. And why do they choose such careers? One of the primary reasons is because of whom they know rather than what they know. In 1999, after resigning from the House of Representatives, where he served as Speaker of the House, Louisiana Congressman Bob Livingston began a consulting firm with several of his former aides. Almost immediately, the Livingston Group had amassed a client base from Louisiana's business community.* By the end of 1999, the Center for Responsive Politics was reporting a lobbying income for the Livingston Group of over a million dollars.** The former member of Congress has also been successful at luring six-figure clients like Lockheed Martin and the Oracle Corporation. More recently, the Livingston Group, in conjunction with Gerald Solomon—the former House Rules Committee

---

*Stone, Peter H. 2000. "Starting Over," *National Journal,* February 25, 2000.
**See *http://www.opensecrets.org/lobbyists/firm.asp?ID=95002&year=1999.*

Chair—and Stephen Solarz—the former congressman from New York signed a $1.8 million contract with the government of Turkey, which among other things, would like to purchase military equipment as well as build an oil pipeline with U.S. help. The Livingston Group's success can be explained by a variety of factors, but certainly one of the most important is the cordial relationship that the Speaker has with his former colleagues. Congressman Livingston freely admits that the fortune of the Livingston Group has been due to this cordial relationship. "We've been blessed," he states, "to have good relationships with most members on the Hill" (Stone, 2000).

Repeatedly, one finds that those former members of Congress who served on the more powerful congressional committees are the ones more likely to be hired as lobbyists. This means that they are favored as lobbyists even over those former members of Congress who have policy expertise, that is, those who served on the policy committees like agriculture and armed services. Those who served on committees like Ways and Means, Appropriations, and Budget are more likely to become lobbyists. Those who become lobbyists are the members who, while not policy experts, are certainly power brokers.

As a consequence of the representative nature of American democracy, political institutions have been created to take complete advantage of the ambitious nature of human beings. While this system has helped to create a phenomenally representative political system, it has also led to the consequence described above. Namely, that it has failed to limit the discrete ambitions of men and women who represent the American people. To what an extent discrete ambition undermines public policy, and thus representation, remains to be seen. But, it is quite likely that the harm may outweigh the benefit.

References

Abramson, Paul R., John H. Aldrich, and David W. Rohde. 1987. "Progressive Ambition among the United States Senators: 1972–1988," *Journal of Politics* 74:3–35.

Borders, Rebecca, and C. C. Dockery. 1995. *Beyond the Hill: A Directory of Congress from 1984 to 1993 Where Have All the Members Gone?* Lanham, MD: University Press of America.

Brace, Paul. 1984. "Progressive Ambition in the House: A Probabilistic Approach.," *The Journal of Politics* 46:556–571.

Burke, Edmund. [1790] 1950. *Reflections on the Revolution in France.* London: Oxford University Press.

———. [1791] 1962. *Appeal from the New to the Old Whigs.* Indianapolis: Bobbs-Merrill.

Cooper, Joseph, and William West. 1981. "The Congressional Career in the 1970s." In Lawrence C. Dodd and Bruce I. Oppenheimer, eds., *Congress Reconsidered,* 2nd ed. Washington DC: Congressional Quarterly.

Downs, Anthony. 1957. *An Economic Theory of Democracy.* New York: Harper and Row.

Groseclose, Timothy, and Keith Krehbiel. 1994. "Golden Parachutes, Rubber Checks and Strategic Retirements From the 102d House," *American Journal of Political Science* 38:75–99.

Hain, Paul L. 1974. "Age, Ambitions, and Political Careers: The Middle Age Crisis," *The Western Political Quarterly* 27:265–274.

Hall, Richard L., and Robert P. Van Houweling. 1995. "Avarice and Ambition in Congress: Representatives' Decisions to Run or Retire from the U.S. House," *American Political Science Review* 89:121–135.

Hibbing, John R. 1982a. "Voluntary Retirements from the House in the Twentieth Century," *The Journal of Politics* 44:1020–1034.

———. 1982b. *Choosing To Leave: Voluntary Retirement from the U.S. House of Representatives.* Washington DC: University Press of America.

Hibbing, John R. 1986. "Ambition in the House: Behavioral Consequences of Higher Office Goals Among US Reps," *American Journal of Political Science* 30:651–665.

Mayhew, David R. 1974. *Congress: The Electoral Connection.* New Haven, CT: Yale University Press.

Moore, Michael K., and John R. Hibbing. 1998. "Situational Dissatisfaction in Congress: Explaining Voluntary Departures," *Journal of Politics* 60:1088–1107.

Pitkin, Hanna F. 1967. *The Concept of Representation.* Berkeley: University of California Press.

Polsby, Nelson W. 1968. "The Institutionalization of the House of Representatives," *American Political Science Review* 62:146–147.

Prewitt, Kenneth, and William Nowlin. 1969. "Political Ambitions and the Behavior of Incumbent Politicians," *The Western Political Quarterly* 22: 298–308.

Rohde, David W. 1979. "Risk-Bearing and Progressive Ambition: The Case of Members of the United States House of Representatives," *American Journal of Political Science* 23:1–26.

Schlesinger, Joseph. 1966. *Ambition and Politics: Political Careers in the United States.* Chicago: Rand McNally.

Stone, Peter H. 2000. "Turkey Signs up Big Guns in D.C.," National Journal. February 2.

Theriault, Sean M. 1998. "Moving Up or Moving Out: Career Ceilings and Congressional Retirement," *Legislative Studies Quarterly* 23:419–433.

Bureaucracy in a More Positive Light
Ronald Belair

Speaking out in defense of the bureaucracy is not an easy exercise. Most everyone has, at one time or another, had to deal with the variety of bureaucratic rules and procedures that are commonly referred to as red tape. Ronald Belair argues here below that the bureaucracy—both in practice and as a concept—is often misunderstood. As an institution charged with the implementation of governmental policies, bureaucracies wield power. To ensure that this power is not abused, there are built-in mechanisms of checks and balances. Among them are demands for responsibility and accountability. Compliance with these demands requires standardized and systematic processes. It is such processes that are often decried as red tape. With this in mind, it would appear that red tape is not so much a connotation of inefficiency as it is a connotation of responsibility and accountability. Most people who work in the bureaucracy are skillful and highly competent professionals. If one keeps this mind, those outside of bureaucracy may come to have a more favorable view of the bureaucratic establishment.

The word *bureaucracy* sounds intimidating. It certainly conjures up negative reactions to big, bloated public agencies that are neither friendly nor accommodating. Bureaucrats deal with the reality of the daily routines, processes, and procedures of the business of governing and carrying out the laws and policies enacted by our elected leaders. Yet, routines and adherence to certain processes and procedures are important safeguards against the opposite that can lead to unbounded discretion, arbitrary enforcement, and abuse. A balanced understanding of bureaucracy is crucial to a fuller understanding of how government actually works and is essential for any student who aims for a career in government or in the nonprofit sector. Many features of bureaucracy are understandable and acceptable if not necessary.

This essay on bureaucracy is focused especially on mid and senior management level administrators in public agencies. These are supervisory level professionals who lead the agencies of government. While they have a variety of titles across governmental agencies, they will be referred to as "administrators" throughout. While there are many more people who serve in government in lower status positions, it is this senior corps who determine the success or the failure of policies and their implementation. These are the people who are generally highly dedicated to their profession, loyal to their agency superiors, and accountable to the legislated mandates. They broker multiple interest group pressures (both supporting and interfering in nature); mediate conflicting interpretation; and interface with colleagues in other agencies, branches, and levels of government. They are "bureaucrats" to be sure. They serve a vital service, are highly trained in their respective fields, are guided by both written and unwritten codes of ethics, and usually readily adapt to frequent changes in higher level leadership and to revisions in law. While they may falter, they are subject to several oversight mechanisms to assure appropriate implementation of the law or policy.

There are numerous frustrations associated with the many tasks undertaken daily by public agencies at all levels—national, state, and local. And these frustrations often originate not only from the shear complexity of getting the job done with the desired results, but also from frequent ambiguity in the legislated intent in addition to the constraints of collective bargaining agreements of lower level employees and resource limitations. How the law or policy should be applied at the street level is always in question. Someone needs to exercise good judgment in responding to the expectant service recipient and interest group who was the target of relief and instrumental in the law's passage. This in effect is the task of the administrator. It is not likely that the legislator nor the high level policymaker will want to be involved in writing the procedures on how the law should be implemented.

The dictionary defines *bureaucracy* as an organizational entity with a large staff whose purpose is to implement a program with objectives and desired results that are guided by a set of procedures and routines to assure consistency in the application of the task at hand. A bureaucracy, then, is the totality of government employees and generally referring to any inefficient organization steeped in red tape and a rigid set of procedural rules. It is composed of a cadre of appointed (*not elected*) officials who are organized in a pyramidal hierarchy and who function under uniform rules and procedures. In the public sector, there are some 2.8 million civilian employees who work for the national government with fewer than 12 percent working in Washington, D.C. In addition, more than 16 million work among the 85 thousand subnational levels of government—*all bureaucrats working within bureaucracies*. They represent virtually all disciplines of study and expertise. Bureaucracies and bureaucrats can be either public or private—although we generally refer to and identify "bureaucracy" with government because it is unquestionably the largest. Large companies in the private sector exhibit all the characteristics of bureaucracy, both positive and negative. A bureaucracy is seen as a rational, logical, efficient way of organizing human effort to get the job done in an efficient and impartial manner. Simply stated, a bureaucracy is a natural consequence of complexity and they evolved both naturally and deliberately as far back in history as one wishes to go.

The theme of this essay is that the "bureaucracy" and the professional core of "administrators" (the focus group of this essay) are unfairly demeaned and derided, and do not deserve the negativism often directed their way. Administrators have been and continue to be at the forefront of making difficult matters work.

Administrators are career public servants almost always holding a bachelor's degree in a field consistent with the work environment of their employing agency. They often have an advanced degree in public administration (a subfield of political science), management, or public policy. Since they are at senior management levels, they generally have many years of public service and are very familiar with the operations of their agencies and of government in general. As professionals, they are conscious of their professional codes of behavior, both written and unwritten. Administrators at these levels are not members of collective bargaining groups (unions).

The "Blame Game"

Bureaucracies and administrators have for a century received a fair share of blame for every conceivable ill befalling our society. Presidents, governors, and mayors campaign successfully by blaming bloated bureaucracies for everything and promise relief. Both Republicans and Democrats heave disparaging missives at them. Yet, in large organizations—both public and private—things often don't happen as intended. There are always *unintended* or *unanticipated* consequences. One cannot anticipate in advance all the possible contingent events and circumstances that might affect the implementation of a law or rule. The almost constant plea from all sectors is for change, reduction, or elimination. Bureaucracies are subjected to the disdain of legislators, judges, interest groups, and the general public for thwarting the intent of the law whatever that intent was at the point of enactment. Bureaucracy is what we love to hate!

By the late 1960s, ideological disenchantment with government generally was rampant due largely to an unpopular war in Southeast Asia that seemed to have no end, and to Great Society initiatives to end poverty that promised more than could reasonably be achieved. Sit-ins and demonstrations all signaled serious disaffection with a seemingly unsympathetic and insensitive "system." Both conservatives and liberals alike sought desperately some entity to blame. This disenchantment reached its peak with the Reagan administration and later when the Republicans captured control of Congress for the first time since the New Deal and elected Newt Gingrich as Speaker of the House of Representatives. Gingrich championed the cause of dismantling the size and reach of the federal government. A succession of national leaders from all segments and levels of our society proclaimed that the era of big government was over. The age of the "devolution revolution" (i.e., the transfer of government functions from national to state and local government) and of cut-back management continues to dominate the national agenda to this day.

Even with a Herculean attempt to anticipate the unanticipated, the unexpected always happens and well-laid plans need to be adjusted. It is the line staff who must adjust, improvise, and make due in keeping the overall objective in focus. Bureaucracies must behave and react to the present situation by sometimes improvising in order to achieve the objectives of the legislated intent. They must be loyal to the intent of the law (however imprecise that may be), while being sufficiently flexible to adjust to the unexpected on a daily basis. They have multiple, often conflicting, interests to balance. So, given the environment, can they be blamed or be fairly subjected to the negatives leveled their way?

Bureaucracy is explainable by appreciating how it evolved the way it did and why. Theories about administrative management have roots in three converging events: the growth and complexity in what organizations needed to do; reaction to the "spoils system" era of the nineteenth century with its abuses; and the development of management science in the early twentieth century. In regards to the first event, the vast majority of what government did was routine. With the second, government needed to administer fairly, openly, and consistently. Finally, the evolving science of task analysis, workplace improvement, and organizational form to enable these two were seen as essential to efficiency and economy.

Tension, Tension, Everywhere! Policy vs. Administration: The Root Causes

There always has been and always will be tension and contention between those who have the *responsibility and authority to make policy* (elected and politically appointed officials) and those who *administer to or carry out those policies* (administrators). Indeed, examples of this tension are unlimited. The fundamental understanding—indeed, basic principle of government—is that those who are elected to office in this democratic form of government are those who determine and select policy choices through the enactment of laws. They represent the will of the people. Once policy is set and laws enacted, however, it is the responsibility of the executive branch of government to administer or implement the law. In reality, however, it is not uncommon for the administrator to exercise a considerable amount of discretion during the policy implementation phase, thus occasioning the success or the failure of intended policy objectives. Additionally, administrators not only affect policy outcome at the point of implementation, but also influence policy development at the front end through their informal association with colleagues in allied agencies, elected officials, and interest groups, thereby forming what is commonly referred to as the *Iron Triangle*. It is not insignificant to note that the administrative arm of governing drafts the rules and regulations stating exactly how the law will be implemented in great detail. These rules and regulations once published and made official carry the full force and effect of law. How can this be? These are not elected officials and therefore ought not be involved in making law or policy. This involvement of administrators in both policy and administration is the cause of tension between policy and administration, and raises questions about how our government actually operates and how representative of the popular will it actually is. This area of concern is the subject of a considerable amount of literature and debate in the theory and practice of public administration.

For example, exactly what administrative steps need to be taken to demonstrate that concerted affirmative action steps have been taken to achieve diversity in hiring practices or admission to universities? Although the objective is clear and adherence broadly accepted, uncertainty and debate on how best to achieve the intended result administratively is unresolved and may remain so pending rulings in federal courts. The difficulty that the administrator encounters in knowing how best to implement the intent of the policy is not unusual. It illustrates the tension that is always prominent between policy and administration. It might also be argued that this tension is desirable however. It highlights ambiguity between the intent and how implementation might best be guided to achieve the objective. It in effect might be seen as a check and balance at both ends, that is, policy and implementation.

The tension in politics and administration can be traced back to the 1880s when the early political scientists saw the need for the study of *how government ought to work,* but struggled with the interference of administration in politics because politics is the exclusive role of duly elected officials. While we can go back to ancient times to view the origins of management and administration, our focus here is on the discipline and professional specialization of modern management and how the relevant theorists give us clues to the better understanding of bureaucracy. Of particular note and interest are the principles advanced by selected theorists whose founding principles are seminal and enduring albeit revised and updated to fit the times and advancements in management technology. Admittedly, there is a risk in choosing any one or a few over others. It is not intended as a slight of something that may be of equal value.

By the late 1880s and in reaction to the excesses of the "spoils system" of the nineteenth century, there was the need for a new field of study—public administration, now a subfield of political science. The role and significance of government was changing and there was the urgent need to make governing both efficient and effective while combating the excesses and abuses that were characteristic of the earlier period. Without elaborating at length on what administrative theorists have written,[1] it is useful to understand that their contribution to the debate explains the evolution of public administrative principles and how advances in management science in general have defined bureaucratic behavior. Woodrow Wilson, as a young professor of political science at Princeton who would later become president of the nation, advocated that political science devote attention to the study of how governments should be administered. Wilson, although primarily concerned with matters of economy and efficiency in government, was first to recognize that a distinction existed between politics (policy) and administration. It seemed clear to him and others to follow that governing meant much more than merely passing laws. There was an urgent need for staffing the expansion of public agencies with a professional corps to administer to the business of running the government. "Administration lies outside the proper sphere of government," Wilson said. Others soon followed emphasizing the critical need to separate politics from administrative management in government. During this early period, in addition to the need for staffing the growing bureaucracy and repudiating the past practices of abuse, there was considered to be a one best way to get the work done in the workplace. Fred Taylor, the "father of scientific management," was influential in applying the rigors of what is now known as industrial engineering concepts to the details of the work unit production. These notions were important in advancing many critical themes of study in modern public management and administration and the application of administrative theory in the real world.[2]

During and between the World Wars, management science came to fruition as did the need for mass production. America had changed dramatically moving from an agrarian to an urban industrialized society. The concern now was with organizational structure and workplace control to assure that "policy" was indeed implemented as intended by instituting prescribed workplace routines and procedures to enhance efficiency and desired results. There was the need for the precise definition of tasks, work units, and procedures. Further, the administrator should be aware of the interdependence of the formal and the informal organization where the latter represents those unofficial associations within organization that are formed naturally among colleagues in the workplace. These associations were essential because they enhanced efficiency and short-circuited the suffocating influences of the bureaucracy. By this point, increased interaction and interpersonal relations in the workplace as well as the desirability of encouraging grassroots input and involvement of workers received increased attention.

New Deal initiatives during the Roosevelt administration ushered in the need for a strengthened and expanded executive to carry out the many new roles of government. It was recognized that the laws as passed often represented a complex series of compromises among the many interest groups, thereby leaving to the administrator by default the job of providing definition to the enacted law or policy. Therefore, it is incumbent upon the administrator to *broker* and *mediate* the law's meaning in its application.[3] This was very important! Subsequent theorists in the field built on these notions in advancing the study and application of public administration and recognized the important role of the administrator.

While the early theorists embraced the authoritarian military model with rigid, top-down structures, the focus changed from this "mechanistic" belief to an "organic" analogy. This broader view not only valued the active participation of the administrators, but also adapted other evolving modern management applications of systems analysis, management by objectives, and total quality management, etc. Notions of the self-correcting and learning organizations encouraged workers to confer and decide not only the best way of getting the job done, but also how to work beyond the rigors of the bureaucracy—or, how to work "outside the box" in forming task groups and quality circles.

Continued Reasons for Concern

As a consequence of the considerable administrative discretion, administrators in effect "make law" as they go along their daily routines. The central issue that remains is how to make the bureaucracy accountable to the popular will and to control the possible ill effects of stepping beyond its scope of authority? Are there continued risks to our democratic system?

In the post–World War II era especially, the bureaucratization of more and more human effort and the increased role of the public sector in our economy and daily lives make the need for close scrutiny imperative. How can the dual, yet often conflicting objectives of economy and efficiency on the one hand, and accountability to the legislated mandate on the other be achieved? We've expanded the role of government and want its work done well and achieved economically. We want the administrator to be a good agent for the policymaker, but not to be the policymaker. In his quest to achieve the objectives of the legislated mandate there is concern over the incestuous relationship that is formed among fellow bureaucrats, with members of the legislature and their staffs, and with other agencies or external entities including interest groups. This may not be undesirable.

There are some who fear that we are advancing toward an administrative state or a ministerial class often found in other democracies. Others say that the movement in that direction is overstated and that administrators play an essential role in our complex society where results are demanded and policies merely state a desired goal already affirmed during legislative enactment.

If there is reason for continued concern, what are the checks, balances, and oversight?

Administrators are not without controls or restraints on unbounded actions and interpretation. There are many limitations and checks. While there is the expectation that the agency—the administrator—will act as the legislature wishes, a law can be amended to make its intent more precise. There is always the possibility that an administrator will be called to hearings and investigations to answer questions about operations and complaints. Funding can be reduced or eliminated in subsequent appropriations by the legislature. The Office of Management and Budget in the office of the president, and the General Accounting Office that is answerable to Congress play important oversight and controlling roles in checking the bureaucracy. These same oversight vehicles are also present at the state and local levels. Before a new law or amended law is implemented, the administrator develops rules and regulations that spell out all the particulars of how the law will be carried out. These are subject to strict administrative procedure dictates that require, among other things, publication of the intended rules and regulations and provide for fair hearings and comment by all interested and affected parties. Once the rules are implemented, aggrieved parties have ample occasion to have their complaints addressed both administratively and judicially. Additionally, the criticism of experts, the press, interest groups, and the role of professional ethics all have a role in lessening the possible ill effects of excessive or improper action. In fact, these safeguards are quite visible and effective in causing change in administrative actions when warranted.

Additionally, agencies have constituencies, that is, advocates, interest and clientele groups, that follow closely and champion the efforts of the bureaucracies. They maintain a watchful eye on the progress of legislation and its implementation. They lobbied and presented testimony at committee hearings. They reviewed and commented extensively on the proposed rules and regulations written by the agencies. These interests will not allow the administrator to stray from the policy's intent.

Where from Here?

Recent commentators have asked that we accept the reality that the administration of the public's business has far outpaced theory. The practice of public administration is beyond theoretical debate because the past theories that may have served us well are ill suited for the new challenges of the new century.[4] Our federal government has worked rather well when we consider, for example, air traffic control, our national park service, or the mailing of social security checks on the first of every month.

With the trend in the last two decades at a diminished national role and increased subnational responsibility, the real challenge now rests at the lower subnational levels of governing where activity is closer to the people and more nearly in tune with local needs. Closer means better achievement of objectives and closer scrutiny by service recipient groups. If the old concern with the policy-administration dichotomy remains, the violations that existed in the past are less likely and responsiveness to the popular wishes more likely. The administrator in the field and closer to the people is now better trained and better able to turn the aspirations of the popular will into the reality of daily implementation. With the budget restrictions at the dawn of the twenty-first century, it is likely that there will be a reemphasis on efficiency and restructuring leading to better and smarter governing.

Community leaders are now being elected in greater numbers who are more inclined to reach out to include all segments of the community and involving them in policymaking and policy implementation. Right-sizing government increasingly includes the very bureaucrats who were once maligned. No longer are they seen as under-caffeinated automatons.

Endnotes

1. For a comprehensive compendium of most major authors of public administration, see Jay Shaftritz and Albert Hyde, *Classics in Public Administration,* 2nd ed. Belmont, CA: Wadsworth, 1992.

2. See: Woodrow Wilson, "The Study of Administration," pp.11–24; Frank Goodnow, "Politics and Administration," pp. 25–28; Frederick Taylor, "Scientific Management," pp. 25–28; and Mary Parker Follett, "The Giving of Orders," pp.66–74. In Shafritz and Hyde (1992).

3. E. Pendleton Herring, "Public Administration and the Public Interest," pp. 75–79. Ibid.

4. Donald Kettl, "Challenges for 21st Century Governance," p. 27. In Howard R. Balanoff, ed., *Public Administration—Annual Editions 01/02.* Guilford, CA: McGraw-Hill/Dushkin, 2001.

Let's Make a Deal: Courts and Plea Bargaining in American Criminal Justice

Kenneth L. Manning

Most of us try not to spend too much time in courtrooms. Unless we work there, a courtroom for most people is a place where we are inconvenienced by jury duty, accused of a crime, or providing testimony in some cause of action. Kenneth Manning reveals that many attorneys and prosecutors also try to minimize their time in court, and they do so through the process of plea bargaining. Though plea bargaining is often criticized and may pose some very substantial problems, Manning tells us that the process also offers a number of distinct advantages to virtually everyone involved. Criminal justice actors have come to rely so heavily upon plea bargaining that he suggests a costly overhaul of the system would be necessary if we were to abolish the practice.

Most everyone has seen television programs showing courtroom scenes of high drama. Pseudo-lawyers on NBC's hit program *Law and Order* are often shown working a courtroom like Tiger Woods handles a golf club. These dramas depict legal excitement and intrigue, and they help to reinforce the mythical view that much of the public has about court procedure in the United States.

If one were to believe television, most criminal cases eventually erupt in a courtroom battle. Clever TV lawyers are shown parading around the courtroom making emotional appeals to stone-faced juries while the fate of a defendant hangs in the balance. It makes for great television.

But it's not the way most criminal cases are handled. The vast majority of people who are accused of crimes in the United States don't see such drama. Relatively few criminal cases result in full jury trials because most criminal cases are plea-bargained. In a behind-the-scenes process that is often misunderstood, plea bargaining has become central to handling criminal cases in the United States judicial system.[1]

Students of government and politics spend considerable time discussing criminal justice and the criminal procedure in the United States, yet the "oil" and the "glue" of the criminal justice system in the United States—plea bargaining—are rarely discussed. This oversight is unfortunate because plea bargaining has become critically important to American criminal procedure. We may call plea bargaining "oil" because the efficiencies associated with plea bargaining work to keep the criminal justice system running smoothly. And we might consider plea bargaining the "glue" that arguably holds the current system together because plea bargaining is a process that has become very important to American criminal justice.

Plea Bargaining: An Exchange

Plea bargaining consists of a negotiation between a criminal defendant (usually through their lawyer) and a prosecutor. Both sides have the opportunity to get something they want. For prosecutors, a guilty plea by the accused assures conviction. For defendants, the bargain provides the opportunity to avoid a more severe penalty. At the most fundamental level, therefore, plea bargaining represents a classic *quid pro quo*.[2]

The most obvious thing a defendant can offer to the prosecution is a plea of guilty to a crime, thus allowing the prosecutor to achieve his or her goal of obtaining a just conviction while averting a full-blown trial. On some occasions, particularly instances involving some type of organized criminal activity, defendants may also be able to provide testimony that supports the prosecutor's case against another defendant.

Of course, prosecutors have a key incentive that may entice a defendant—the opportunity to avoid a harsher sentence that they might face should they be found guilty at the end of a trial. The chance to "get off easy" (relatively speaking) provides a powerful motivation to take a deal if it is offered.

There are a host of incentives that prosecutors may tender to defendants. Prosecutors possess wide discretion in bringing charges against defendants since that's the basic responsibility of the prosecution. This means that the prosecutor makes direct decisions about the severity of the charge, and consequently the potential punishment a defendant may face.

But prosecutors may also sway the sentence handed down by a judge. Judges often seek input from the prosecution on recommended punishments, and though they are not required to comply with the prosecution, they frequently do. Furthermore, in the plea-bargaining process, it is generally understood that judges will typically defer to the prosecutor's recommendations if a plea deal has been made. Again, they're not required to do so, but jurists will usually agree to the prosecutor's suggestion. An effective plea-bargaining strategy may involve an agreement by the prosecutor to request a lighter sentence in exchange for a statement of guilt. The prosecutor gets what they want—a conviction—while the defense achieves their goal—a lighter punishment.

It is important to note, however, that while this process is common in state cases, it is forbidden in federal courts. In federal courts, the Federal Sentencing Guidelines[3] provide fairly rigid rules for determining punishments based upon the crime and the defendant's record. Consequently, federal prosecutors (i.e., the U.S. Attorney's office) and federal jurists must usually look to other avenues to strike plea deals.

As an incentive to elicit a guilty plea, prosecutors may agree to a reduction of the charge leveled against the accused to a less serious but related offense. If a defendant is accused of felony assault, for example, the prosecutor might agree to reduce the charge to a misdemeanor in exchange for a guilty plea. Misdemeanors typically carry a lighter penalty than felonies and felony records are often more difficult—even impossible in many states—to expunge from one's record than are misdemeanor convictions. Thus, a plea bargain involving a reduction in change offers the prosecutor a quick and easy case resolution while the defendant avoids a more onerous punishment. As one might imagine, a reduction in charges is one of the most common forms of plea bargaining.

Prosecutors might also offer to delete tangent charges. This process involves an agreement by the prosecutor to drop other charges pending against a defendant (or their friend or family member) in exchange for a plea of guilty. There are, furthermore, two types of tangent charge deletion.

An agreement not to prosecute vertically involves a pact to charge a defendant with only one offense when his or her action may in fact have involved multiple crimes. Imagine a hypothetical defendant "George" who is accused of the following: While strolling along a downtown sidewalk, "Laura" was assaulted and her handbag was stolen. George then forged a check from Laura's bank account to purchase items at a local store. In this act, the defendant committed a number of offenses—assault, theft, and check forgery. A vertical deletion of tangent charges in this case might involve a proposal by the district attorney to drop the felony forgery and assault charges in exchange for a guilty plea to the theft charge. This would allow the accused to face a significantly less severe sentence.

On the other hand, agreement not to prosecute horizontally involves bringing only one charge (or a small number of charges) against a defendant when he or she has engaged in numerous identical violations over time. Imagine that our hypothetical criminal, George, this time used a stolen credit card to illegally make purchases. Over a two day period, George used the card ten times. George has committed ten offenses because each use was a separate violation of the law. An agreement not to prosecute horizontally may involve an agreement by the prosecutor not to seek charges in all ten counts in exchange for a guilty plea on one count, thus allowing hapless George to avoid a stiff fine or sentence.

Defendants accused of multiple crimes may receive an offer from the prosecutor to consolidate the cases and request concurrent sentencing. Imagine this time that George robbed three different convenience stores all on the same day. If the sentence for each offense is 5 years in prison, consecutive sentencing of all three offenses would result in a 15 year penalty. However, concurrent sentencing would allow George to serve 5 years in prison for all three offenses.

Another means of plea bargaining involves an exchange that includes a promise by the accused to provide prosecutors with information that might be used in other cases. This is frequently used in cases involving drug dealing and organized crime activities. Prosecutors will sometimes offer one or more of the previously mentioned incentives to individuals in exchange for a guilty plea and a promise to provide information about the criminal operations in which the individual was involved. This gives prosecutors valuable information about criminal activities and usually provides testimony that may aid prosecutors in related cases.

The methods of plea bargaining offer prosecutors and defendants a number of ways to negotiate. Prosecutors and defenders will bargain using any of the numerous tools available to them to reach a settlement, all in a process that is remarkably quick and easy. It may not be surprising, therefore, that the process is used so frequently.

One can imagine, however, that the plea-bargaining process—like any bargaining process—involves a certain level of gamesmanship. Strategy on the part of both sides is definitely at play. Prosecutors generally attempt to convict defendants of the most serious crime and harshest penalty applicable. At the same time, however, they must offer a deal attractive enough to the defendant for him or her to take it. On the other hand, the defense typically seeks to reduce charges and potential punishments as much as possible while not "low balling" the prosecutor to the point that he or she decides to go to trial. Since approximately 90 percent of defendants charged with a felony in the United States are convicted (Carp and Stidham, 2001), the defense faces challenging odds in the courtroom. They have a powerful incentive to avoid going to trial. On the other hand, prosecutors are generally overworked and face enormous time constraints. Though the odds may be in their favor if they go to trial, they know that they realistically cannot have every case develop into a full-blown courtroom battle. They, too, have an incentive to cut a deal.

Thus, the process of reaching a plea-bargain agreement can involve calculated risks for both sides. Neither defense nor prosecution wants to offer something too favorable to their opponent, yet at the same time each side seeks to further their own interests. In this manner, the plea-bargaining process can turn into something akin to a high-stakes poker match or haggling over the price of a used car, with both sides continually evaluating one another to determine if they receiving the best deal possible. There may even be a certain level of posturing or brinksmanship by either side about how far they are really willing to negotiate.[4]

Who Wins, Who Loses?

One can identify a number of potential problems that may be associated with plea bargaining, and these ills might lead some to reject the process. But plea bargaining has assumed a central role in criminal procedure because it offers benefits to virtually all criminal justice participants. It must be kept in mind that, as with virtually all public policies, there are both costs and benefits associated with plea bargaining.

Opponents of plea bargaining level a number of charges against the process. Some protest that plea bargaining can pose a disadvantage to defendants. The pressure to plead guilty may lead some who are innocent to avoid the costs and risks of going to court. Additionally, prosecutors who have weak cases may have an incentive to press strongly for a guilty plea to prevent the case from going to court. Knowing that they stand a good chance of losing at trial, prosecutors might be under increased pressure to obtain guilty pleas in the very instances when defendants might be better off going to court. Some contend, therefore, that in their quest for conviction, prosecutors may unjustly lead defendants to plead guilty. Indeed, criminal justice history has seen a number of instances in which innocent people caved in to enormous pressure to admit guilt. In the notorious case of the Central Park jogger, in which a woman was brutally beaten and raped in New York in 1989, police arrested and interrogated a number of suspects, at least one of whom confessed to the crime. However, subsequent investigations revealed that the police used improper tactics in securing the confession and DNA testing ultimately revealed that someone else had actually committed the felony.[5] One scholar has suggested that plea bargaining is akin to torture in that it constitutes an enormous pressure to plead guilty to a crime, even if one is innocent (Langbein, 1978).

Some have also questioned the pressure defendants may face if the individual offers to provide testimony in exchange for some benefit. Defendants who are asked to make statements that may be used in the prosecution of others are often faced with a difficult choice: face a long time in jail or tell a court what the prosecutors want to hear. One can easily envision, therefore, that this pressure might lead to instances in which a defendant either embellishes the truth—or even lies—in order to protect himself. Furthermore, since these instances often involve individuals who have been deeply involved in organized criminal activity, these defendants aren't usually candidates for sainthood. Their character and truthfulness is invariably called into question.

It may also be argued that plea bargaining places too much emphasis on substantive justice rather than procedural justice, and violates the spirit of due process. Instead of ensuring justice through a fair, consistent, and rigorous application of the law, critics of plea bargaining contend that the process is ultimately a haphazard game. Opponents suggest that the plea-bargaining process thus reduces the noble pursuit of justice to something akin to quibbling over junk at a rummage sale.

Perhaps the most controversial aspect of plea bargaining is its influence on the victims of crime. Some may criticize plea bargaining as a perversion of justice. As a result of bargaining, criminals may not face the full repercussions of their actions. Some might say that this means there is little, if any, justice for the victims of crime. In some instances, plea bargaining may lead to criminals quickly returning to criminal behavior. An especially gruesome example of this occurred when, because of a plea bargain and criminal justice system errors, a mentally disturbed piano teacher spent a mere five years in prison for murdering one of his students. Upon release, he killed again (Tanenbaum and Greenberg, 2001).

It might also be argued that plea bargaining undermines confidence in the criminal justice system. The entire process is reduced to a series of quiet negotiations and thus renders the criminal justice process little more than a simple negotiated game of give-and-take. Others might counter, however, that since plea bargaining involves assured conviction, it directly benefits the victims of crime.

But while there may be disadvantages to the plea-bargaining process, it clearly offers a number of advantages as well.

It is obvious that those who are accused of crimes have the potential to benefit at some level from plea bargaining. The possibility of a reduced sentence or punishment is a strong incentive for defendants to seek a deal. However, those who plea-bargain may benefit in other ways as well. The plea bargain offers defendants the opportunity to avoid a significant amount of publicity associated with a trial. This is particularly important in smaller communities where personal reputation may matter a great deal in civic life. The plea bargain offers defendants the ability to minimize negative publicity associated with some criminal activity. Imagine, for example, a case where a person is accused of engaging in sexual activity in a public restroom. The publicity associated with such a case being heard in court would be tremendous in a tight knit community. However, a plea bargain might allow the defendant to plead guilty to a public lewdness charge, keep the issue off the front page of the local newspaper, and permit the defendant to save some face.

Those who plead guilty may also benefit from the recognition of a problem that an admission of guilt inevitably suggests. This may be especially valuable in alcohol- or drug-related offenses, allowing individuals and/or their families to recognize a chemical dependency problem and seek proper treatment. Thus, plea bargaining may be, at least for some, the first step toward recovery.

Plea bargaining also provides benefits for those who work in the criminal prosecution system. The certainty of conviction is a strong incentive for prosecutors to bargain. Prosecutors frequently boast of their high conviction rate, a rate that is usually the result of plea-bargained cases. Nevertheless, the high conviction rate associated with plea-bargaining large numbers of cases allows district attorneys and other prosecutors to present themselves to the public as effective, tough-on-crime arbiters of justice. Of course, plea bargains also require less work on the part of prosecutors and staff. Not that prosecutors are lazy and underworked—quite the contrary. Most prosecutors face enormous workloads, and plea bargaining allows them to focus their limited time and resources on the most serious cases. In plea-bargaining many lesser crimes, prosecutors may focus their efforts on cases involving the most dangerous defendants.

The speed of plea bargaining also benefits the state because delays tend to favor defendants. Over time, evidence can be lost and witnesses' memory becomes less clear. Plea bargains also allow the state to be less concerned with loopholes in the law and case technicalities and more concerned about the substance of crime and punishment. By quickly handling cases through plea bargaining, the state is assured of conviction and is freed to work more quickly and efficiently.

The lawyers who defend those accused of crimes also have a strong incentive to seek a plea bargain. Criminal defendants are rarely people with "deep pockets." As a result, many private lawyers who handle criminal cases do so on a flat fee basis, rather than billing their clients per hour as is commonly done in civil matters. Given this reimbursement method, therefore, there is usually a strong desire on the part of attorneys to resolve cases quickly. It's not hard to see why plea bargaining can be an appealing option for defense lawyers since the process is not especially time-consuming. Deals between lawyers and prosecutors can be struck over a cup of coffee, in a hallway conversation, via a telephone call, or a brief office visit. Compare that to the many hours—or even days—that a criminal case may tie up if it goes to trial and one can easily see the incentive an lawyer has to plea out a case. Thus, the plea-bargaining process enables a defendant's attorney to provide a valuable and quick service to his client. There is little incentive for lawyers to prepare a case and spend a day (or more) in court on cases for which their fee is relatively low.

It might also be argued that society benefits from the plea-bargaining process. Perhaps the most obvious benefit offered to society is the lower criminal justice costs. While the figure varies, it is estimated that at least 90 percent of all state and federal criminal cases never go to trial because a deal is struck beforehand.[6] Were all cases tried, there would have to be a five or tenfold increase in the sheer number of courtrooms to accommodate the exponentially larger number of trials. Courts, with all of the professional labor associated with running them, are costly institutions for society to support. And, of course, citizens would be called for jury duty much more often than they are now if there were a larger number of trials. By trying fewer cases, we are able to maintain fewer courts, and fewer courts means lower taxes for citizens and fewer inconveniences of serving on juries. Would you be willing to go to jury duty ten times as often in order to abolish plea bargaining? And pay higher taxes as well?

Another reason plea bargain may be considered beneficial is that it allows for greater police efficiency, allowing officers to spend less time in court and more time on the street. Were police to spend significantly more time in court testifying in a greater number of trials, we would either have fewer police patrolling American streets or added costs associated with the hiring, training, and pay of more law enforcement officials just to maintain current policing levels. Either way, there would be added societal costs. It isn't too hard to see that there are distinct benefits associated with a quick and efficient criminal justice system, and plea bargaining is critical to making this happen.

While the process may be criticized, there has been little effort to fundamentally change or restrict plea bargaining in the United States. For the most part, the public is generally unaware of the importance of plea bargaining in the criminal justice system, clinging to an inaccurate popular perception of courtroom drama that is not found in the vast majority of criminal cases. Because so many involved benefit from the process, the costs of plea bargaining are so diffuse, and the alternative is so costly, the important but often misunderstood process of plea bargaining continues to thrive.

References

Carp, Robert A., and Ronald Stidham. 2001. *Judicial Process in America*, 5th ed. Washington, DC: CQ Press.

Fisher, George. 2003. *Plea Bargaining's Triumph: A History of Plea Bargaining in America*. Palo Alto, CA: Stanford University Press.

Heumann, Milton. 1981. *Plea Bargaining: The Experiences of Prosecutors, Judges, and Defense Attorneys.* Chicago: University of Chicago Press.

Langbein, John. 1978. "Torture and Plea Bargaining," *University of Chicago Law Review* 46: 4.

Tanenbaum, Robert, and Peter Greenberg. 2001. *The Piano Teacher: The True Story of a Psychotic Killer.* New York: Pocket Books.

United States Sentencing Commission. 1998. *Guidelines Manual.* (November).

Vogel, Mary E. 2003. *Coercion to Compromise: Social Conflict and the Emergence of Plea Bargaining, 1830–1920.* Oxford: Oxford University Press.

Endnotes

1. For a history of plea bargaining, see Vogel 2003 and Fisher 2003.
2. Latin for "something for something."
3. The guidelines are set by the United States Sentencing Commission, an independent agency in the judicial branch. The goal of the commission is to establish fair and consistent policies and practices for the federal criminal justice system (United States Sentencing Commission 1998).
4. For more on the bargaining process and the actors involved, see Heumann 1981.
5. See PBS *NewsHour* Online (http://www.pbs.org/newshour/bb/law/july-dec02/centralpark_12-24.html).
6. Carp and Stidham 2001.

People and Politics:
Political Behavior

Political Party Platforms:
Democrats and Republicans

Excerpted below are the Democratic and Republican Party platforms, approved by party delegates at their respective conventions in 2000. The party platforms, which are customarily revised and approved by convention delegates at their national meetings every four years, are a significant statement of a political party's core beliefs. Note the adoption of positions that clearly stake the parties on different sides of some key issues.

Democratic Party Platform: *Prosperity, Progress, and Peace*

Introduction

Today, America finds itself in the midst of prosperity, progress, and peace. We have arrived at this moment because of the hard work of the American people. This election will be about the big choices we have to make to secure prosperity that is broadly shared and progress that reaches all families in this new American century. In the year 2000, the Democratic Party stands ready to meet that challenge and to build on our achievements.

Let us not forget that America's future did not always seem so bright. Under the Bush-Quayle administration, America was suffering through economic stagnation. Businesses were failing. Jobs were disappearing. The welfare rolls swelled. Crime exploded in the streets. Hope and optimism were scarce. Most Americans felt that the American Dream was endangered—if not extinct.

But in 1992, Americans elected Bill Clinton and Al Gore with a mandate to turn America around. And that's just what they did. They took on the old thinking that had come to dominate politics and offered new ideas—new ideas that met the challenges of the day, new ideas that kept faith with America's oldest values, new ideas that worked.

Eight years later the record is clear: the longest economic expansion in American history. The most jobs ever created under a single administration. The first real wage growth in 20 years. The highest home ownership rate ever. The lowest African-American and Hispanic-American unemployment rates in American history. The lowest crime rate in 25 years. The lowest number of people on welfare since the 1960's. The largest drop in poverty in nearly 30 years. The lowest level of child poverty in 20 years. And after 15 painful years when the rich were getting richer and the poor were getting poorer, America is finally growing together instead of growing apart.

Prosperity

The road to long-term prosperity starts with embracing fiscal discipline. Unfortunately, the Republicans eschew fiscal discipline and offer up nothing less than fiscal disaster. They would squander the surplus on a more than trillion-dollar federal government tax giveaway for the well-off and well-connected, while failing to eliminate the national debt, neglecting to shore up Social Security and Medicare, and shirking the need to invest in the education of America's children and the skills of her workers.

The Bush tax slash takes a different course. It would let the richest one percent of Americans afford a new sports car and middle class Americans afford a warm soda. It is so out-of-step with reality that the Republican Congress refused to enact it. It would undermine the American economy and undercut our prosperity. Democrats seek the right kind of tax relief—tax cuts that are specifically targeted to help those who need them the most. These tax cuts would let families live their values by helping them save for college, invest in their job skills and lifelong learning, pay for health insurance, afford child care, eliminate the marriage penalty for working families, care for elderly or disabled loved ones, invest in clean cars and clean homes, and build additional security for their retirement.

To build on the success of Social Security, Al Gore has proposed the creation of Retirement Savings Plus—voluntary, tax-free, personally-controlled, privately-managed savings accounts with a government match that would help couples build a nest egg of up to $400,000. Separate from Social Security, Retirement Savings Plus accounts would let Americans save and invest on top of the foundation of Social Security's guaranteed benefit. Under this plan, the federal government would match individual contributions with tax credits, with the hardest-pressed working families getting the most assistance.

The Republicans have a far different idea—a scheme that would come not in addition to Social Security but at the expense of it. Their Social Security privatization plot would siphon $1 trillion in payroll taxes away from the Social Security trust fund, take 14 years off the life of Social Security, eliminate the fundamental guarantee of retirement security, and raise the specter of massive government bail-outs. And, according to independent analyses, the Republicans' privatization plan would cut the guaranteed benefits for young workers by as much as 54 percent. It would take the "security" out of Social Security.

Democrats understand that America will not long remain first in the world economically unless we become first in the world educationally. We cannot continue to generate a fifth of the world's economic output if a third of our students do not meet basic reading standards. We cannot stay number one in high technology jobs if we remain last in the percentage of degrees awarded in science. In today's knowledge-based economy, it's just that simple. Education leads to the future success and security of our country and citizenry.

The time for tinkering around the edges has long passed. We need revolutionary improvements in our public schools. This requires a major national investment; a demand of accountability from all; a genuine expansion of public school choice; and a renewed focus on discipline, character, and safety in our schools.

Far too many teachers are overstressed and overworked, underpaid and underappreciated. We need to treat teachers like professionals—pay them like professionals and hold them to professional standards. All qualified teachers should get a raise and master teachers should get the biggest raise. We need to provide professional development, training, and support so that all teachers can succeed.

We should rebuild and modernize our school buildings to assure students can attend schools that are modern, safe, and well-equipped for learning. And we need to construct more new schools to meet the needs of the largest generation of students in American history. We cannot convince our children to value education when they are packed into crammed classrooms like sardines in a can and when their facilities are falling down.

Strengthening small business is a vital component of economic innovation, job creation, and supporting entrepreneurship. Small businesses have accounted for more than 90 percent of the 22 million new jobs created with Democratic leadership. The Democratic Party is committed to sustaining and adding to that level of growth of small businesses, including home based businesses. Democrats believe that strengthening small businesses is a vital component of strategies to create opportunity and community economic development.

Exports sustain about 1 in 5 American factory jobs—jobs that pay more than jobs not tied to the global economy. Open markets spur innovation, speed the growth of new industries, and make our businesses more competitive. We must work to knock down barriers to fair trade so other nation's markets are as open as our own.

Trade has been an important part of our economic expansion—about a third of our economic growth in recent years has come from selling American goods and services overseas. There is no doubt that with trade—and with investments in giving American workers the skills they need—we can out-compete workers anywhere in the world.

We need to make the global economy work for all. That means making sure that all trade agreements contain provisions that will protect the environment and labor standards, as well as open markets in other countries.

Progress

We will fight to increase the number of community police on our streets. We will fight to give police the high-tech tools and the training they need to keep our streets safe and our families secure. We will toughen the laws against serious and violent crime to restore the sense of order that says to children as well as to criminals: don't even think about committing a crime here. We will reform a justice system that spills half a million prisoners back onto our streets each year—many of them addicted to drugs, unrehabilitated, and just waiting to commit another crime. We will make schools safe havens for students to learn and teachers to teach. We believe that in death penalty cases, DNA testing should be used in all appropriate circumstances, and defendants should have effective assistance of counsel. In all death row cases, we encourage thorough post-conviction reviews. We will put the rights of victims and families first again. And we will push for more crime prevention, to stop the next generation of crime before it's too late.

Democrats believe that we should fight gun crime on all fronts—with stronger laws and stronger enforcement. That's why Democrats fought and passed the Brady Law and the Assault Weapons Ban. We increased federal, state, and local gun crime prosecution by 22 percent since 1992. Now gun crime is down by 35 percent.

Now we must do even more. We need mandatory child safety locks, to protect our children. We should require a photo license I.D., a full background check, and a gun safety test to buy a new handgun in America. We support more federal gun prosecutors, ATF agents and inspectors, and giving states and communities another 10,000 prosecutors to fight gun crime.

Government does not raise children, families do. But government can help make the hardest job in the world—being a parent—a little easier. Today, families come in all different shapes and sizes, but they all face similar challenges. Government should be on the side of parents—making it easier for them to raise their children and pass down their values.

We need to find new ways to help parents balance work and family so that they will have time to pass on the right values to their children. Already millions of Americans have benefited from the Family and Medical Leave law, now we need to expand it so that it covers parent-teacher visits and children's routine medical appointments. And we will extend the law to cover more employers so that more working families enjoy this vital protection during times of family and medical need.

For fifty years, the Democratic Party has been engaged in a battle to provide the kind of health care a great nation owes its people. We reaffirm our commitment to take concrete, specific, realistic steps to move toward the day when every American has affordable health coverage. And we will not rest until the job is done.

Instead of the guaranteed, universal prescription drug benefit that Democrats believe should be added to Medicare, Republicans are proposing to leave to insurance companies the decisions about whether and where a drug benefit might be offered, what it would include, and how much it would cost. Studies suggest that less than half of seniors will be able to use this benefit.

There is much more left to do. We must redouble our efforts to bring the uninsured into coverage step-by-step and as soon as possible. We should guarantee access to affordable health care for every child in America. We should expand coverage to working families, including more Medicaid assistance to help with the transition from welfare to work. And we should also seek to ensure that dislocated workers are provided affordable health care. We should make health care accessible and affordable for small businesses. In addition, Americans aged 55 to 65—the fastest growing group of uninsured—should be allowed to buy into the Medicare program to get the coverage they need. By taking these steps, we can move our nation closer to the goal of providing universal health coverage for all Americans.

The Democratic Party stands behind the right of every woman to choose, consistent with *Roe v. Wade,* and regardless of ability to pay. We believe it is a fundamental constitutional liberty that individual Americans—not government—can best take responsibility for making the most difficult and intensely personal decisions regarding reproduction. This year's Supreme Court rulings show to us all that eliminating a woman's right to choose is only one justice away. That's why the stakes in this election are as high as ever.

Our goal is to make abortion less necessary and more rare, not more difficult and more dangerous. We support contraceptive research, family planning, comprehensive family life education, and policies that support healthy childbearing. The abortion rate is dropping. Now we must continue to support efforts to reduce unintended pregnancies, and we call on all Americans to take personal responsibility to meet this important goal.

The Democratic Party is a party of inclusion. We respect the individual conscience of each American on this difficult issue, and we welcome all our members to participate at every level of our party.

Democrats know that for all of us there is no more solemn responsibility than that of stewards of God's creation. That is why we have worked for eight years to produce the cleanest environment in decades: with cleaner air, cleaner water, and a safer food supply; a record number of toxic waste dumps cleaned up; new smog and soot standards so that children with asthma and the elderly would be able to live better lives; and a strong international treaty to begin combating global warming—in a way that is market-based and realistic, and does not lead to economic cooling.

Democrats believe we must give Americans incentives to invest in driving more fuel-efficient cars, trucks, and sport utility vehicles; living in more energy-efficient homes, and using more environmentally-sound appliances and equipment. We need to clean up aging power plants. We must invest in rebuilding and improving our transportation infrastructure and ensure that we adequately maintain these systems for the future. Americans need and rely on diverse transportation sources, and our public infrastructure priorities should reflect that diversity.

And we must dramatically reduce climate-disrupting and health-threatening pollution in this country, while making sure that all nations of the world participate in this effort. Environmental standards should be raised throughout the world in order to preserve the Earth and to prevent a destructive race to the bottom wherein countries compete for production and jobs based on who can do the least to protect the environment. There will be no new bureaucracies, no new agencies, no new organizations. But there will be action and there will be progress. The Earth truly is in the balance—and we are the guardians of that harmony.

Peace

The Democratic Party believes that America's peace and security depend on our unflagging leadership and engagement in global affairs—and that Forward Engagement is the strategy that must guide us. We must maintain America's economic and military strength. We must also form partnerships to help solve global problems and take advantage of new global opportunities. That means we must deepen our key alliances, develop more constructive relationships with former enemies, and bring together diverse coalitions of nations to deal with new problems. America has a responsibility to lead—and should lead from within the international community.

A strong, flexible, and modern military force is the ultimate guarantor of our physical survival and the protection of our interests and values. Today, America's military is the best-trained, best-equipped, most capable, and most ready fighting force in the world. With Bill Clinton and Al Gore in the White House, Democrats reversed a decline in defense spending that began under President Bush, boosted pay and allowances, and provided the funding for a new generation of weapons.

The lessons of the past eight years show that the nation must be prepared to use force when American interests and values are truly at stake. We cannot be the world's policeman, and we must be discriminating in our approach. But where the stakes are high, when we can assure ourselves that nothing short of military engagement can secure our national interest, when we know that we have the military forces available for the task, when we have made our best efforts to join with allies, and when the cost is proportionate to the objective, we must be ready to act.

We reject Republican plans to endanger our security with massive unilateral cuts in our arsenal and to construct an unproven, expensive, and ill-conceived missile defense system that would plunge us into a new arms race. Al Gore and the Democratic Party support the development of the technology for a limited national missile defense system that will be able to defend the U.S. against a missile attack from a state that has acquired weapons of mass destruction despite our efforts to block their proliferation. A decision to deploy such a system should be made based on four criteria: the nature of the threat, the feasibility of the technology, the cost, and the overall impact on our national security, including arms control. The Democratic Party places a high value on ensuring that any such system is compatible with the Anti-Ballistic Missile Treaty. We also support continued work in significantly reducing strategic and other nuclear weapons, recognizing that the goal is strategic nuclear stability at progressively lower levels.

Forty years ago, John F. Kennedy came to Los Angeles to accept the Democratic Party's nomination for president. In doing so, he pointed America towards new frontiers at home and abroad. In the year 2000, Al Gore comes to Los Angeles to accept that same nomination and renew our party's determination to accept big challenges and make bold choices. At the edge of a new century, Democrats stand united in our determination to offer prosperity to all who are willing to work for it, to provide progress to all who are willing to live by the values that have made America great, and to bring peace to all those willing to embrace democracy all over the world.

For eight years, the Democratic Party's new thinking has helped America reach unparalleled heights of prosperity, progress, and peace. Now, we say that this is the time to move forward—not to go back. Now, we say that Democrats have just yet begun to fight for a better America and a brighter future. Now, we say to America, "You ain't seen nothing yet."

Republican Party Platform: *Renewing America's Purpose. Together.*

Preamble

We meet at a remarkable time in the life of our country. Our powerful economy gives America a unique chance to confront persistent challenges. Our country, after an era of drift, must now set itself to important tasks and higher goals. The Republican Party has the vision and leadership to address these issues.

Our platform is uplifting and visionary. It reflects the views of countless Americans all across this country who believe in prosperity with a purpose—who believe in Renewing America's Purpose. Together.

The American Dream: Prosperity With A Purpose

When the average American family has to work more than four months out of every year to fund all levels of government, it's time to change the tax system, to make it simpler, flatter, and fairer for everyone. It's time for an economics of inclusion that will let people keep more of what they earn and accelerate movement up the opportunity ladder.

We therefore enthusiastically endorse the principles of Governor Bush's Tax Cut with a Purpose:

- Replace the five current tax brackets with four lower ones, ensuring all taxpayers significant tax relief while targeting it especially toward low-income workers.

- Help families by doubling the child tax credit to $1,000, making it available to more families, and eliminating the marriage penalty.

- Encourage entrepreneurship and growth by capping the top marginal rate, ending the death tax, and making permanent the Research and Development credit.

- Promote charitable giving and education.

- Foster capital investment and savings to boost today's dangerously low personal savings rate.

Small businesses are the underlying essence of our economy. They deserve far better treatment from government than they have received. We will provide it through many of the initiatives explained elsewhere in this platform: lower tax rates, ending the death tax, cutting through red tape, legal and product liability reform, and the aggressive expansion of overseas markets for their goods and services.

We must secure America's competitive advantage in the New Economy by preventing other countries from erecting barriers to innovation. For American producers and consumers alike, the benefits of free trade are already enormous. In the near future, they will be incalculable.

Education and Opportunity: Leave No American Behind

It's long past time to debate what works in education. The verdict is in, and our Republican governors provided the key testimony: strong parental involvement, excellent teachers, safe and orderly classrooms, high academic standards, and a commitment to teaching the basics—from an early start in phonics to mastery of computer technology. For dramatic and swift improvement, we endorse the principles of Governor Bush's education reforms, which will:

- Raise academic standards through increased local control and accountability to parents, shrinking a multitude of federal programs into five flexible grants in exchange for real, measured progress in student achievement

- Assist states in closing the achievement gap and empower needy families to escape persistently failing schools by allowing federal dollars to follow their children to the school of their choice.

- Expand parental choice and encourage competition by providing parents with information on their child's school, increasing the number of charter schools, and expanding education savings accounts for use from kindergarten through college.

- Help states ensure school safety by letting children in dangerous schools transfer to schools that are safe for learning and by forcefully prosecuting youths who carry or use guns and the adults who provide them.

- Ensure that all children learn to read by reforming Head Start and by facilitating state reading initiatives that focus on scientifically based reading research, including phonics.

Governor Bush and congressional Republicans have given priority to programs that increase access to higher education for qualified students. The centerpiece of this effort has been education savings accounts—the ideal combination of minimal red tape and maximum consumer choice.

At many institutions of higher learning, the ideal of academic freedom is threatened by intolerance. Students should not be compelled to support, through mandatory student fees, anyone's political agenda. To protect the nation's colleges and universities against intolerance, we will work with independent educators to maintain alternatives to ideological accrediting bodies. We also support a reasonable approach to Title IX that seeks to expand opportunities for women without adversely affecting men's teams.

We renew our call for replacing "family planning" programs for teens with increased funding for abstinence education, which teaches abstinence until marriage as the responsible and expected standard of behavior. Abstinence from sexual activity is the only protection that is 100 percent effective against out-of-wedlock pregnancies and sexually transmitted diseases, including HIV/AIDS, when transmitted sexually. We oppose school-based clinics that provide referrals, counseling, and related services for contraception and abortion. Because many youngsters fall into poverty as a result of divorce, we also encourage states to review their divorce laws and to support projects that strengthen marriage, promote successful parenting, bolster the stability of the home, and protect the economic rights of the innocent spouse and children.

Renewing Family and Community

The family is society's central core of energy. That is why efforts to strengthen family life are the surest way to improve life for everyone. We support the traditional definition of "marriage" as the legal union of one man and one woman, and we believe that federal judges and bureaucrats should not force states to recognize other living arrangements as marriages. We rely on the home, as did the founders of the American Republic, to instill the virtues that sustain democracy itself. That belief led Congress to enact the Defense of Marriage Act, which a Republican Department of Justice will energetically defend in the courts. For the same reason, we do not believe sexual preference should be given special legal protection or standing in law.

The Supreme Court's recent decision, prohibiting states from banning partial-birth abortions—a procedure denounced by a committee of the American Medical Association and rightly branded as four-fifths infanticide—shocks the conscience of the nation. As a country, we must keep our pledge to the first guarantee of the Declaration of Independence. That is why we say the unborn child has a fundamental individual right to life which cannot be infringed. We support a human life amendment to the Constitution and we endorse legislation to make clear that the Fourteenth Amendment's protections apply to unborn children. Our purpose is to have legislative and judicial protection of that right against those who perform abortions. We oppose using public revenues for abortion and will not fund organizations which advocate it. We support the appointment of judges who respect traditional family values and the sanctity of innocent human life.

We defend the constitutional right to keep and bear arms, and we affirm the individual responsibility to safely use and store firearms. Because self-defense is a basic human right, we will promote training in their safe usage, especially in federal programs for women and the elderly. A Republican administration will vigorously enforce current gun laws, neglected by the Democrats, especially by prosecuting dangerous offenders identified as felons in instant background checks. Although we support background checks to ensure that guns do not fall into the hands of criminals, we oppose federal licensing of law-abiding gun owners and national gun registration as a violation of the Second Amendment and an invasion of privacy of honest citizens.

Our country's ethnic diversity within a shared national culture is unique in all the world. We benefit from our differences, but we must also strengthen the ties that bind us to one another. Foremost among those is the flag. Its deliberate desecration is not "free speech" but an assault against both our proud history and our greatest hopes. We therefore support a constitutional amendment that will restore to the people, through their elected representatives, their right to safeguard Old Glory.

Another sign of our unity is the role of English as our common language. It has enabled people from every corner of the world to come together to build this nation. That is why fluency in English must be the goal of bilingual education programs. We support the recognition of English as the nation's common language.

Our Republican governors, legislators, and local leaders have taken a zero tolerance approach to crime that has led to the lowest crime and murder rates in a generation.

A Republican president will advance an agenda to restore the public's safety:

- No-frills prisons, with productive work requirements, that make the threat of jail a powerful deterrent to crime.
- Increased penalties and resources to combat the dramatic rise in production and use of methamphetamine and new drugs such as ecstasy.
- An effective program of rehabilitation, where appropriate.
- A constitutional amendment to protect victims' rights at every stage of the criminal justice system.

Retirement Security And Quality Health Care: Our Pledge To America

[The Republican Party will] keep faith with both the past and the future by saving Social Security. Now a Republican president will forge a national consensus on these principles to protect this national priority:

- Anyone currently receiving Social Security, or close to being eligible for it, will not be impacted by any changes.
- Key changes should merit bipartisan agreement so any reforms will be a win for the American people rather than a political victory for any one party.
- Real reform does not require, and will not include, tax increases.
- Personal savings accounts must be the cornerstone of restructuring. Each of today's workers should be free to direct a portion of their payroll taxes to personal investments for their retirement future.
- Choice is the key. Any new options for retirement security should be voluntary, so workers can choose to remain in the current system or opt for something different.

Medicare, at age 35, needs a new lease on life. It's time to bring this program, so critical for 39 million seniors and individuals with disabilities, into the Twenty-First Century. To do that, we need to build on the strengths of the free market system, offer seniors real choices in coverage, give participants flexibility, and make sure there are incentives for the private sector to develop new and inexpensive drugs.

After eight years of pressure from the current administration, the foundations of our health care system are cracking. There are currently 44 million uninsured Americans, an increase of one million for each of the past eight years.

More than 100 million American workers and their families have sound health insurance through their places of employment. The job-creating dynamism of our free economy has thus done more to advance health care than any government program possibly could. The tie between good jobs and good insurance coverage is the single most important factor in advancing health care for those who need it.

Truly positive market forces occur when individuals have the ability to make individual marketplace decisions. We therefore strongly encourage support of the emerging concepts of defined contribution plans and medical savings accounts. Individuals should be free to manage their own health care needs through Flexible Savings Accounts (FSAs) and Medical Savings Accounts (MSAs).

American Partners In Conservation And Preservation: Stewardship Of Our Natural Resources

Today's Republican party stands in the proud tradition of Teddy Roosevelt, the first president to stress the importance of environmental conservation.

The way current laws have been implemented has often fostered costly litigation and discouraged personal innovation in environmental conservation. We need to get back on a common track, so that both the people and their government can jointly focus on the real problems at hand. As a basis for that cooperation, we propose these principles:

- Economic prosperity and environmental protection must advance together. Prosperity gives our society the wherewithal to advance environmental protection, and a thriving natural environment enhances the quality of life that makes prosperity worthwhile.

- Scare tactics and scapegoating of legitimate economic interests undermine support for environmental causes and, what is worse, can discredit actual threats to health and safety.

We believe the government's main role should be to provide market-based incentives to innovate and develop the new technologies for Americans to meet—and exceed—environmental standards. Wherever it is environmentally responsible to do so, we will promote market-based programs that are voluntary, flexible, comprehensive, and cost-effective.

Affordable energy, the result of Republican policies in the 1980s, helped create the New Economy. If we do not carefully plan for our energy needs, the entire economy could be significantly weakened. America needs a national energy strategy—and a Republican president will work with congressional Republicans to enact their National Energy Security Act. That strategy will:

- Increase domestic supplies of coal, oil, and natural gas. Our country does have ample energy resources waiting to be developed, and there is simply no substitute for an increase in their domestic production.

- Improve federal oil and gas lease permit processing and management, including coalbed methane.

- Provide tax incentives for production.

- Promote environmentally responsible exploration and development of oil and gas reserves on federally-owned land, including the Coastal Plain of Alaska's Arctic National Wildlife Refuge.

- Offer a degree of price certainty to keep small domestic stripper producers in operation.

- Advance clean coal technology.
- Expand the tax credit for renewable energy sources to include wind and open-loop biomass facilities, and electricity produced from steel cogeneration.
- Provide a tax incentive for residential use of solar power.

Government For The People

A Republican president will run the federal government much as the Republican governors run state agencies. Bureaucracy will be reduced and trimmed in size at its upper echelons. If public services can be delivered more efficiently and less expensively through the private sector, they will be privatized. A Republican president will establish accountability, reward performance, put civility back into the civil service, and restore dignity and ethics to the White House.

The Republican party affirms that any regulation of the political process must not infringe upon the rights of the people to full participation in the political process. The principal cure for the ills of democracy is greater participation in the political process by more citizens. To that end, we have one guiding principle in the development of laws to regulate campaigns: Will any particular proposal encourage or restrict the energetic engagement of Americans in elections? Governor Bush's agenda for more honest and more open politics meets that standard. It will:

- Stop the abuses of corporate and labor "soft" money contributions to political parties.
- Level the playing field by forbidding incumbents to roll over their leftover campaign funds into a campaign for a different office.
- Require full and timely disclosure on the Internet of all campaign contributions—so the media and the public can immediately know who is giving how much to whom.
- Encourage all citizens to donate their time and resources to the campaigns of their choice by updating for inflation the quarter-century-old limits on individual contributions.

Principled American Leadership

A Republican president will identify and pursue vital American national interests. He will set priorities and he will stick to them. Under his leadership, the United States will build and secure the peace. Republicans know what it takes to accomplish this: robust military forces, strong alliances, expanding trade, and resolute diplomacy.

A Republican president and a Republican Congress will transform America's defense capabilities for the information age, ensuring that U.S. armed forces remain paramount against emerging dangers.

The new Republican government will renew the bond of trust between the Commander-in-Chief, the American military, and the American people. The military is not a civilian police force or a political referee. We believe the military must no longer be the object of social experiments. We affirm traditional military culture. We affirm that homosexuality is incompatible with military service.

A Republican president, working in partnership with a Republican Congress, will push beyond marginal improvements and incorporate new technologies and new strategies—spending more and investing wisely to transform our military into a true twenty-first century force.

America must deploy effective missile defenses, based on an evaluation of the best available options, including sea-based, at the earliest possible date. These defenses must be designed to protect all 50 states, America's deployed forces overseas, and our friends and allies in the fellowship of freedom against missile attacks by outlaw states or accidental launches.

International organizations can serve the cause of peace, but they can never serve as a substitute for, or exercise a veto over, principled American leadership. The United Nations was not designed to summon or lead armies in the field and, as a matter of U.S. sovereignty, American troops must never serve under United Nations command. Nor will they be subject to the jurisdiction of an International Criminal Court.

Republicans support a response to terrorism that is resolute but not impulsive. The most likely highly destructive terrorist attack remains a large bomb hidden in a car or truck. Yet, as with the rest of our defense posture, we must prepare for the most dangerous threats as well as the most likely ones. Therefore the United States must be extremely vigilant about the possibility that future terrorists might use weapons of mass destruction, which are increasingly available and present an unprecedented threat to America.

Republicans have a strategy. It is a strategy that recalls traditional truths about power and ideals and applies them to networked marketplaces, modern diplomacy and the high-tech battlefield. A Republican administration will use power wisely, set priorities, craft needed institutions of openness and freedom, and invest in the future. A Republican president and a Republican Congress can achieve the unity of national governance that has so long been absent. We see a confident America united in the fellowship of freedom with friends and allies throughout the world. We envision the restoration of a respected American leadership firmly grounded in a distinctly American internationalism.

Lobbyists and the Equality
of the Political Process

MARK S. HYDE AND JOHN J. CARROLL

As their introductory quote suggests, Mark Hyde and John Carroll report that lobbyists are complex figures. Often reviled by the public as dishonest power-brokers, lobbyists nevertheless bring a very valuable asset—knowledge—to the policymaking process. Hyde and Carroll's study looks at different types of lobbyists and the distinctions between these professionals. Though each type of lobbyist can draw on different strengths in being effective in their job, this study suggests that not all lobbyists are created equal. Ultimately, contract lobbyists may be most advantageously positioned to exert influence.

"*A lobbyist is a cross between a teacher and a used car salesman.*"

Texas Lobbyist

Information about individuals who lobby can help clarify normative issues about representation and the institutions of democracy. Many people seem to have a general image of a myriad of lobbyists swarming—or individual lobbyists lurking—around state capitol buildings waiting for an opportunity to cajole or threaten a public official into serving their special interests. This image of the lobbyist, common in the popular press and popular imagination, sees lobbying as a perversion of the public interest, which is regularly abandoned when the interests of special and narrow groups are advocated persuasively.

Those who are knowledgeable about state politics know lobbyists testify at hearings, speak informally with legislators in hallways about the merits of proposed legislation, and represent the views of their organizations. From this vision of the lobbyist, common in the academic literature, comes the idea that lobbyists serve the public interest by providing public officeholders with specialized information they would not otherwise have, information that allows them to perfect legislation. These two images—the interest group as democratic facilitator versus lobbyists as protectors of the powerful—are in collision, and the data in this reading provide some analysis that speaks to this.

As one way to understand lobbying and interests—who participates, how, why, and to what end—previous studies have tended to emphasize the group and its place within the system. In this approach the unit of analysis is the interest group, such as the labor unions; professional associations like nurses or psychologists; industry alliances like truckers, lumber, or petroleum; reform-minded citizens allied together like the Sierra Club or Common Cause; individual corporations like General Motors; and government groups, including associations of counties or school committees. This approach provides an appreciation of which groups are active in the system, the issues of concern to them, the resources they commit, their reputation for influence, and the tactics they use. These have been the recurring themes in the literature describing interest group systems in the American states (Zeigler and Baer, 1969; Thomas and Hrebnar, 1996).

The group approach to the study of lobbying has its intellectual origins in what Paul Lazarsfeld and his colleagues called the "dynamic social research," which emerged before and shortly after World War II (Lazarsfeld, 1944). These innovative scholars de-emphasized institutional analysis and legal doctrine to take what seemed to be a more realistic approach to understanding politics, the study of groups in action (Latham, 1952; Truman, 1951). They believed the American political system was linked to the larger social system through a network of secondary groups—schools, neighborhoods, religion, work, ethnic clubs—to which large numbers of individuals belonged.

In this view, American democracy depended on the operation of groups in which individuals merged their influence and worked together for common policy goals. Some of the groups, especially labor unions and corporations, gathered enormous numbers of Americans under their organizational roofs and claimed to speak for them. Groups provided an alternative avenue for democratic participation for individuals who wished to be politically active; they served as outlets for the expressions of grievances, thus reducing social stress; they informed political leaders of the bewildering array of interests in the larger society; and they bargained with other groups and interests during the policy-making process. In a sense, groups perfected the democratic system by cumulating interests, articulating those interests and representing them at the seat of government in a timely and continuous fashion (Dahl, 1961).

The focus on groups was particularly helpful to democratic theorists who sought to explain and rationalize the democratic system in the face of troubling findings in the voting literature. Voting studies conducted in the late 1940s and 1950s were the first to demonstrate that large segments of the voting public were uninformed of the choices before them and others seemed to be responding mechanically to campaign stimuli (Lazarsfeld, Berelson, and Gaudet, 1944; Campbell, Gurin, and Miller, 1954). Many voters, it seemed, could not identify the names of competing candidates for high public office and had even less information about the policies that candidates advocated (Campbell, Gurin, Miller, and Stokes, 1960). These findings were so disturbing that they provoked a respected scholar of parties and interest groups, V. O. Key, Jr., to publish a defense of democratic elections under the title *The Responsible Electorate*. Key ruefully observed that "The perverse and unorthodox argument of this little book is that voters are not fools" (Key, 1966).

From another perspective, because elections of persons to government offices took place only once every few years, they seemed to have a limited use in providing control to democratic majorities over the activities of government officials. As a consequence, the suspicion grew that elections did not play the central role in the public control of public policy they were once thought to have, and the system must somehow be more complex (Dahl, 1956). Groups provided a key answer to the democratic riddle once they were conceptualized as mediating influences. Groups, it was argued, presented officeholders with the plurality of demands in the society at large and argued for them, gave close attention to the policy decisions made by public and party officeholders, and reported those decisions to their members and the public at large. Seen in this light, groups were a positive democratic influence because they provided a check on the system, and a continuing avenue for the expression of the popular will within a system in which a plurality of groups slugged it out in the arena of politics. Out of the interest-group conflict between labor and capital, rich and poor, soldier and civilian, the public interest was somehow identified and public policy forged.

For several decades the interest group system has come under withering attack in mass media and from critics on the left who charge that interest groups overrepresent some interests at the expense of others, and reinforce the power of already influential segments (for example, Birnbaum and Pooley, 1996; Updegrave, 1966; McMenamin 1997). These critics are skeptical that the outcomes and processes associated with interest group activity are fair in any sense but the Darwinian, and charge that the interest system reinforces the inequitable distribution of resources within the system as a whole. Consequently, the interest system is thought to advantage those already in superior positions, while disadvantaging those who are not; unlike the ballot box, the interest group system does not reflect the democratic ideal of a level playing field in which every citizen has an equal opportunity to influence policy with every other.

The popular hypothesis is that power follows money and this article takes a closer look at that simple but provocative idea. We use a national sample of approximately fifteen hundred state lobbyists covering all of the fifty states. The randomly drawn sample is drawn from the lists of registered lobbyists maintained by the states.

In thinking about who exercises power in the interest group system, the popular hypothesis implies that individuals who are paid to work as professional lobbyists will have advantages over others. It suggests that the more professional the lobbyists the more money they will have to spend, the more time they can devote to lobbying, and the more skills they will have acquired through education. In *The Third Branch* (1993), Alan Rosenthal concentrated on the lobbyists he believed to be the most influential in their states, and for the most part they seem to be paid lobbyists working for clients. Even so, there has been no systematic analysis of these differences between state lobbyists and what that entails for power and its exercise.

Lobbyists and Their Work

We classify lobbyists by their relationships to the interests they represent into three distinct categories: contract, in-house, and volunteer. This typology is organized around the common ways the job of lobbyist is structured. We suspect the typology will allow us to identify patterns among lobbyists in revealing ways, especially if the popularly held assumption that there is a close connection between power and money is correct.

The first group of lobbyists, at 24 percent of our national sample, is the **contract lobbyists,** who hire out their professional services for a fee. Because of the costs associated with hiring professional representation, contract lobbyists tend to represent commercial interests, which have the resources to afford them. Consequently, contract lobbyists typically represent large firms whose enterprises are national in scope, such as insurance, banking, natural resources and chemicals, or firms that play, or would like to assume an important role in a state's economy. Even though we are talking about lobbyists working in state capitols, these are professionals at the work of lobbying: they make their living representing interests and many of them have multiple clients, including some with a long list of Fortune 500 firms. For example, a New Mexico contract lobbyist with 25 years experience represents a typical assortment of groups: liquor interests, health care providers, grocery and convenience stores; a 50-year-old Illinois lawyer and contract lobbyist represents tobacco, Shell Oil, Amoco, radiologists, and riverboat gambling operators, among others. Such lobbyists are found in every state, the small and rural as well as the large and urban. Lobbyists of this sort are typically lawyers, the head of their own firm or partners in a larger practice, who often represent their clients in other contexts, defending them from suit and speaking on their behalf to the press and public. The concentration of their clients in the business world is remarkable: 82 percent of contract lobbyists are employed by business, while less than 2 percent worked for labor unions, 5 percent for government, with the rest scattered among farm and other interests.

The most common relationship between lobbyists and the groups they represent is that of the **in-house lobbyists,** who account for 66 percent of our sample. In-house lobbyists are employees, proprietors, or executives of their interest group whose work responsibilities include lobbying the Assembly or the governor's office. Such a person may be the executive director of a regional chamber of commerce, the public relations representative for a medium-sized retailer, an employee of a labor union, or the director for a state affiliate of a citizens' group, such as a small ACLU affiliate or conservation advocates. Typically, government (86 percent) and labor (88 percent) use in-house lobbyists; even so, slightly more than half of all in-house lobbyists (51 percent) work for business.

In-house lobbyists provide important advantages to groups working with limited budgets or to those who believe their interests are only marginally threatened or advanced by state public policy. In-house lobbyists are already on the payroll where they are usually assigned additional tasks for their firms or organizations, but take on the lobbying effort as a part of their job, most commonly when the legislature is in session. This type of lobbyist often finds the task to be a substantial added burden because the work associated with the nonlobbying part of their job tends to pile up and run late when the legislature is sitting, and they are distracted from their normal office routines. While this group of lobbyists often has the advantage of knowing their issues well, most are disadvantaged by lobbying part-time. This means they may have difficulty keeping on top of the legislative process and may not know all of the key players.

The third group, and the smallest among registered lobbyists nationwide, are the **volunteers,** who make up just 10 percent of the sample. The volunteer lobbyists are persons whose efforts are expended on behalf of causes they support, typically for nonprofit organizations, good government groups, churches, or professional associations with limited budgets. As might be expected from amateurs, very few report that they lobby the equivalent of a full workweek when the legislature is in session (6 percent), more typically they spend a few hours a week, squeezed in among their other avocations, domestic responsibilities, or job. Of all the groups, volunteers report expending the least time on the job, and considerably so, which has important negative ramifications for access to decision-makers and the ability to influence policy. In terms of the major vested interests, about a third of the volunteers (32 percent) lobby for business interests, but only 4 percent for labor and 11 percent for government. As a group, their numbers are small and their interests diverse.

Lobbying and Their Use of Time

How lobbyists use their time provides important clues about their ability to lobbying effectively and to represent their interests. Obviously, the more time spent at the state house, the more likely it is that the lobbyists will form personal relationships with officeholders, be able follow the course of legislation, and develop access to processes and people who determine the outcomes of policy decisions.

As independent professionals working for clients wealthy enough to pay them, contract lobbyists have substantial advantages in the amount of time they are able to dedicate to their lobbying work. Almost half of the contract lobbyists reported that they spent the equivalent of a full workweek lobbying, 38 or more hours, when the legislature was in session (Table 1). This is almost twice the proportion of in-house lobbyists, and far more than our third group, the volunteers. In all, contract lobbyists averaged 31 hours of lobbying a week when the legislature was in session, compared to 24 hours for in-house lobbyists and only 11 hours for volunteers.

TABLE 1   **Type of Lobbyist and Time Devoted to Lobbying While Legislature Is In and Out of Session**

	Contract Lobbyists	In-House Lobbyists	Volunteer Lobbyists
Average No. of Hours per Week (Legislature in Session)	31.0 hours n=348	23.9 hours n=951	10.9 hours n=133
Average No. of Hours per Week (Legislature out of Session)	11.7 hours n=313	7.8 hours n=856	4.7 hours n=109

When the legislature is out of session, the contract lobbyists continue to be the most active group. This can be a most important time in many state legislative assemblies, even though the rank-and-file membership may have gone home for the summer or the balance of the year. There are often interim committees at work preparing reports and the agenda for the next session. Members of the legislative leadership, including party leaders and the committee chairs, may be active at the capitol meeting with legislative staff and executive branch officials and organizing party fundraising efforts. At the other end of the capitol building, the executive branch is still at work, administering state government, implementing legislation, and dealing with those lobbyists who are still around. During this period, contract lobbyists devote an average of 12 hours a week to their lobbying work, compared to eight hours for the in-house and less than five hours for volunteers.

Who Are They?

There are important and significant differences between the various groups of lobbyists, which shed light on how the lobbying profession is structured and the social strata from which they are drawn. Education distinguishes the three groups, providing advantages to contract lobbyists (Table 2). Among contract lobbyists, 68 percent hold a law or other graduate degree, compared to less than half of the in-house and a third of the volunteers. The volunteers emerge again as a group less well situated to perform the lobbying function because they are also considerably less likely to have completed the four-year degree than the other groups. Contract lobbyists also tend to be significantly more experienced in the work than the other two groups (Table 2). Contract lobbyists are more likely than the other groups to have worked in the profession for more than

TABLE 2 Type of Lobbyist by Education and Experience

	Contract Lobbyists	In-House Lobbyists	Volunteer Lobbyists
Percentage with Graduate Degree	68.1 % *n*=367	47.0 % *n*=1013	36.4 % *n*=15
Average No. of Years Lobbying	11.2 years *n*=363	9.1 years *n*=1004	7.7 years *n*=15

ten years, and considerably less likely to have less than five years of experience. In contrast, volunteers again emerge as the weakest group. Among them, only a fifth have more than ten years experience, while 44 percent have less than five. This contrasts starkly with the numbers for the contract lobbyists, among whom the relationship was precisely reversed. The in-house lobbyists were spread quite evenly between the categories of experience, with 31 percent having less than five years, 30 percent more than ten, and the rest falling between.

Resources and Tactics

One of the central themes of the interest groups literature has been the techniques or tactics that lobbyists use in their work. There is little difference between the types in their use of three of the traditional lobbying techniques (Table 3). Helping to create the record on a bill by giving testimony at committee hearings responds to a formal opportunity, which the legislative process has structured, and it emerges as a nearly universally used technique. Personal contact between lobbyist and public official also emerges as a near universal technique with no discernible differences among the groups. Mobilizing grassroots efforts is a strategy reported by fewer lobbyists, between 50 or 60 percent rather than 90 percent, but again the reported differences among the groups is slight, although statistically significant. In-house lobbyists utilize this technique more often than other groups, drawing on their close relationship to the group membership, although the contract lobbyists are not far behind. That the volunteers are least likely to use this technique is a surprising finding, since one might have assumed that volunteer lobbyists would be closer to their memberships than contract lobbyists, and more likely to mobilize them.

There are significant and substantial differences in the use of the two techniques that require the expenditure of funds: campaign contributions and social activities. By a substantial margin, contract lobbyists are the most likely to use these techniques, but they are also used by significantly more in-house lobbyists than volunteers.

At least in the popular imagination, parties and junkets sponsored by lobbyists are viewed as a prime opportunity to schmooze legislators and other offi-

TABLE 3   Percentage of Lobbyists Reporting Use of Lobbying Technique

	Contract Lobbyists	In-House Lobbyists	Volunteer Lobbyists
Providing Testimony	94%	92.7%	87.7%
Making Personal Contact	95.9%	92.6%	92.3%
Grassroots Efforts	62.6%	65.1%	54.8%
Engaging in Social Activities	62.9%	59.4%	43.2%
Making Campaign Contributions	71.1%	54.7%	40%
	n=364	n=1012	n=155

cials. The dynamic of these social events is an exchange of food, drink, warmth and sociability for access and familiarity. By any calculation, social familiarity with the customer and the memory of pleasant times are assets useful to any salesperson, including the lobbyists with a point of view to market. Campaign contributions are one side of an exchange in which cash is given for a mutually understood but unstated agreement to provide access for the lobbyist and support where possible for the lobbyist's policy positions. Many of our contract and in-house lobbyist respondents made the particular point that the purpose of contributions and other spending was to buy access, not votes. As a Maine lobbyist put it, "Dollars may gain some access but do not ensure votes or success."

Contract lobbyists have an edge over their in-house and volunteer rivals in the use of both techniques. Almost three-quarters of contract lobbyists report making campaign donations, to about half of in-house and 44 percent of volunteers. Social activities are sponsored by contract and in-house lobbyists in approximately the same proportions, but more often than the volunteers. Again, the greater resources at the disposal of contract, and to a lesser extent in-house lobbyists are apparent.

Many of the volunteer and in-house lobbyists are acutely aware of the advantages that come with the ability to spend money on entertainment and contributions. An environmental lobbyist from a Rocky Mountain state commented: "I lobby for a grassroots organization . . . [and] our strength lies in individual commitment and the zeal of our members. Our finances are meager. . . . Our opponents have lots of money and exert tremendous influence on state government, so our victories are few. . . ." A Florida lobbyist commented that "Over the years the role [of lobbyist] has really changed. Now you really have to have the dollars for political campaigns or you need not ask for votes when they are in [session]." An Illinois lobbyist said, "I do agree that at times, when groups are in competition on an issue, the group with the more dollars has a decided advantage." And a Virginian made the following observations: "Unfortunately our all-volunteer, grass-root group has only sufficient funds to lobby completely by the U.S. mail, while our opposition has a lobbyist representative on the scene in Richmond who throws an expensive dining bash for legislators—something we cannot afford to do. They out spend us about 40 to one! We make a bit of headway each session . . . [but] under funded lobbying is a *great* handicap against moneyed—business and professional—groups."

The Hierarchy of Lobbyists

There is a hierarchy within the ranks of lobbyists in which contract lobbyists hold substantial advantages over in-house lobbyists, who in turn are advantaged as a group over the volunteers. The hierarchy among lobbyists is constructed upon both who they are and the resources they command.

As to who they are, contract lobbyists tend to be better educated, more experienced in the work of lobbying, and more likely to be at the midpoint of their careers. As to the resources at their disposal, contract lobbyists have the comparative advantage of spending substantial time at the job when the legislature is in session, as well as the money to make campaign contributions and host social events. On all these measures, in-house lobbyists fall between the contract lobbyists and the volunteers, with the latter group typically spending only a few hours a week on the job, and more than half reporting that they make neither campaign contributions nor host social events.

The consequence of this hierarchy is that some lobbyists within the interest group system are systematically advantaged over others, with those representing business groups holding the major advantage, and those representing noneconomic interests, such as government, nonprofits and citizens' groups at a disadvantage. That vested economic interests will seek and hold advantages over others in a capitalist system is not a new argument (Lindblom, 1977). The implications of this argument are that the lobbying system does not present a level playing field for all groups, and that well-represented but relatively narrow interests will trump more broadly based interests, some of which are not adequately represented in the interest group system.

These are conclusions with which lobbyists, including contract lobbyists, tend to agree (Table 4). A majority of all lobbyists agree that "It is rare for opposing groups to be evenly matched in influences and resources on a particular issue." Only the contract lobbyists are closely divided on this question, which may reflect the high stakes for which they work, and the findings of Hunter, Wilson, and Brunk (1991) that most group competition at the state level occurs within rather than between categories of groups. From this perspective, contract lobbyists who spend more time and resources than other types of

TABLE 4 Lobbyists on Lobbying: Inequalities in the System

		Contract Lobbyists	In-House Lobbyists	Volunteer Lobbyists
"It is rare for opposing groups to be evenly matched in influences and resources on a particular issue." Do you agree or disagree with this statement?	Agree	44.40%	53.10%	60.00%
	No Opinion	13.10%	12.90%	19.40%
	Disagree	42.50%	34.00%	20.60%
		n=360	*n*=992	*n*=155
"Sometimes lobbyists and interest groups convince public officials to support legislation that is not in the public interest." Do you agree or disagree with this statement?	Agree	83.2%	83.8%	87.7%
	No Opinion	6.2%	7.3%	6.5%
	Disagree	10.6%	8.9%	5.8%
		n=357	*n*=990	*n*=155

lobbyists may be reacting to competition from other contract lobbyists with nearly equal resources, while volunteers and the comparatively resource-poor in-house lobbyists may seem peripheral to them. Even so, most lobbyists believe that most of the time the competing interests within the system are not engaged in an equal contest.

Equally persuasive is agreement by lobbyists on the widely held view that "Sometimes lobbyists and interest groups convince public officials to support legislation that is not in the public interest" (Table 5). On this issue, there are no significant differences between groups and the levels of agreement among lobbyists approach consensus. The views of lobbyists on this matter reflect the widely-held popular perception that "special interest" lobbyists have more than their share of power in the state capitols and that the broader public interest is often ignored. That lobbyists themselves share this view reinforces the weight of that analysis. We conclude that there is considerable validity to the popular critique that the playing field is strongly tilted in the direction of those interests who can afford to hire a contract lobbyist. The contract lobbyist brings advantages of experience and education, while the contractor provides resources lobbyists need to do the job well—time and money.

References

Birnbaum, Jeffrey H., and Eric Pooley. 1996. "New Party Bosses," *Time* 147 (15): 218–232.

Campbell, Angus, Gerald Gurin, and Warren E. Miller. 1954. *The Voter Decides.* Evanston, IL: Row, Peterson.

Campbell, Angus, Philip E. Converse, Warren E. Miller, and Donald E. Stokes. 1960. *The American Voter.* Chicago: University of Chicago Press.

Dahl, Robert A. 1956. *Preface to Democratic Theory.* Chicago: University of Chicago Press.

———. 1961. *Who Governs? Democracy and Power in an American City.* New Haven: Yale University Press.

Gardner, John W. 1972. *In Common Cause.* New York: Norton.

Hunter, Kenneth G., Laura Ann Wilson, and Gregory G. Brunk. 1991. "Societal Complexity and Interest-Group Lobbying in the American States," *Journal of Politics* 53: 488–503.

Key, V.O., Jr. 1966. *The Responsible Electorate: Rationality in Presidential Voting.* Cambridge, MA: Belknap Press of Harvard University Press.

Latham, Earl. 1952. *The Group Basis of Politics: A Study in Basing-Point Legislation.* New York: Octagon Books.

Lazarsfeld, Paul. 1944. *The People's Choice: How the Voter Makes Up His Mind in a Presidential Campaign.* New York: Duell, Sloan and Pearce.

Lazarsfeld, Paul, H. Gaudet and B. Berelson. 1944. *The People's Choice.* New York: Columbia University Press.

Lindblom, Charles E. 1977. *Politics and Markets: The World's Political-Economic Systems.* New York: Basic Books.

McFarland, Andrew S. 1984. *Common Cause: Lobbying in the Public Interest.* Chatham, NJ: Chatham Press.

McMenamin, Brigid. 1997. "Senators for Sale," *Forbes* 159 (11): 47–48.

Rosenthal, Alan. 1993. *The Third House: Lobbyists and Lobbying in the States.* Washington DC: CQ Press.

Thomas, Clive S., and Ronald J. Hrebnar. 1996. "Interest Groups in the States." In Virginia Gray and Herbert Jacob, eds., *Politics in the American States,* 6th ed. Washington, DC: CQ Press.

Truman, David B. 1951. *The Governmental Process: Political Interests and Public Opinion.* New York: Alfred A. Knopf.

Updegrave, Walter L. 1996. "Stacking the Deck," *Money* (8): 50–63.

Zeigler, Harmon, and Michael A. Baer. 1969. *Lobbying: Interaction and Influence in American State Legislatures.* Belmont, CA: Wadsworth Publishing Co.

Piety and Politics: The Christian Right and American Politics in the Twentieth Century and Beyond

Franklyn C. Niles

The Religious (or Christian) Right has been a potent force in American politics for some time, as Franklyn Niles reports. Praised by its supporters and vilified by opponents, conservative religious organizations have sought to make a mark on American politics and policy. A distinguishing characteristic of conservative religious interest group activity, when compared to many other special interest participations, is the grassroots nature of the movement. Rather than being major players at the nexus of money and politics, social conservatives have found their power through votes and active participation. This has meant, however, that the group has seen dramatic ebbs and flows in the level of influence it has had. Niles suggests that after a period of steep decline, the Christian conservative movement may be in the early stages of a political rebound.

Introduction

Throughout the twentieth century, the Christian Right has been a social movement intent on infusing conservative religious values (often called "family" or "traditional" values) into the policy process. In addition to pursuing a conservative policy agenda in recent years, the movement has also sought to mobilize and represent evangelical Christians in the electoral arena (Wald, 2003; Wilcox, 2003). With roots in the Fundamentalist Movement of the 1920s, the contemporary Christian Right, typically labeled the New Christian Right (NCR), includes other conservative Protestants, such as evangelicals and Pentecostals/charismatics, as well as some traditionalist Catholics and mainline Protestants.[1] Although there is some evidence of a broader religious coalition, historically, most political action has occurred among theologically conservative Christians.

During the 1970s, political observers were shocked, and often dismayed, by the reemergence of Christian conservatives into the political realm. Long thought to be of diminishing relevance in political life, especially after the failure of William Jennings Bryan at the Scopes "Monkey Trial" and after the decline of communism as an international threat—two issues the fundamentalist Christian Right focused on—evangelicalism reemerged again as an important political force. During the late 1970s and early 1980s, Christian conservatives built a web of successful grassroots organizations, such as the National Christian Action Coalition (1978), Jerry Falwell's Moral Majority (1979), and

Pat Robertson's Christian Coalition (1989), each of which lobbied conservative causes and mobilized conservative voters. During this period, the movement experienced electoral success, evidenced, perhaps, most notably by the two-term presidency of Ronald Reagan. In addition, the Christian Right achieved some success in the policy arena, "winning votes on constitutional amendments to ban abortion and to permit prayer in schools in the 98th Congress (1983–1984)" (Moen, 1994: 77). Even though overlooked by many scholars, more than simply winning elections and achieving some policy objectives, the Christian Right helped set the terms of national political debate.

However, by the mid-1990s, many scholars and journalists concluded that the influence of the Christian Right in American politics had run its course. Owing to a series of missteps, one of which was an amateur approach to lobbying in Congress that created an inhospitable bargaining environment, by the late 1980s, nearly every Christian Right organization had dissolved, merged with another group, or had become moribund (the Moral Majority disbanded in 1989 amid increased difficulty in raising money through direct mail). Additionally, despite helping to secure a more conservative Supreme Court and mobilizing evangelical voters, in terms of achieving its policy objectives, the Christian Right of the 1980s can hardly be considered a success (Wilcox, 1994: 154). To date, its policy agenda remains unfulfilled. President Reagan was more interested in pursuing conservative fiscal policy rather than the moral agenda favored by evangelicals, and Bill Clinton rescinded most pro-life policies enacted by executive order. Moreover, abortion remains legal, homosexuals have been increasingly successful at securing policy objectives, prayer in schools is still disallowed, and the Christian Right has lost influence in its adopted home, the Republican Party. Combined, these occurrences led many observers in the 1990s to consider the Christian Right to be largely irrelevant and moving toward extinction.[2]

However, as the 2000 general election drew near, it became readily apparent that predictions concerning a decline in the influence of the contemporary Christian Right needed to be reconsidered.[3] Despite the fact that the national organization of the Christian Coalition, faced with a wave of resignations, low morale, membership decline, and growing debt, crumbled in 1999, the Christian Right was able to mobilize enough conservative voters in the GOP primaries to secure a victory for a candidate they believed would support their legislative agenda and return "morality" to the presidency. Evidencing some strategic forethought, during the primary season most activists in the Christian Right rejected ideologically conservative candidates, including Gary Bauer, Pat Buchanan, and Alan Keyes in favor of the more moderate, yet electable, George W. Bush. According to exit poll data, George W. Bush beat out rival John McCain among Republican voters who identified themselves with the Christian Right and lost among nonreligious voters. Given the large percentage of religious conservatives in the Republican primary electorate, political scientist Clyde Wilcox in 2002 declared, "In the final analysis, Bush won the GOP nomination because of the Christian Right" (112).

The success of George W. Bush and the support he received from the Christian Right in 2000 suggest that the movement is not in a period of decline. At the same time, it would be too premature to conclude that the Christian Right has entered a period of ascendancy. As we begin the new millennium, the question remains, what is the future of the Christian Right in American politics? Will the Christian Right likely fade into history, only to be remembered as a failed social movement, or will the movement reinvent itself with new organizations and activism? Answers to these questions are, of course, necessarily tentative, if not impossible. Still, we can gain an understanding of challenges and opportunities that face the Christian Right in the new millennium by viewing the movement through the lens of social mobilization theory, and by examining the trends in Christian Right development during the twentieth century. One of the central tenets of social movement theory is that groups evolve (or perhaps, devolve) over time in response to organizational and contextual demands (Morris and Mueller, 1992; Moen, 1997). Applied to the Christian Right, one implication of this theory is that if the movement is to persist, it must anticipate contemporary challenges and exploit opportunities (Bruce, 1988). At the same time, another implication is that current leadership decisions are shaped by precedents and patterns established in previous epochs. According to Lienesch (1997: 17), these precedents might include "repertoires, networks, frames, and opportunities," each of which influences subsequent strategic choices.

The goal of this chapter is to describe the evolution of the Christian Right in the twentieth century with the purpose of understanding how organizational goals and political contexts—both past and present—influence the types of strategies (and their consequences) employed by leaders in the New Christian Right.

The Origins of the Christian Right: Fundamentalism v. Evolution

Until the 1920s, evangelical Protestantism was an animating force in the political and social life of America.[4] Believing in the need to pursue individual and social pietism, in the years following the Civil War, evangelicals engaged in a wide range of campaigns to reform society. Often with measured success, the movement battled deism and Roman Catholicism, and championed temperance and immigration restrictions. As the twentieth century approached, evangelicals defended against what they perceived to be encroaching modernism, liberalism, and corruption in American politics, the latter of which, ultimately resulted in the Progressive reforms of the 1890s, spearheaded by William Jennings Bryan. While it would be incorrect to claim that evangelicalism was the only religious perspective represented in American politics at the beginning of the twentieth century, it clearly played a central role in the nation's political and cultural life.

The cultural dominance of evangelicals, however, ended in the 1920s. In response to industrialization, urbanization, the development of science and technology, and rapid birth rates in non-Protestant immigrant communities, the environment that had favored traditional Protestant religious values began to erode (Wald, 2003: 202; Leuchtenburg, 1958). The weakening of traditional values was seen by many evangelicals as contributing to a host of social problems, including the growth in women's employment, the loosening of sexual restraint, the publishing of "hedonistic" literature, and the pursuit of material goods. During this time, conflict also developed within Protestantism between the *fundamentalists,* who promoted a literal interpretation of the Bible and emphasized piety and the need for personal conversion, and the *modernists* or *theological liberals*—individuals who interpreted scripture with less certainty and used religion to pursue social goals.

Faced with the threat of modernism, fundamentalists in the North pursued an agenda that sought to stem the tide of theological liberalism. In addition, in an effort to resist the intrusion of secularism in the political realm, fundamentalists attacked what they perceived to be a grave social evil: the teaching of evolution in public schools. During this period, fundamentalists founded organizations, such as the Bible League of North America, the Bible Crusaders of America, and the Defenders of the Christian Faith. Using a variety of tactics, these organizations tried to encourage state lawmakers to pass laws banning the teaching of evolution in schools. Leaders of these organizations also attempted to bolster support for their cause by holding large antievolution rallies (Wilcox, 2003). In the end, the fundamentalist antievolution crusade ended in disaster at the famous Scopes Trial in 1925, where William Jennings Bryan defended the fundamentalist's view of evolution only to be humiliated by the questioning of Clarence Darrow, an ACLU attorney. Although the Scopes Trial did not end the debate over evolution, it did end the organized involvement of fundamentalists in the antievolution activism. Ultimately, the fundamentalist crusade failed because it was a movement that pursued an agenda that turned out to be contrary to the values and beliefs of most Americans.

After the Scopes Trial, and because of the failure of Prohibition, many fundamentalists and evangelicals retreated from politics. While a group of purists joined forces with other religious leaders, most notably Father Charles Coughlin, an anti-Semitic priest, and Gerald Smith, a mainline Protestant minister, in protest against Franklin Roosevelt and the New Deal, most fundamentalist leaders withdrew from politics and focused on religious matters. Far from being institutionally quiescent, however, during this period fundamentalists regrouped and built Bible colleges, churches, new organizations, and publishing houses— the infrastructure that would play a key role in future Christian Right political activities.

Fundamentalists and the Anticommunism Crusade

In the late 1940s, a second wave of fundamentalist activism occurred with the target this time being communism. With the specter of communism looming after World War II, new fundamentalist groups formed in support of Senator Joseph McCarthy's attacks on communism in America. Anticommunism was a natural rallying point for many fundamentalists who believed that Armageddon, the final battle between good and evil, would occur in Israel when Antichrist forces from the Soviet Union attack the forces of Christ. Under the leadership of political entrepreneurs, such as Carl McIntire and his American Council of Christian Churches and Billy James Hargis of the Christian Crusade, a host of anticommunist organizations were founded that, like their antievolution predecessors, used lobbying, conventions, and public speeches to warn against the threat of domestic communism. These efforts were eventually supplemented by radio broadcasts and anticommunist publications. While these groups recruited members (as well as financial resources) from fundamentalist churches, many of the new organizations downplayed their fundamentalist roots. As a result, they were able to attract secular anticommunist groups, such as the John Birch Society (founded in 1958). With the aid of nonreligious groups, fundamentalists pursued an issue agenda that was broader than that pursued by the antievolution groups of the 1920s. For example, the Christian Anticommunism Crusade, in addition to focusing upon the "Red Menace," also opposed Medicare (calling it socialized medicine) and sex education (Wilcox, 2003). Other groups opposed fluoridation of water and zoning. Regardless of the issue, however, fundamentalist leaders believed each to be part of a broad communist conspiracy that was attempting to weaken the nation's moral resolve, thus, making it easier for a communist takeover.

Despite a prolonged period of activity, the fundamentalist anticommunism crusades were largely unsuccessful at attracting a large following or mobilizing voters. And, after the censure of Joseph McCarthy by the Senate in 1954 concerning his inquiry into suspected communists in the military, and the landslide defeat of Barry Goldwater in 1964, the fundamentalist anticommunism movement rapidly declined.

When the forces that animated the anticommunist movement faded away, their constituency did not. Indeed, during the late 1950s and 1960s, working through their congregations, local pastors continued to build Bible colleges, Bible bookstores, and camps and established a wide range of conservative magazines, newspapers, and radio broadcasts. Each of these outlets provided fundamentalist leaders with access to a broader audience. For example, Fred Schwarz, the founder of American Anti-Communism Crusade (AACC) in 1953, wrote a weekly newsletter in which he warned of the evils of communism. Still active, the AACC makes available anticommunism information through *The Schwarz Report,* a monthly publication, and in books available for purchase through the organization's web site.

During the 1950s and early 1960s, to the extent the Christian Right participated in national politics, it was in partnership with the Democratic Party. The regional and ethnic lines of the fundamentalists that, after the 1930s, were primarily located in the South, perhaps, best explain this alliance. However, after Barry Goldwater's failed presidential bid in 1964—evangelicals were drawn to his anticommunist stance and conservative domestic agenda—and when the party nominated John F. Kennedy, a Catholic, for president, the alignment between evangelicals and the Democratic Party began to erode. In addition, during the 1960s, the party was seen as increasingly moving in the liberal direction on race and social welfare issues. Even with the election of Jimmy Carter, a Democrat who was also a moderate evangelical, by the mid-1970s, the Christian Right was increasingly associated with the more socially conservative Republican Party.

The Roots of the New Christian Right

Perhaps not surprisingly, a third wave of fundamentalist Christian Right activism emerged in the 1970s. As with earlier fundamentalist movements, activists in the 1970s mobilized in response to what they perceived to be a wide array of liberalizing and secularizing trends in American society, including the removal of religion from schools, the increased ease of securing abortions, and the demands of gays and women for equal rights. Many fundamentalist leaders saw these trends as reflecting the influence of secular humanism in society, which they believed to be the primary challenge to orthodox Christian values.

Making use of infrastructure developed by earlier fundamentalist movements, as well as new technologies, the Christian Right in the 1970s made a rapid ascent. Numerous fundamentalist organizations were founded, such as National Christian Action Coalition, the Religious Roundtable, and Christian Voice (1979) that used radio, television, and publications to broadcast their messages. Among these organizations, the most visible was the Moral Majority, founded by Jerry Falwell, a Baptist Bible Fellowship pastor who built a large church in Lynchburg, Virginia. The Moral Majority drew most of its supporters from independent Baptist churches, and in combination with Falwell's recruitment of leaders within the Baptist Bible Fellowship, state and county organizations quickly developed. During the 1970s and 1980s, the Moral Majority and other Christian Right organizations had a much broader issue agenda than their predecessors, and included opposition to abortion, gay rights, and the Equal Rights Amendment. During this time, the Christian Right also campaigned in support of school prayer. In an effort to broaden its constituency, leaders in the Moral Majority also promoted conservative economic policy, including a sub-minimum wage and cuts in welfare spending.

The Christian Right achieved some initial success in fulfilling their goals, such as contributing to the defeat of the Equal Rights Amendment in 1972, winning votes on constitutional amendments to ban abortion, lobbying for legislation permitting prayer in schools in the 98th Congress (Moen, 1994), and by Falwell's account, helping to elect Ronald Reagan in 1980. These successes, however, were costly. Often using moralistic language to describe their positions on issues, such as opposing pornography because it is "sinful," and their tendency to declare the "correct" position on an issue by using scripture, Christian Right lobbyists created a hostile bargaining environment on Capitol Hill that would limit their influence in the future. Additionally, because fundamentalist activists were often antagonistic toward divergent theological viewpoints, they also tended to alienate potential evangelical and Pentecostal allies.

Because of failed political strategies, inflammatory rhetoric, and the inability to raise enough money through direct mail, by the late 1980s, nearly every Christian Right organization had closed its operations or became moribund, including the Moral Majority, which disbanded in 1989 (Moen, 1994: 350).

With social threats still perceived to be present at the end of the 1980s, and electoral success a seeming possibility, out of the ashes of the final wave of fundamentalist activism, the New Christian Right emerged. However, because of the relatively unsuccessful foray by Jerry Falwell into the political arena, and the belief by many political observers that Christian Right leaders would decrease activism once they vented their grievances, this transformation went largely unnoticed. Even the Republican presidential campaign of Pat Robertson in 1988, an ordained minister and founder of the Christian Broadcasting Network, failed to generate a groundswell of interest. Yet, it was during the late 1980s and early 1990s, that the Christian Right retrenched, matured, and became politically active once again.

While national support for Robertson never materialized, Robertson's campaign was an important first step in the institutionalization of the NCR. Unlike Falwell, Robertson broadened his constituency by appealing to Pentecostal and charismatic Christians, and was more successful at raising money than previous Christian Right leaders. In addition, Robertson developed a core of skilled political workers who worked to gain influence in state and local GOP party committees, an important first step in the strengthening of ties between the Christian Right and the Republican Party.

In 1989, Pat Robertson founded the Christian Coalition, the most visible of the NCR organizations. Distinct in terms of strategies, goals, and resources from that of previous fundamentalist organizations, the Christian Coalition represented an important shift in the level and type of evangelical activism in the United States. Using a cadre of skilled activists, the Christian Coalition focused primarily on electoral politics using a multi-pronged strategy. First, the Coalition pursued building grassroots organizations at the state and precinct level. Second, the Coalition downplayed its religious roots by avoiding explicitly religious language. Instead, leaders couched argument in the "rights" language of liberalism, so, for example, abortion became an affront to "fetal rights" rather than murder (Moen, 1994). Third, Coalition workers distributed voter guides in churches around the country. While supposedly nonpartisan, these guides typically presented a Republican bias. Fourth, leaders within the Christian Coalition endeavored to strengthen their ties with the Republican Party by campaigning for GOP candidates, gaining control of state and local party committees, and serving as convention delegates. Fifth, unlike the Moral Majority, the Christian Coalition formed state and local chapters around an activist core, rather than among preachers. This contributed significantly to the professionalism of the organization and the resolve of the movement's leadership. In addition, leaders within the Coalition developed an ecumenical constituency by appealing directly to conservative Catholics, African Americans, and Jews. Finally, in an effort to mobilize voters, the Christian Coalition pursued a wide policy agenda that included domestic policy positions on health care, tax policy, and crime. Even with a broadened agenda, however, most activists were still concerned with abortion and education reform (Wilcox, 2003).

The Christian Coalition illustrates well the state of the NCR during the early 1990s. As a movement, the NCR avoided many of the missteps that plagued prior movements. For example, most groups within the NCR relied upon membership dues, rather than on uncertain direct mail solicitations, to defray operating costs, and as a result experienced a great deal of financial stability. Most organizations also represented a wide range of theological orientations, and had relatively strong representation at the grass roots (Moen, 1994).[5] When compared to its fundamentalist predecessors, the NCR of the 1990s seemed to have created for itself a political encampment from which it could launch a succession of legislative and electoral attacks.

However, following a cyclical pattern characteristic of previous Christian Right movements, by the late 1990s, the Christian Coalition found itself in disarray. In 1999, Ralph Reed resigned to pursue other political endeavors, and most of the organization's state and local chapters disbanded. This allowed Pat Robertson to assume a more active role in the Coalition, which, in response to his increasingly moderate position on abortion and public statements that offended many Republicans—Robertson suggested that President Clinton had won the public relations battle during his impeachment trial—resulted in the resignation of many state and national activists. Another blow to the Christian Coalition occurred in the aftermath of President Clinton's impeachment acquittal. Believing they had lost the "culture war," a group of leaders in the Christian Coalition came to believe that organized political action was futile and as a result publicly advised evangelical Christians to withdraw from political activism (Thomas and Dobson, 2000). Before the 2000 election, the Coalition also had to defend itself against the Federal Election Commission who accused the Coalition of illegally spending money to promote Republican candidates. As of 2003, the Christian Coalition has not disbanded like many previous Christian Right organizations. The organization still maintains a World Wide Web presence, organizes voter registration drives, and lobbies Congress for pro-family causes. Nevertheless, the events of the late 1990s clearly diminished the influence of the Christian Coalition within the Republican Party, Congress, and the electorate at large.

The Christian Right in the New Millennium: Challenges and Opportunities

As the New Christian Right enters the twenty-first century, its fate is uncertain. Contrary to expectations, the movement was unable to establish organizations in every precinct by the year 2000, and moderates in the Republican Party continue to be hostile to the agenda of the NCR. Moreover, the movement's close ties with the GOP may limit potential support among African Americans and Catholics, two groups that polls indicate tend to support some key provisions of the conservative agenda. Internally, the movement lacks a clear leader—this makes sustained, ideologically consistent, growth difficult. The movement is also experiencing an ongoing debate among activists over whether political action is actually effective. Clearly, the NCR faces some daunting challenges, both internally and externally, as it strives for continued development and political influence in the twenty-first century.

At the same time, as the results of the 2000 general election suggest, the NCR was successful at electing a Republican candidate who publicly attested to his Christian faith and campaigned on a conservative platform. Rejecting more ideologically conservative candidates (such as Gary Bauer) in favor of George W. Bush suggests that the NCR is willing to make strategic concessions in order to win important political battles.

In terms of the legislative and policy impact of the NCR, however, the results remain mixed. Clearly, the appointment of John Ashcroft as Attorney General was a victory for the NCR. However, conservative House Republican Dan Coats was rejected by the administration as a possible candidate for Secretary of Defense because of his opposition to gays in the military, and Bush has found himself embroiled in a fight with Senate Democrats over his judicial appointees. Previously, Bush was also seen as backing away form his socially conservative agenda when he eliminated school vouchers from his education reform bill, and took a moderate position on stem-cell research. Each of these "defeats" suggests that the NCR has less of an influence in the policy process than it has in the electoral arena. Ultimately, the election of President Bush suggests that the NCR is a pragmatic movement that is capable making political compromises in the pursuit of its electoral objectives. Whether or not the NCR is capable of achieving the same strategic viewpoint in the legislative arena remains to be seen.

While the ultimate success or failure of the NCR is beyond the horizon, the Christian Right has historically demonstrated an uncanny ability to adapt to new political contexts (often through ideological moderation and organizational innovation), and in the process, reinvent itself. No doubt, the NCR will likely continue using strategies that have worked previously, while also seizing unforeseen opportunities. In this way, the Bush administration and the Republican-dominated Congress may play a pivotal role in the immediate future of the Christian Right (Wilcox, 2003). If leaders in the NCR are emboldened by recent legislative activity aimed at eliminating "partial-birth" abortions,[6] then they will likely increase their efforts to achieve one of the movement's primary agenda items: the elimination of abortion rights. However, if Bush fails to achieve (or pursue) a conservative agenda that is amenable to most in the NCR, the forces within the movement favoring a withdrawal from the political realm may prevail, and once again, the Christian Right will retreat into an era of passivity.

Perhaps the greatest challenge the NCR faces as it enters the twenty-first century is to move from a position of cultural isolation to cultural leadership (Atwood, 1990). The NCR's inability to achieve most of its policy objectives suggests that the movement has yet to convince voters that its vision of the "good society," which includes restrictions on abortion and social welfare programs, educational choice in the form of school vouchers, and limited gay rights, possesses moral veracity. In an increasingly religiously and ethnically pluralistic society, this seems like a daunting task. Nevertheless, if history teaches us anything, as a critiquing force in society, the Christian Right will likely continue to use a combination of lobbying, grassroots development, party activism, and voter mobilization in an effort to ply its vision of society for some time.

References

Atwood, Thomas C. 1990. "Through a Glass Darkly. Is The Christian Right Overconfident It Knows God's Will?" *Policy Review* (Fall): 44–52.

Bruce, Steve. 1988. *The Rise and Fall of the New Christian Right.* New York: Oxford University Press.

———. 1994. "The Inevitable Failure of the Christian Right," *Sociology of Religion* 55(3): 229–242.

Jelen, Ted G. 1991. *The Political Mobilization of Religious Beliefs.* New York: Praeger.

Leuchtenburg, William E. 1958. *The Perils of Prosperity, 1914–1932.* Chicago, IL: University of Chicago Press.

Lienesch, Michael. 1997. "The Origins of the Christian Right: Early Fundamentalism," In Corwin E. Smidt and James M. Penning, eds., *Sojourners in the Wilderness. The Christian Right in Comparative Perspective.*

Moen, Matthew C. 1994. "From Revolution to Evolution: The Changing Nature of the Christian Right," *Sociology of Religion* 55(3): 345–357.

———. 1997. "The Changing Nature of the Christian Right: 1970s–1990s." In Corwin E. Smidt and James M. Penning, eds., *Sojourners in the Wilderness. The Christian Right in Comparative Perspective.*

Morris, Aldon D., and Carol McClurg Mueller. 1992. *Frontiers in Social Movement Theory.* New Haven, CT: Yale University Press.

Smidt, Corwin E., and James M. Penning. 1997. *Sojourners in the Wilderness. The Christian Right in Comparative Perspective.* Lanham, MD: Rowman & Littlefield Publishers.

Thomas, Cal, and Ed Dobson. 2000. *Blinded by Might.* Grand Rapids, MI: Zondervan.

Wald, Kenneth D. 2003. *Religion and Politics in the United States,* 4th ed. Lanham, MD: Rowman & Littlefield Publishers.

Wayne, Stephen J., and Clyde Wilcox. 2002. *The Election of the Century and What It Tells Us About the Future of American Politics.* Armonk, NY: M.E. Sharp.

Wilcox, Clyde. 1994. "Premillennialists at the Millennium: Some Reflections on the Christian Right in the Twenty First Century," *Sociology of Religion* 55(3): 243–261.

———. 2002. "Whither the Christian Right? The Elections and Beyond. " In Stephen J. Wayne and Clyde Wilcox, eds., *The Election of the Century and What It Tells Us About the Future of American Politics.* Armonk, NY: M.E. Sharp.

———. 2003. "Laying Up Treasures in Washington and in Heaven: The Christian Right and Evangelical Politics in the Twentieth Century and Beyond." *OA H Magazine of History,* January 23–29.

Endnotes

1. For those unfamiliar with Protestant religious categories, fundamentalists believe that the Bible is literally, word-for-word true (called inerrantists) and are separatists. Other than for evangelistic purposes, they avoid social, religious, or political connections with nonfundamentalists. Fundamentalists are located in many conservative Protestant denominations, such as the Southern Baptist Convention. Pentecostals believe they are recipients of spiritual gifts from the Christian Holy Spirit, which might include the ability to "speak in tongues" (glossolalia), prophecy, and healing. Pentecostal Christians are primarily found in the Assemblies of God denomination. Charismatics, much like Pentecostals, also believe in the "gifts of the Spirit," but they belong to many different

denominations and often worship in large, nondenominational churches. In addition, unlike Pentecostals, who tend to be relatively poor and white, charismatics are much more ethnically diverse and often of higher socioeconomic status. Evangelicals, sometimes referred to as neo-evangelicals, are theologically conservative much like fundamentalists, but are often less separatist toward things secular and less theologically dogmatic. Evangelical denominations include Evangelical Free Church and Presbyterian Church America. Evangelicalism is often used when referring to any conservative Protestant. Finally, mainline Protestant denominations, which include Methodists, Presbyterian Church USA, and Episcopalians, are theologically liberal—they do not believe the Bible to be inerrant—and they place a heavier emphasis upon pursing social justice than evangelism.

2. Illustrative of this point of view, Steve Bruce in an article in the *Sociology of Religion* titled "The Inevitable Failure of the New Christian Right," argued that "much of what the NCR [New Christian Right] wants to change is a near-inevitable consequence of cultural pluralism in a democratic industrialism" (1994: 241). As a result, he predicted that the New Christian Right would decline in political and social relevance.

3. The discussion in this section draws heavily from Wilcox (2002).

4. The cultural and political influence of evangelicals in the nineteenth century has been written about extensively. Interested readers should refer to *The Political Culture of the American Whigs* by Daniel Walker Howe (1984) and *Chariot of Fire: Religion and the Beecher Family* by Marie Caskey (1978).

5. Recognizing its limited role in national politics, many leaders in the NCR shifted their emphasis to building grassroots organizations, and focusing on local political battles, such as outlawing books in schools that they deemed offensive, campaigning for local and state candidates, and filling school boards with Christian conservatives.

6. On June 4, 2003, the House passed a bill (HR 760) restricting physicians from performing a certain type of late-term abortion procedure that opponents have termed "partial-birth" abortions. As of this writing, the Senate has yet to vote on the measure.

Elections and Electoral Systems in a Democracy: *How* You Vote Matters

Michael A. Baum

Voting matters, but so does the electoral context in which one casts their vote. This is the point that Michael Baum makes when he suggests that differing electoral methods can produce very different election outcomes, even while adhering to the principles of political equality and one person–one vote. Americans often have a difficult time understanding that there are other—perhaps fairer—ways of conducting elections than the system widely used here in the United States.

Until the United States presidential elections of 2000, and in particular the events that took place in the state of Florida, most Americans pretty much took our elections for granted— so much so that a majority of the voting age population routinely opted not to bother going to the polls.[1] Among many young voters—the least likely group to vote[2]—the election really only got interesting in the days and weeks after election day.

Whatever their political persuasion, individuals in Florida and in several other tight races around the country soon learned that the old adage about "making your vote count" was hardly empty rhetoric. Several contests were decided by mere hundreds of votes. But what was especially unsettling to many Americans was the notion that maybe they had been lied to. All their lives they had been told by both of the major political parties that the United States was "the greatest democracy in the world," some even said "in the history of the world"! And now politicians and newspaper editors from all over the world were asking whether the United States might in fact need their help with election monitoring. After all, many foreigners asked how was it possible that the election for the most powerful office in the world was being decided by local officials staring at punch cards and state officials nominated by the brother of one of the candidates? It sounded more like an election process in a struggling democracy in the developing world, not the advanced democracy of the United States!

Despite the controversy, at least one positive outcome of the election was a broad reassessment by elected officials, political parties, nongovernmental organizations, and the citizens themselves about the need for election reforms in the United States. People finally started to ask some classic questions of comparative politics: "Is this really the best way to elect a President?" "Are there other options?" "What about our other elected officials, shouldn't we also reconsider how they are elected?" This chapter seeks to go beyond questions of merely updating voting technologies (always a good idea), or the issue of campaign finance (most developed countries have much stricter regulations than the

United States), to sketch some very broad outlines regarding the larger debates about the purpose of democratic elections, the various ways they are presently conducted around the world, and the predictable outcomes implied by each of these choices.

The Role of Elections

So what is the purpose of free and fair elections in a democracy? According to G. Bingham Powell, Jr. (2000), one of the foremost writers on electoral systems, elections are "instruments of democracy." Although the word *democracy* can mean many different things depending upon the context; in large polities such as the modern nation-state it has generally come to be associated with "government by the people," only now "the people" are represented *indirectly* through a competitive appeal for their vote. This is the essence of representative government. Elections thus serve as "instruments of democracy" insofar as they provide a way for the people to influence policymaking. Electoral systems, as we learned in the elections of 2000, are critically important because they are the system of rules that govern how people's votes are turned into seats. These rules also determine, to a very large degree, the number of political parties that are likely to get seats in the legislature. As such, electoral systems are crucially important for understanding a country's political system.

Although there are about as many varieties of democracy as there are days in the year, Powell and others (see Dahl, 1971; Lijphart, 1984, 1999) have helped us make a basic distinction between two types of democratic government: *majoritarian* and *proportional*. At the risk of some oversimplification, this distinction is as old as democracy itself. Is democracy simply, as Alexis de Tocqueville ([1835], 1990) would argue, the tyranny of the majority (or majority rule if you prefer), or is it about limiting majority tyranny and reflecting as accurately as possible the range of policy preferences that exist in a polity at a given time? As John Stuart Mill (1861) said, rule "by a mere majority of the people, exclusively represented, is synonymous with a government of privilege, in favour of the numerical majority, who alone possess practically any voice in the State. This is the inevitable consequence of the manner in which the votes are now taken, to the complete disfranchisement of minorities."[3]

In the majoritarian view, elections allow the citizenry to *tightly control* policymakers. If there is a clear majority that comes out of the election, then responsibility is clear and voters can either reward or punish the incumbent party at the next elections. In this case, elected officials are more directly accountable to voters. If voters are unhappy with their representative's performance, they can "throw the rascal out" at the next election. The proportional view, on the other hand, opts for allowing citizens to influence policymaking, but they do not control it to nearly the degree as in the majoritarian vision. Instead, democracy in the proportional vision is inclusive of minorities, bringing all or nearly all representatives of the various factions in society into the policymaking arena. There, these representatives will bargain and cajole each other in a flexible manner, the policy outcomes from which are more difficult to predict. In this way, elections are more *indirect* instruments for citizen control over policy. Democracy in the proportional vision is about the people's elected representatives bargaining with each other in an arena of shifting policy coalitions. According to this view, the preferences of all citizens, not just an electoral majority, should be taken into account for policymaking (Powell, 2000: 6).

Two Types of Electoral Systems

This very brief sketch of two competing visions of democracy can now help us understand why there are broadly two very different types of electoral systems in the world today—these are *plurality,* or winner-take-all (WTA) systems, and their polar opposite, *proportional representation* or PR.[4] Here it is important to note that the choice of electoral system is not the same thing as *type* of political system. For example, both the United Kingdom (UK) and the United States use plurality electoral systems for electing their legislatures (House of Commons and Congress, respectively). However, the United Kingdom is a *parliamentary* system whereas the United States is a *presidential* democracy.[5] In the discussion that follows, I will concentrate primarily on the electoral rules that govern the election of legislatures. Presidential elections are by definition winner-take-all, but variations in this type of election will be covered afterwards.

Winner-take-all (WTA) elections are really very simple to understand and since this is the system used in the United States, we will begin here. The most important defining characteristic of this type of election is that for each district there can be only one winner. That is, there is only one seat representing the people who live in that district (*single-member districts or single-seat constituencies*). Scholars of electoral systems use the term *district magnitude* to refer to the average number of seats in each district. In the United States and the UK, the district magnitude is the lowest possible—one (1.0), since there is only one winner per district. For example, the U.S. House of Representatives has 435 seats. This means that there are 435 congressional districts in the United States. Britain has 659 seats in its House of Commons, and thus 659 electoral districts (or constituencies).[6]

PR systems, on the other hand, have *multi-member districts*. This means that instead of there being only one winner in each district, there can be several. For example, in this type of system, residents of New Bedford, Massachusetts, who belong to the Massachusetts 4th congressional district would be represented in Washington by more individuals than just Congressman Barney Frank. Instead, depending on the population of the district, they might have 2, 3, or 10 or more representatives working for their policy preferences in Washington (depending on their district magnitude). In this type of system, Republicans living in New Bedford would be likely to elect their own representative(s) and would not have to tolerate a liberal Democratic Congressman like Frank speaking on their behalf.

So how do these respective electoral systems work in practice? WTA systems are simple. Political parties list the names of their candidate on the ballot and voters choose that person/party that they think best represents their interests. At the end of the day, the ballots are tabulated and the person who wins the *most* votes, *even if they do not win a majority of the votes*,[7] wins the seat and becomes the representative for all the residents of that district. If there are only two serious candidates, this seems rather straightforward. But what happens if there is a serious third-party candidate, like say a Green Party candidate, fighting it out in New Bedford with a Republican and a Democratic candidate?

In this hypothetical case, let's imagine that 42 percent of the voters voted Republican (highly unlikely in a heavily Democratic area like New Bedford, but this is just for illustration!), 41 percent voted Democratic, and the remaining 17 percent voted Green. In this case, the Republican candidate would become the Congressman/woman for the district despite only winning 42 percent of the popular vote, that is, a *plurality*. Fifty-eight percent of the voters of New Bedford would have voted for someone else! Now, imagine public opinion polls prior to the election indicated that the Greens and Democrats were badly splitting the leftist vote and that a Republican might possibly win the district for the first time in living memory. In this case, Green Party voters would probably have to suffer terrible pangs of conscience as they entered the voting booth. The WTA system forces them to think "should I vote my preferred policy preference, which is the Green Party, or should I try to block the evil Republican candidate, whose policies I dislike much more than the Democratic candidate?" In other words, WTA systems tend to hurt third-party voters by frequently forcing them to vote *strategically,* rather than in accord with their true wishes. Likewise, one can easily see how this type of system would make it very difficult for smaller parties to ever gain a foothold nationally. As a matter of fact, WTA electoral systems tend to produce legislatures with fewer political parties, and typically two main parties tend to control the overwhelming majority of seats in the legislature.

PR-list systems, on the other hand, are much fairer to the voters of smaller minority parties. In this system, voters see a ballot similar to the one in a WTA system, only now instead of each party listing only one person as its candidate, there are lists of candidates for each party (in rank order), the number of which corresponds to how many seats are available. So if the New Bedford district has, let's say, a total of say 10 seats to send to Washington, then each party on the ballot will have a list of 10 candidates on the ballot. Now, using the hypothetical results mentioned above, the seats would be distributed *proportionately* to how each party did in the popular vote. Thus, the Republicans with 42 percent of the vote would get 4 of the 10 seats; the Democrats with 41 percent of the vote would also get 4 of the 10 seats; and the Green Party voters with 17 percent of the vote would send 2 representatives from the district.[8] This means that the first 4 people on the Republican and Democratic lists would become congressmen/women, and only the top 2 people on the Green list would become representatives.

What are the implications of these electoral system choices for a political system? First, more parties (voices) are likely to win official representation in the country's legislature if PR is used, and thus if one's vision of democracy is the one that stresses the accurate reflection of the various factions of the electorate, then PR is the more representative system. But does that make it a more *democratic* system? That depends on which vision of democracy you prefer. Since more parties get into the legislature in a PR system, it is mathematically less likely for any one party to succeed in winning a majority of the *seats* in the legislature.[9] This has especially important implications for the formation of governments in parliamentary systems, but presidential governments are also greatly impacted by the presence or absence of majority parties in the legislature.

In a parliamentary system like the United Kingdom's, governments are formed after the parliament has been elected by the people. Typically, the leader of the party with the most seats becomes prime minister. He/she then forms the government by selecting who the cabinet ministers will be, and the government remains responsible to parliament (which was itself elected by the people). Since the United Kingdom uses the same type of electoral system as the United States, relatively few seats get awarded to third parties and the parliament tends to be dominated by the two main political parties, in this case New Labour and the Conservatives.[10] One of these two parties has almost always held a majority of the seats (*majority government*) and thus voters know whom to hold responsible for policymaking. However, in the Netherlands, which also uses a parliamentary system, the choice of PR means that many more parties tend to get seats in the parliament. It is also less common for any one party to win a majority of the seats. When no one party wins a majority, *coalition governments* are more likely to occur. A coalition government is simply when two or more parties agree to share decision-making power together, until such time as the coalition collapses due to disagreements, or new elections are held.[11] Although it is possible for countries to be governed in a stable fashion for years by coalition governments, due to their greater potential for disagreements, this type of government tends to fall apart more frequently than majority governments.

Thus, it is fair to say that WTA tends to produce more stable political systems at the cost of less fair representation of minority interests, whereas PR systems tend to elect more representative legislatures, but at the cost of greater instability and less direct party accountability to voters. Furthermore, since PR systems more accurately reflect the electorate's policy preferences, strategic voting is less common and voter turnout is higher than in majoritarian electoral systems.[12] PR systems also produce higher rates of female representation than majoritarian systems (Matland, n.d.). On the other hand, James Madison argued vehemently against the dangers of "factionalism" in the *Federalist Papers,* and the two-party system effectively guards against narrowly ideological parties, thereby promoting greater centrism and moderation in party programs. Likewise, voters who lament the "boring stability" of two-party systems would do well to study the history of extremely proportional voting systems in intensely divided societies, such as Weimar Germany prior to the rise of Hitler, or Italy after World War II.[13]

Choosing Executives

The discussion so far has focused on the impact of electoral rules for choosing legislative bodies. But how do other countries that have directly elected presidents conduct their executive-branch contests? First, we must recognize that most presidential or dual-executive systems (often referred to as semi-presidential systems, like in France) do not use an Electoral College, nor do most countries use the primaries system that we are accustomed to in the United States. Due to spatial constraints I cannot discuss the full rationale for these institutions here, but suffice it to say that both institutions do in fact reflect certain elements of the proportional vision of democracy alluded to above. That is, our electoral college overrepresents less populous districts (like Rhode Island) in the interests of giving minorities a stronger voice in national campaigns than they might have otherwise. Similarly, by holding electoral primaries in less populous states like New Hampshire and Iowa, candidates are forced to campaign in districts that they might otherwise choose to ignore, due to their small weight in the national tally.

That said, how do other presidential systems carry out their direct presidential elections?[14] The most common system is the one used by France, Portugal, Brazil, Russia, and a host of other presidential (or semi-presidential) democracies.[15] It is called a *run-off election* and it ensures that whoever the winner is, they will have a mandate based on the majority will of the voters. Very simply, if no candidate wins a majority of the national vote in the first round of elections, then everyone except the top two candidates are excluded and voters go to the polls again (a week or two later) to choose between these two candidates.

Now imagine if the United States had this type of presidential electoral system in place during the 2000 campaign! In this case, neither Gore, who won the plurality of the vote nationwide (with 48.4 percent), nor Bush (47.9 percent) received a majority of the popular vote. Nader, the Green Party candidate (with 2.75 percent) clearly cost Gore the win in Florida (and thus the election) and Buchanan (with .47 percent) also siphoned off some of the natural Bush vote. Had we used the run-off system, Nader and Buchanan would not have necessarily been seen as "spoilers" and their voters (and potential voters) could have freely voted for their first-choice candidates without worrying too much about "throwing their vote away." They could do this because if they suspected that no one candidate would win a majority in the first round, then they would have an opportunity in the second round to express their "least worst" preference.

Some would argue that this type system is more democratic because it allows for a fuller expression of preferences and more varied opinions get aired during the campaign. It also encourages people with good ideas (but little chance of winning) to nevertheless run for office, rather than discouraging them for being "spoiler candidates." This brings new ideas into the political system, possibly getting young people more interested in politics, and their issues are given greater national attention. Others worry that run-off elections can lead to "voter fatigue" and thus much lower turnout in the second round, increased expenses for taxpayers, and in very close races between second and third place, it can lead to dramatic exits for the third place candidate![16]

There are, however, ways of avoiding these problems. Take for example *Instant Runoff Voting or IRV.*[17] In this system, the rules are the same as those described above, a winner is required to have more than half the votes. However, here if nobody wins a majority of the vote in the first round, voters do not have to physically go to the polls a second time. Instead, voters use *preference voting* to rank their choices on the ballot (say 1-2-3-4). Thus, if no one wins a majority, then the least popular candidate is eliminated and her supporters' second-choice preferences are added to the total instantly. If her supporters' second-choice votes are enough to take one of the other candidates to a majority, then a winner is declared. That person wins because a majority of the voters actually preferred that candidate to some other. To illustrate this, let's use the example again of the 2000 U.S. presidential election in Florida.[18] The actual results were as follows:

Buchanan	.38%
Bush	48.95%
Gore	48.94%
Nader	1.73%

Given our actual rules, Bush won at least 1 more vote than Gore and thus he got all the electoral college votes from Florida and won the election (despite losing the popular vote in Florida and nationwide by about 500,000 votes). However, let's pretend that IRV was in place and run-offs were needed. In this case, Buchanan, since he had the least votes, is eliminated. But instead of throwing his supporters' (only .38 percent of all voters) second-choice preferences away, let's assume that .33 percent of those people would have preferred Bush as their second choice, .04 percent for Gore, and .01 percent for Nader. By adding these to the totals from the first round, we now have the following:

Bush	49.28%
Gore	48.98%
Nader	1.74%

Yet again, however, no candidate has a majority and so we must now eliminate the third-place candidate—Nader. In this, the second instant run-off election, the preferences of the eliminated candidate are added to those above. Of Nader's 1.74 percent, let's assume that only .17 percent would have preferred

Bush, while 1.57 percent would have said Gore was their second choice. We now end up with the following totals:

Bush	49.45%
Gore	50.55%

Now we have a clear majority winner who is preferred by more than half the electorate in Florida. No votes were "wasted" and if your preferred candidate was eliminated, your votes went on to select the person you preferred second best.

Of course, the choices discussed here are only a tiny fraction of those available and in use by different countries around the world. If any of these sound reasonable to you, you should spend some time studying them in more detail. Even some U.S. city councils (including Cambridge, MA, and San Francisco) and universities are now adopting PR and IRV. However, without a major push from civil society, the two-party "duopoly" in Washington is highly unlikely to alter a system that clearly benefits them. This is why one of the chief programs of smaller parties tends to be electoral system reform, since they would prefer a more proportional vision of democracy.

References

Dahl, Robert. 1971. *Polyarchy: Participation and Opposition.* New Haven: Yale University Press.

Lijphart, Arend. 1984. *Democracies: Patterns of Majoritarian and Consensus Government in Twenty-One Countries,* 1st ed. New Haven, CT: Yale University Press.

Lijphart, Arend. 1994. *Electoral Systems and Party Systems: A Study of Twenty-Seven Democracies, 1945–1990.* Oxford: Oxford University Press.

Lijphart, Arend. 1999. *Patterns of Democracy: Government Forms and Performance in Thirty-Six Countries.* New Haven: Yale University Press.

Manuel, Paul Christopher, and Anne Marie Cammissa. 1999. *Checks & Balances: How a Parliamentary System Could Change American Politics.* Boulder, CO: Westview Press.

Matland, Richard. n.d. *IDEA, Women in Parliament: Beyond the Numbers* [accessed June 6, 2003]. Available from *http://www.idea.int/women/parl/ch3c.htm.*

Shugart, Matthew Soberg, and John M. Carey. 1992. *Presidents and Assemblies : Constitutional Design and Electoral Dynamics.* Cambridge [England]; New York: Cambridge University Press.

Tocqueville, Alexis de. 1990 [1835–40]. *Democracy in America, Vols. I & II.* Trans. H. Reeve and F. Bowen, P. Bradley and D. J. Boorstein. *Vintage Classics.* New York: Random House.

Endnotes

1. In the 2000 presidential election, voter turnout was 50.4 percent of the voting age population (according to US Census figures) and 67.1 percent of the registered voters. For all federal elections, turnout has varied between a high of 63 percent of the voting age population in 1960 to a low of 36 percent in 1986 and 1990. http://www.fec.gov/pages/htmlto5.htm Turnout in mid-term Congressional elections is typically much lower than for presidential elections. In 1998, turnout rates among the voting age population ranged from 60 percent in Minnesota to only 24 percent in Tennessee. See, for example: http://www.fec.gov/pages/reg&to98.htm

2. See, for example: http://www.fec.gov/pages/agedemog.htm

3. Quoted from http://worldpolicy.org/globalrights/democracy/democracy.html.

4. In actuality there are many more varieties of electoral systems than can be discussed here, due to spatial constraints. Interested readers should see Lijphart (1994) for more details.

5. For an interesting look at how a parliamentary system could change American politics, see Manuel and Cammisa (1999).

6. For up-to-date electoral statistics on every country in the world, see http://www.electionworld.org/

7. This is important. A plurality means simply "the most votes." A majority, however, implies that the winner got at least 50.1 percent of the votes cast. If a district has 3 or more serious candidates running, it is quite possible that the person with the most votes may not win a majority of the votes.

8. The rules for what to do with the fractions of percentages are complex. See Lijphart (1994) for details.

9. Recall that there is a very important difference between winning a majority of the popular vote and how many seats this translates into in the legislature. It is perfectly possible that a party might win less than a majority of the popular vote nationwide, but still end up with a majority of the seats in the legislature.

10. Britain, like the United States, is generally understood to be a "two-party" political system; not because there are only two political parties with seats in the legislature (actually, as of 2003 there are 10 parties with at least one seat), but because more than 85 percent of the seats are typically won by the top two parties.

11. Voters typically have no say in which parties will join a coalition government, that is negotiated by the party elites behind closed doors in the weeks following an election. Similarly, the policy choices that come out of coalition governments will always be a compromise between the members of the government, and thus the biggest party in the coalition must often compromise on its ideals to satisfy the junior partner in the coalition. This fact gives even very small parties tremendous potential to influence legislation, far above what would be expected in a WTA system, where they might not even get seats in the legislature!

12. See, for example, http://www.idea.int/voter_turnout/voter_turnout8.html

13. Readers who are interested in exploring in greater detail the intense debate about majoritarian versus proportional visions of democracy should visit sites like: www.idea.int; www.fairvote.org; and http://worldpolicy.org/globalrights/democracy/democracy.html. See also Lijphart (1994) and Powell (2000).

14. Note that I am using this section to talk about different types of presidential elections, but run-offs (instant or otherwise) are also used for electing legislators.

15. For more information on presidential systems worldwide, see Shugart and Carey (1992).

16. For example, in the stunning French presidential elections of 2002, the second place candidate was an extreme right-wing racist ideologue named Jean Marie Le Pen, who barely beat out the standing prime minister, Lionel Jospin. Of course, in the second round of voting, the French overwhelmingly voted to support the more moderate right-wing candidate, the incumbent Jacques Chirac. In this case, the French were deprived of the typical choice between "left" and "right" candidates, one of the risks of the run-off system.

17. For more details on this choice, see www.fairvote.org. An excellent computer animation of how this system works in Australian elections can be found at: http://afr.com/election2001/graphics/2001/12/06/FFXCIEIVURC.html

18. I thank Chris Gates and his wonderful flash animation, available at: http://www.chrisgates.net/irv/.

Bush v. Gore

UNITED STATES SUPREME COURT

The Supreme Court's December 2000 ruling in Bush v. Gore *was one the
most awaited and debated decisions the High Court has ever handed down.
The following text is excerpted from the controversial ruling, with the majority
opinion written by Justice Anthony Kennedy. Republicans hailed the decision
as a fair end to the recount controversy, while Democrats sharply condemned
the decision as a blatant and unjust political act. Whether one agrees or dis-
agrees with the Court's reasoning, one fact is perfectly clear: the Supreme
Court's decision handed the election to George W. Bush.*

Governor Bush and Richard Cheney, Republican Candidates for the Presidency and Vice Presidency, filed an emergency application for a stay of this
mandate. On December 9, we granted the application, treated the application
as a petition for a writ of certiorari, and granted certiorari

The petition presents the following questions: whether the Florida Supreme
Court established new standards for resolving Presidential election contests,
thereby violating Art. II, Section1, cl. 2, of the United States Constitution and
failing to comply with 3 U. S. C. Section 5, and whether the use of standardless
manual recounts violates the Equal Protection and Due Process Clauses.

The Supreme Court of Florida has said that the legislature intended the
State's electors to 'participate fully in the federal electoral process' . . . as provided in 3 U.S.C. 5.

That statute, in turn, requires that any controversy or contest that is
designed to lead to a conclusive selection of electors be completed by December 12. That date is upon us, and there is no recount procedure in place under
the State Supreme Court's order that comports with minimal constitutional
standards.

Because it is evident that any recount seeking to meet the December 12
date will be unconstitutional for the reasons we have discussed, we reverse the
judgment of the Supreme Court of Florida ordering a recount to proceed.
Seven Justices of the Court agree that there are constitutional problems with the
recount ordered by the Florida Supreme Court that demand a
remedy. . . . The only disagreement is as to the remedy.

Because the Florida Supreme Court has said that the Florida Legislature
intended to obtain the safe-harbor benefits of 3 U. S. C. 5, Justice Breyer's proposed remedy remanding to the Florida Supreme Court for its ordering of a
constitutionally proper contest until December 18—contemplates action in violation of the Florida election code, and hence could not be part of an 'appropriate' order. . . .

None are more conscious of the vital limits on judicial authority than are the members of this Court, and none stand more in admiration of the Constitution's design to leave the selection of the President to the people, through their legislatures, and to the political sphere.

When contending parties invoke the process of the courts, however, it becomes our unsought responsibility to resolve the federal and constitutional issues the judicial system has been forced to confront. The judgment of the Supreme Court of Florida is reversed, and the case is remanded for further proceedings not inconsistent with this opinion.

From Justice Breyer's dissent:

The Court was wrong to take this case. It was wrong to grant a stay. It should now vacate that stay and permit the Florida Supreme Court to decide whether the recount should resume.

The political implications of this case for the country are momentous. But the federal legal questions presented, with one exception, are insubstantial. The manual recount would itself redress a problem of unequal treatment of ballots . . . I fear that in order to bring this agonizingly long election process to a definitive conclusion, we have not adequately attended to that necessary 'check upon our own exercise of power,' 'our own sense of self-restraint.' Justice Brandeis once said of the Court, "The most important thing we do is not doing." What it does today, the Court should have left undone. I would repair the damage done as best we now can, by permitting the Florida recount to continue under uniform standards. I respectfully dissent.

From Justice Ginsburg's dissent:

Time is short in part because of the Court' s entry of a stay on December 9, several hours after an able circuit judge in Leon County had begun to superintend the recount process. More fundamentally, the Court's reluctance to let the recount go forward, despite its suggestion that 'the search for intent can be confined by specific rules designed to ensure uniform treatment' ultimately turns on its own judgment about the practical realities of implementing a recount, not the judgment of those much closer to the process.

Justice Souter's dissent, with whom Justices Breyer, Stevens and Ginsburg join:

If this Court had allowed the State to follow the course indicated by the opinions of its own Supreme Court, it is entirely possible that there would ultimately have been no issue requiring our review, and political tension could have worked itself out in the Congress following the procedure provided in

3 U.S.C. 15. The case being before us, however, its resolution by the majority is another erroneous decision . . .

As will be clear, I am in substantial agreement with the dissenting opinions of Justice Stevens, Justice Ginsburg and Justice Breyer. I write separately only to say how straightforward the issues before us really are. . . . In deciding what to do about this, we should take account of the fact that electoral votes are due to be cast in six days. I would therefore remand the case to the courts of Florida with instructions to establish uniform standards for evaluating the several types of ballots that have prompted differing treatments, to be applied within and among counties when passing on such identical ballots in any further recounting (or successive recounting) that the courts might order. Unlike the majority, I see no warrant for this Court to assume that Florida could not possibly comply with this requirement before the date set for the meeting of electors, December 18.

From Justice Stevens, with whom Justice Ginsburg and Justice Breyer join, dissenting:

When questions arise about the meaning of state laws, including election laws, it is our settled practice to accept the opinions of the highest courts of the States as providing the final answers. On rare occasions, however, either federal statutes or the Federal Constitution may require federal judicial intervention in state elections. This is not such an occasion. The federal questions that ultimately emerged in this case are not substantial. . . .

Nor are petitioners correct in asserting that the failure of the Florida Supreme Court to specify in detail the precise manner in which the "intent of the voter," Fla. Stat. 101.5614(5) (Supp. 2001), is to be determined rises to the level of a constitutional violation." . . .

The Florida statutory standard is consistent with the practice of the majority of States, which apply either an 'intent of the voter' standard or an 'impossible to determine the elector's choice' standard in ballot recounts. . . .

Admittedly, the use of differing substandards for determining voter intent in different counties employing similar voting systems may raise serious concerns. Those concerns are alleviated, if not eliminated, by the fact that a single impartial magistrate will ultimately adjudicate all objections arising from the recount process. . . .

In the interest of finality, however, the majority effectively orders the disenfranchisement of an unknown number of voters whose ballots reveal their intent, and are therefore legal votes under state law, but were for some reason rejected by ballot-counting machines.

Finally, neither in this case, nor in its earlier opinion in Palm Beach County Canvassing Bd. v. Harris . . . did the Florida Supreme Court make any substantive change in Florida electoral law. Its decisions were rooted in long-established precedent and were consistent with the relevant statutory provisions, taken as a whole. It did what courts do—it decided the case before it in light of the legislature' s intent to leave no legally cast vote uncounted. . . .

What must underlie petitioners' entire federal assault on the Florida election procedures is an unstated lack of confidence in the impartiality and capacity of the state judges who would make the critical decisions if the vote count were to proceed. Otherwise, their position is wholly without merit. The endorsement of that position by the majority of this Court can only lend credence to the most cynical appraisal of the work of judges throughout the land. It is confidence in the men and women who administer the judicial system that is the true backbone of the rule of law. Time will one day heal the wound to that confidence that will be inflicted by today's decision. One thing however is certain. Although we may never know with complete certainty the identity of the loser is perfectly clear. It is the Nation's confidence in the judge as an impartial guardian of the rule of law.

Who Rules?: The Impact of Public Opinion in America

DAVID PRENTISS

The role of public opinion in driving the political debate has been the source of much controversy throughout American history. In the article below, David Prentiss tells us that the nation's founders gave a lot of thought toward public opinion. As is often noted, the founders were skeptical of a political system that is too responsive to public mood. This, they feared, would lead to political fads and fashions that would result in political instability. On the other hand, the founders were true democrats and clearly wanted ultimate political power to rest with the people. The question from the founders' perspective rested on how to include the opinions of the public in the political process but at the same time fashion a political system that somehow tempered or filtered these views.

Who should be in charge of the United States, and who actually is? In 2001, a public opinion survey explored Americans' views on these questions and came up with some interesting answers.

On the question of who should elected and government officials be influenced by when making important decisions, 68 percent of Americans stated that the views of the majority should have a great deal of influence. But when asked how much influence majority views actually have on officials, only 9 percent of Americans thought that the people have a great deal of influence. (The most popular answers to the question of who had a lot of influence were campaign contributors, lobbyists, and special interest groups). In a related question, the poll asked whether officials should make decisions based on what the majority wants or should they make decisions using their own judgment on what is best for the people. Fifty-four percent of Americans answered in favor of what the majority wants and 42 percent for officials using their own judgment. However, when asked about cases where officials think that the majority is wrong, 51 percent of Americans stated that officials should do what they think is right and disregard the wishes of the majority. Even still, in such cases 40 percent of Americans felt that the officials should follow what the majority wants, notwithstanding the officials' belief that the majority is wrong (*Public Perspective*, July/August 2001).

These poll numbers show that the answer most Americans give to the question of who is actually in charge of the United States is a clear and resounding "not us!" Yet the answer they give to the question of who should be in charge is a bit more complicated. Almost half of Americans believe that the majority view should prevail even when government officials believe it is wrong. A slight majority, however, believes that officials should follow their own judgment, in contravention to majority sentiment, if those officials think that the majority view is wrong. Given that the overwhelming majority of Americans believe that their views should have a great deal of influence on officials in Washington, the slight majority of Americans who are willing to have their views ignored when officials think they are wrong seem to answer the question of who should be charge of the United States with the reply, "it depends." It depends, they apparently are saying, on whether officials agree with the people's views or not. They want the people's views to have a significant amount of influence on the decisions of officials—hence, the people are in charge. However, if those officials believe the people's views are wrong, then they are willing to let the officials ignore those views—hence, the officials are in charge (at least for that instant).

The issues raised by this poll are not new. In 1792, James Madison—as a member of the U.S. Congress—was embroiled in a political dispute over the economic policies of the United States. Madison opposed the proposals of Secretary of the Treasury Alexander Hamilton and he sought to mobilize public opinion against them. Madison believed that if the public expressed its opposition to the policies proposed by Hamilton, then the government was obligated to heed the wishes of the people and retract the proposals. Hamilton insisted that government officials were obligated to implement the policies they judged were best, even if opposed by the people. These different views about public opinion's role in the political system were an ever-present theme in the political battles between Madison and Jefferson's Republican Party and Hamilton's Federalist Party for the next 20 years (Buel, 1972).

Perceptions of who actually is in charge in United States and varying views regarding the question of who should be in charge are not disconnected phenomena, given the nature of the American political system. To see how they are connected, and to begin to assess the perceptions and views themselves, one must go back to the beginning.

The Declaration of Independence states that legitimate government must be based on the consent of the governed. It does not specify, however, exactly what that consent must consist of or extend to. While it was universally recognized that the genius of the American people required a republican form of government, the details were left to be worked out later. One could say that the American people have been working out those details ever since.

At the 1787 Constitutional Convention in Philadelphia, the role of public opinion in American democracy was very much on the minds of the delegates. In the course of their deliberations, there were more than three-dozen statements by delegates specifically referring to whether the proposals they were considering would be acceptable to the people. Some delegates were also quite explicit about the people's ability to understand political issues and form political judgments. Roger Sherman from Connecticut argued that the House of Representatives should not be elected by the people. He asserted "the people . . . , immediately should have as little to do as may be about the Government. They [lack] information and are constantly liable to be misled" (Farrand, 1966). On the other hand, James Wilson, a delegate from Pennsylvania, argued "the national legislative powers ought to flow immediately from the people, so as to contain all their understanding, and to be an exact transcript of their minds" (Farrand, 1966).

While it is important to consider the differing views of individuals expressed in debates as the Constitution was being constructed, it is also necessary to understand the rationale presented for the finished product that was the result of those debates. The best source for this is *The Federalist,* the collection of essays written by Hamilton, Madison, and John Jay under the pen name of Publius to win public support for the Constitution. In a number of key passages in *The Federalist,* the question of public opinion is discussed as a fundamental issue concerning the character and operation of the constitutional system.

For example, in *Federalist No. 63,* the following observation is made about public opinion when discussing the advantages of the Senate:

> To a people as little blinded by prejudice or corrupted by flattery as those whom I address, I shall not scruple to add, that such an institution [the Senate] may be sometimes necessary as a defense to the people against their own temporary errors and delusions. *As the cool and deliberate sense of the community ought, in all governments, and actually will, in all free governments, ultimately prevail over the views of its rulers,* so there are particular moments in public affairs when the people, stimulated by some irregular passion, or some illicit advantage, or misled by the artful misrepresentations of interested men, may call for measures which they themselves will afterwards be the most ready to lament and condemn. (italics added)

The sentence emphasized in the middle of the passage bears careful consideration. Publius declares that the design of the constitutional system is premised on the view that the cool and deliberate sense of the people should prevail in the government but that the system should also be able to block the people's wishes temporarily when those sentiments would lead to harmful policies. Based on this passage it therefore can be said that Publius believed that public opinion is problematic: It may be wise and just on most occasions, but at times it may be unwise or unjust. Publius claims that the constitutional system is designed so that it can both give effect to the former and resist the latter.

This intent is further revealed in *The Federalist No. 49,* where Publius states "it is the reason, alone, of the public, that ought to control and regulate the government. The passions ought to be controlled and regulated by the government." While it might sound a bit simplistic to our modern ears, Publius viewed people as a composite of reason and passion. Depending on the individuals and circumstances involved, the opinions of people may be based on their reason, or based on their passions. According to Publius, this is why public opinion is problematic and why the constitutional system must be designed to both give effect to public opinion and be able to resist it (at least temporarily) when necessary.

One charge leveled at the supporters of the Constitution was that a system designed in this way would allow corrupt public officials to ignore the legitimate interests and well-being of the people and turn the government into a despotism. Publius replied that elections and other provisions in the Constitution would guard against this. Publius also believed that human nature must be taken into account:

> As there is a degree of depravity in mankind which requires a certain degree of circumspection and distrust, so there are other qualities of human nature which justify a certain portion of esteem and confidence. Republican government presupposes the existence of these qualities in a higher degree than any other form. Were the pictures which have been drawn by the political jealousy of some among us faithful likenesses of the human character, the inference would be, that there is not sufficient virtue among men for self-government; and that nothing less than the chains of despotism can restrain them from destroying and devouring one another (*The Federalist No. 55*).

Thus, *The Federalist* offers an explanation of how public opinion should operate in the constitutional system that is ultimately based on a particular view of human nature and the dynamics of political behavior. Part of this view is the belief that representatives are obligated to go against the wishes of the people in those circumstances where the representative believes that what the people want is unwise or unjust.

It is one thing to design a framework of government and explain the rationale behind it. It is another thing to put it into practice. The alliance of Madison and Hamilton aimed at winning approval of the Constitution soon gave way, as mentioned above, to fierce political disputes between them during the Washington administration. In the midst of these partisan battles, Madison expressed his views on the question of public opinion in an essay published in the *National Gazette* in 1792:

> Public opinion sets bounds to every government, and is the real sovereign in every free one. As there are cases where the public opinion must be obeyed by the government, so there are cases, where not being fixed, it may be influenced by government. This distinction, if kept in view, would prevent or decide many debates on the respect due from the government to the sentiments of the people.

It is interesting to compare this passage to the view of public opinion expressed in *The Federalist*. In 1792, Madison was not emphasizing the need or duty for government officials to resist the views of the people. Rather, he introduces the principle that under certain circumstances government is obligated to obey public opinion. He does not, however, elaborate on what those circumstances are. By implication of the next sentence, though, he seems to hold that government must obey public opinion when it is fixed—that is, clearly established. What Madison does not address in this essay is what is the government's obligation when public opinion is fixed and unwise or unjust.

Importantly, Madison makes explicit another dynamic of political behavior: Government officials should endeavor to influence public opinion, at least when it is not fixed. This is exactly what Madison was trying to accomplish in the numerous essays he published in newspapers during the Washington administration. Hamilton, in his own way, also ascribed to this approach as he published a plethora of essays during this period.

While the use of political rhetoric is everywhere evident in the founding period, it is seldom mentioned when the political system is explained or defended. *The Federalist* is an outstanding example of political persuasion, but it never explicitly discusses the topic. Considering its view of public opinion and how the constitutional system is designed to operate, however, one sees the role of political rhetoric quite clearly. In those instances where the government may resist the wishes of the public, officials will have to explain themselves to the people and attempt to convince them of the proper course of action taken if those officials want to be reelected. *The Federalist* therefore envisions communications traveling in both directions between the people and the government.

The attempt to understand the nature of public opinion and place it in its proper role in the political system has continued to capture the interest of political scientists since the founding period. In 1992, two political scientists published a book based on ten years of studying over 10,000 policy preference questions asked in public opinion polls between 1935 and 1990. Their stated purpose was to show that the distrust of public opinion that they see in *The Federalist* and elsewhere was unfounded. Rather than being capricious and arbitrary, they endeavored to prove that public opinion is for the most part stable, sensible, and changes only gradually. They described their main point for presenting their study in this way: "The chief cure for the ills of American democracy is to be found not in less but in more democracy; not in thwarting the public's desires but in providing it with good political information and heeding its wishes" (Page and Shapiro, 1992).

Page and Shapiro also cite studies that indicate that public policy involving major issues corresponds to majority preferences about two-thirds of the time and that significant changes in the public's preferences are followed by congruent changes in policy also about two-thirds of the time. What they do not indicate, however, is what figure would be acceptable. In other words, does their call for more democracy mean that public policy should match majority preferences 75 percent, 90 percent, or 100 percent of the time? (Page and Shapiro, 1992).

Based on the Public Perspective poll taken in 2001, almost half of Americans might want to see that figure at 100 percent inasmuch as they indicated that government officials should follow the view of the majority even when those officials believe the majority view is wrong. Slightly more than half, however, might not see the need for more democracy, as those people want officials to use their own judgment when they think the majority view is wrong. Yet the

68 percent of Americans who want to have a great deal of influence on the decisions officials make must be dissatisfied with their democracy as only 9 percent feel that they have such influence.

While there is no law against holding conflicting opinions, these numbers must be understood in terms of the circumstances and practices created by the American political system. As outlined in *The Federalist,* the system is designed to permit varying degrees of government responsiveness to public wishes. Based on the Public Perspective poll, many Americans seem comfortable with this, but there is a substantial portion of the population that is not. Moreover, even for those Americans who want their representatives to use independent judgment and disregard public opinion under certain circumstances, that is only a general proposition and they can certainly disagree with representatives' conduct in any particular instance.

These disagreements about the role of public opinion seem to be a permanent feature of the American political system: They are as evident in the policy disputes during the Washington administration in 1792 as they are in a poll taken during the Bush administration in 2001. As such, they can be seen as a fundamental and defining tension within the American political system that shapes political practice and policy. This may not be a bad thing. Tensions between different views of public opinion that can nonetheless coexist within a political system foster the kind of flexibility, development, and adjustment that a system needs to survive as times change.

The oldest political question is "who should rule?" At one level the Declaration of Independence answered that question for the United States. Yet it is very clear that certain aspects of the question are unsettled, or at least disputed, and maybe permanently so. By understanding the source of the tension that underlies this question, we will be in a better position to see how the American political system was designed to work, evaluate how it has performed, and consider what political practices can improve it or may harm it.

References

Buel, Richard, Jr. 1972. *Securing the Revolution: Ideology in American Politics, 1789–1815.* Ithaca, NY: Cornell University Press.

Farrand, Max, ed. 1966. *The Records of the Federal Convention of 1787.* New Haven, CT: Yale University Press.

Federalist, The. *The Federalist* papers, 1787.

Page, Benjamin I., and Robert Y. Shapiro. 1992. *The Rational Public.* Chicago: University of Chicago Press.

Public Perspective Magazine, July/August 2001. (http://www.ropercenter.uconn.edu/pp_poll_dem)

Rutland, Robert A., and Thomas A. Mason, eds. 1983. *The Papers of James Madison.* Charlottesville, VA: University of Virginia Press.

Anti-War Sentiment in Bush Country: A Survey of Student Attitudes on the Conflict with Iraq

JOHN LINANTUD, RAYMOND JOHNSON, AND SCOTT MCCLARY

Prior to the U.S. invasion of Iraq in 2003, public opinion throughout the world was extremely divided on the appropriateness of military action. Though numerous public opinion surveys provided indicators of national mood in the Iraq issue, John Linantud, Raymond Johnson, and Scott McClary provide quantitative data on student opinions toward the war. In a survey of campus attitudes, the authors find that students generally opposed war in Iraq. Student opinions~many of them passionately felt~ran counter to national polls which indicated that a majority of Americans supported military action. The data provide telling glimpses of how deeply split opinion was on the war.

In American democracy, the relationship between public opinion, politics, and foreign policy is complex and important for several reasons. Public opinion influences the decision to go to war, how national leaders manage the conflict, and who gets the credit or blame after the shooting stops. Both Republicans and Democrats therefore have much to gain or lose depending on what the American people think about war in Iraq. Of course, war can bring the peoples of a nation together or it can tear them apart, exposing fissures that would have otherwise remained hidden. The attitudes of racial and ethnic minorities toward war are of special importance because they offer a way to assess the legitimacy of our political system among people who have often stood outside the mainstream. And because political values are shaped early in life, the shock of September 11, 2001, the war on terror and subsequent U.S. invasions of Afghanistan and Iraq will likely have the greatest impact on the beliefs and attitudes of younger generations of citizens, whose impressions forged during these events will last a lifetime.

Like almost all policies, the U.S. policy against Iraq and Saddam Hussein was the source of controversy. Both domestically and internationally, there were many different opinions for and against taking out Saddam. But divergent groups felt quite differently about going to war; Republicans, for example, were much more likely to support an Iraqi invasion than the general population at large. In an effort to determine what *students* thought about going to war[1], we conducted a survey and asked college students for their opinions on war in Iraq. Though one student body cannot represent all campuses nationwide, its views may provide valuable insight on how young people, in particular racial and ethnic minorities, perceived the war in Iraq.[2] Furthermore, the survey was conducted in President Bush's home state of Texas, where the President enjoys strong support, and in the city of Houston, the adopted hometown of George W. Bush's parents former President and First Lady George and Barbara Bush. This study provides an excellent opportunity to investigate the level of support for the war among college students in the middle of "Bush country."

Data and Methods

Approximately one month before war in Iraq[3], we distributed a question-naire to students at the University of Houston-Downtown (UHD). The survey was comprised of question items taken verbatim from various national polling organizations. Respondents included 255 students enrolled primarily in intro-ductory United States Government classes that are mandatory for all under-graduates. The focus on required courses made a random sample more likely. As it turns out, the sample of 59 percent women and 40 percent men did match the gender distribution of the undergraduate population. The sampling was also respectable in terms of achieving a sizable representation of member of racial and ethnic minority groups: Hispanics comprise 35 percent of the student body and 45% of survey respondents, African Americans 28 percent and 22 percent, Whites 25% and 18%, and Asian Americans 10 percent and 8 percent.[4]

Overall, we found that students kept abreast of the crisis through the media at the same rate as other Americans. As seen in table 1, 69 percent of students surveyed reported that they followed developments in Iraq somewhat or very closely. But based on a comparison with the results of national surveys com-pleted at roughly the same time, campus support for the way President Bush handled the crisis, and military action taken with or without the support of allies and the United Nations, trailed the rest of the United States (see Tables 2 and 3). Whereas 61 percent of respondents to a national survey approved of the way Bush handled the situation in Iraq, our survey found that only 34 percent of students felt the same way, and the disapproval rate among students was somewhat higher than the nation. But our data also indicate that students

TABLE 1   Levels of Attention to Developments in Iraq

"How closely have you been following the news about the United Nations' inspections for weapons of mass destruction in Iraq—very closely, somewhat closely, not too closely, or not at all?"

	Very Closely	Somewhat Closely	Not Too Closely	Not At All
Students	19%	50%	24%	6%
Nation	25%	42%	24%	9%

Source for USA: Gallup.com, Jan. 9, 2003

TABLE 2   Approval of President Bush's Handling of the Situation in Iraq

"Do you approve or disapprove of the way President Bush is handling the situation with Iraq and Saddam Hussein?"

	Approve	Disapprove	No Opinion
Students	34%	46%	20%
Nation	61%	37%	2%

National polling results source: *Washington Post*, Feb 11, 2003.

appeared to be much more uncertain about the Iraqi situation, with 20 percent of respondents stating that they had no opinion.

When survey respondents were asked qualified questions about military action in Iraqi, the results were similar. Both national respondents and the students we polled tended to be less supportive of military action if it occurred without United Nations approval. However, both students and the nation were more favorably inclined toward military operations if the U.S. garnered some international backing, with 47 percent of students surveyed favoring forceful action if the U.S. obtained key allied support. However, the data overall suggest that the students we surveyed tended to be less approving and more tentative about developments in Iraq. What might explain the gap between students and the rest of the country?

Party Loyalty, Perceptions of Iraq, and Fear of War

Once a person begins to identify with a particular political party, it becomes more likely that we can predict their views of current events. Students are no different. As seen in table 4, our poll found that 51 percent of campus Democrats opposed military action to remove Saddam Hussein from power, but 71 percent of Republicans and 53 percent of Independents supported it. Yet on campus, we found that 51 percent of students identified themselves as Democrats, compared to 32 percent of national respondents (see table 5). Given that there are a greater percentage of Democrats on our campus than that found the across country, coupled with the fact that we identified sharp partisan differences on views about Iraq, we can see that party loyalty helps explain why we found divergent attitudes about war in Iraq and President Bush.

Our survey also revealed that students were less likely than their fellow Americans to see Iraq as a threat. As reported in table 6, we found that 27 percent of students perceived Iraq to be an immediate threat, while 36 percent of national respondents felt the same way. Conversely, 10 percent of those on campus said that Iraq does not pose a threat versus 6 percent nationally.

TABLE 3   Support for Military Action in Iraq

	Favor		Oppose		No Opinion	
	Students	Nation	Students	Nation	Students	Nation
"Would you favor or oppose having U.S. forces take military action against Iraq to force Saddam Hussein from power?"	45%	66%	43%	31%	13%	2%
"What if the United Nations opposes such action? In that case would you favor or oppose having U.S. forces take military action against Iraq?"	38%	50%	49%	47%	13%	2%
"What if the United Nations opposes such action but some U.S. allies such as Great Britain, Australia and Italy support it? In that case would you favor or oppose having U.S. forces take military action against Iraq?"	47%	57%	39%	40%	14%	3%

National polling results source: *Washington Post*, Feb. 11, 2003.

TABLE 4   Student Party Identification and Support for Military Action in Iraq

"Would you favor or oppose having U.S. forces take military action against Iraq to force Saddam Hussein from power?"

	Favor	**Oppose**
Democrats	35%	52%
Republicans	71%	25%

TABLE 5   Student and National Political Party Identification

	Democrat	**Republican**	**Independent**	**Other**
Students	51%	20%	18%	11%
Nation	32%	33%	34%	*

National polling results source: Gallup.com, Jan. 7, 2003.

TABLE 6   Perception of Threat Level Posed by Iraq

"Which comes closest to your view — Iraq poses an immediate threat to the United States, Iraq poses a long-term threat to the United States, but not an immediate threat, or Iraq does not pose a threat to the United States at all"

	Immediate Threat	**Long-Term Threat**	**Does Not Pose A Threat**	**No Opinion**
Students	27%	54%	10%	9%
Nation	36%	56%	6%	2%

National polling results source: Gallup.com, Feb. 11, 2003.

Students we polled also exhibited a slight tendency to exhibit greater fears about the military and economic consequences of an attack on Iraq (see table 7). This might also explain why we identified lower levels of support on campus for war.

In sum, it may be that the psychological loyalty to respondents' political party may have influenced Democrats to not only disapprove of Bush, but also overestimate the anticipated spillover effects of war and underestimate the threat from Iraq. The impact of party loyalty on Republicans, of course, would

TABLE 7   Level of Concern About War Repercussions

"Would you say you are very worried, somewhat worried, not too worried, or not at all worried that a war with Iraq could . . .

	Very Worried		Somewhat Worried		Not Too Worried		Not At All Worried	
	Students	Nation	Students	Nation	Students	Nation	Students	Nation
. . . develop into a larger war that could spread throughout the region and other parts of the world."	39%	39%	45%	37%	13%	16%	3%	8%
. . . lead to further acts of terrorism in the U.S."	55%	53%	33%	34%	10%	9%	2%	3%
. . . lead to an economic recession in the U.S."	48%	34%	29%	35%	18%	21%	4%	9%

be the opposite. This may not the ideal way for individuals to formulate a political opinion, but it is a plausible interpretation of the data nonetheless.

The Impact of Race, Ethnicity, and Gender

"We did not land on Plymouth Rock. Plymouth Rock landed on us." The anonymous student who responded to our survey with this quote from the Malcolm X version of American history provided a telling glimpse of a significant racial dimension on the question of attitudes toward Iraq. We found that race made a substantial difference in party identification, which likely influenced support for the war and President Bush.

As the data presented in table 8 indicate, just 29 percent of African-American students supported military action compared to 49 percent of Hispanics, 50 percent of Asian-Americans, and 64 percent of Whites. Yet we also found distinct differences among different racial groups' party identification. Our poll found that just 18 percent of white students described themselves as Democrats versus 75 percent of African-Americans (see table 9). Conversely, a slim majority of whites identified with the GOP while only 7 percent of African-Americans did so. The black/white partisan divide among students was remarkably profound. Asian-

TABLE 8   Student Race, Gender, and Support For Military Action in Iraq

	Favor	Oppose	Other/Don't Know
African-Americans	29%	50%	21%
Asian-Americans	50%	40%	10%
Hispanics	49%	42%	9%
Whites	64%	34%	2%
Men	55%	38%	7%
Women	39%	45%	16%

TABLE 9   Student Race and Party Identification

	Democrat	Republican	Independent	Other/Don't Know
African-Americans	75%	7%	13%	5%
Asian-Americans	25%	25%	25%	25%
Hispanics	56%	13%	21%	10%
Whites	18%	51%	18%	13%

Americans were the most balanced of all ethnic groups in terms of party support, while Hispanics exhibited a distinct trend toward favoring the Democratic party though not to the same extent as African-Americans.

Despite the best efforts of television programs such as *Buffy the Vampire Slayer, Xena the Warrior Princess,* and like-minded enterprises which present young women as capable of violence, men students at first glance appeared far more warlike than their coed counterparts. As seen in table 8, 55 percent of men favored military action versus 39 percent of women. Interestingly, these results virtually mirrored levels of support for Bush; 53 percent of men approved of the President compared to just 38 percent of women (see table 10).

It is important to remember that the same combination of gender and race may be influential in determining the next presidential election. Not surprisingly, the least amount of support for Bush is among African-Americans. Furthermore, our survey results also suggest that Bush trails significantly among Hispanics. Among whites, however, Bush appears to have high levels of support. We also identified distinct differences between the genders. Male students had higher levels of support for Bush and military action in Iraq. Alternatively, women were much more hesitant to support war and exhibited lower approval levels for President Bush.

TABLE 10   Race, Gender, and President Bush Approval Rating

	Approve	Disapprove
African-Americans	20%	80%
Asian-Americans	45%	55%
Hispanics	48%	52%
Whites	60%	40%
Men	53%	47%
Women	38%	62%

Students Speak Out on War

The most dramatic and emotional feedback we received in our survey came from students who wrote open-ended comments after completing the questionnaire. The fact that over 60 of 255 respondents made the effort to express themselves in their own words indicates how passionate the debate over war became. A great deal of these sentiments assumed a personal, visceral (and occasionally) vulgar opposition to both war and President Bush. Given the more evenhanded support for Bush nationwide, it is noteworthy that we identified far more negative comments personally directed toward Bush.

These comments do not, of course, provide scientific evidence about student levels of support for or opposition to war, but they are nonetheless revealing about individuals' attitudes. Pro-war and pro-Bush comments included:

"Like many others, I don't like war. But in this situation, I feel that if we just keep haggling and give them time, then we are allowing Iraq to build stronger forces against us. I feel we should take them out while they are at their weakest."

"KILL THEM ALL!"

"I think we need to go to war before Iraq has a chance to do anything to us."

"Why is Bush now playing games? He said that we will go to war, but he keeps on giving Iraq chances to disarm, without any deadlines. I say he [Saddam] has had his chances to disarm, and now we have to use force to disarm him . . . Kill! Kill! Kill!"

"Nuke-em!"

"I think Saddam Hussein should be stopped before he goes out and uses weapons of mass destruction. And if that means that the U.S. has to stop him with military action, then so be it."

"We need to hurry up and attack, before its too late—and too hot."

"KILL HIM!!!"

"The U.S. is the big brother of the world and is a leader, not a follower. If there is a legitimate threat we must take action to protect the liberties of the world."

Conversely, there were may deeply held comments on the anti-war and anti-Bush side:

"A small group of neo-conservative fanatics have high-jacked the White House and their contempt for U.S. opinion, let alone world opinion, is disgraceful. God help us."

"President Bush is incapable of building alliances and solving problems diplomatically."

"Fuck George Bush! He should use his own money to fight his oil war."

"Americans in general have very little useful knowledge of the culture and real political situation in the Middle East. The President is ill-advised with respect to the war in Iraq. Long term consequences make the war inadvisable."

"Bush needs to get a hold of himself! Powell seems to have better control and can give the people actual understanding of the situation."

"If there is going to be a war then let there be a war, and we would owe it to that son of a Bush!"

"Bush is displaying fascism at its finest. He only wants to duplicate his father at the expense of the American People. Bush is not the brightest person in the world and should be stopped at any cost."

"Bush is an IDIOT"

"Bush is taking it too personal because of what happened to his Dad. A war will kill a lot of innocent people. And why can't the president's sons or daughters go to war? They always send the minorities."

"Screw John Ashcroft and President G.W. "Gump" Bush"

"I hope that Bush does not take us to war. There has to be other alternatives. Our country is not ready for it, and it is a harsh, irrational decision."

"NO TO WAR!!"

"Why don't we all just get along?"

"This is new generation. We have new dreams and new promises. We don't want to make a decision we are going to regret. Blood causes blood, which causes more blood. Make love, not war."

Some comments were more ambiguous or directed more toward the debate about war rather than the war itself:

"I am in favor removing a killer and a sick rapist from power in Iraq with help, hopefully, from some of his own people. But to act like some superpower, know-it-all, arrogant asshole is not the way Bush needs to gain approval!"

"I think we should find Bin Laden and stop messing with other countries until we catch him."

"I believe that we sat around and did too much talking with these Middle Eastern countries, and that is why we are in this situation now. They don't take us seriously. We're all bark and no bite. Regarding the "peace" demonstrators: most of the people who protest aren't in the military nor have family fighting. They are privileged people who never had to fight for anything in their lives before. When they say, "Don't send our children to fight," it's not their children."

"No war unless we are backed by other nations; then all the responsibility of the outcome will not be on ourselves."

"A U.N. resolution in favor [of war] might change my opposition."

"This survey does not give one an ample amount of room to convey his/her position on war. In brief sum, we should just every careful in this approach. I'm not really convinced either way."

"If you oppose war, do you want to pay $1.60 for gas all the time?"

"We did not land on Plymouth Rock. Plymouth Rock landed on us."

"I do not favor a war with Iraq. However, I do support the threat of war to disarm Saddam. I do understand that this may, and probably will, lead to a war with him."

"The Iraq situation is designed to 1) force the U.N. to take action; 2) employ unemployed Americans; 3) ready Americans for reduced comforts coming in the future; and 4) Soft-shoe the economic recession as caused by war-efforts. This is a diversionary tactic."

The depth of personal feelings behind the comments were inescapable on both sides of the debate. However, we received substantially more comments from those opposed to President Bush and war in Iraq. Regardless of the occasionally creative or imprecise syntax, the greater number of open-ended comments opposed to war tended to reinforce the strength and depth of the anti-war and anti-Bush attitudes among students we surveyed.

Conclusion

Compared to the nation at large, the undergraduate community at we surveyed harbored an unusual degree of antipathy toward both the possibility of war with Iraq and President Bush. That is not say that feeling were unanimous on campus. But we found a clear majority opposed to war. What might account for this finding? On one hand, the students we polled generally perceived Iraq to be a lesser threat to national security than did the population across the U.S. Furthermore, our results indicate that students also feared the consequences of war more than the rest of the country.

Of course, race, party loyalty and antipathy to the President also appear to have had a major influence on student opinions. We found that Democratic students far outnumbered Republicans, and partisanship was clearly a powerful predictor of support for the war. Race and ethnicity were also factors. We identified a substantial gap between African-American and other students and this difference of opinion may be indicative of larger divisions that could have considerable implications for the future of American democracy. Is low African American support for war and George W. Bush another element of a general alienation already evidenced by lower voter turnout, civic engagement, trust in public institutions, and other economic and social indicators? Or does it merely reflect a heartfelt aversion to war, the Republican Party, or Bush himself? This question must not be swept under the rug, because the stakes, from the consolidation of liberal ideals to the realistic need for national cohesion in a time of conflict, are far too high.

Republicans might take heart that Hispanic students appeared more willing than African Americans to support Bush's war effort. This supports the idea that the Hispanic population may constitutes a "swing" vote in upcoming elections. On the other hand, Democrats will surely note that Hispanics still lag behind whites in support for Republican policies and leadership and that Latinos are substantial Democratic party supporters. Since foreign policy problems are unlikely to disappear any time soon, these divisions could be telling in future elections. It is clear, however, that even in the heart of "Bush country," students were generally unsupportive of military efforts in Iraq.

Endnotes

1. The survey was conducted by the Political Science Club at the University of Houston-Downtown (UHD).

2. UHD offers an exceptional opportunity to survey the attitudes of both college students and minorities on the war with Iraq. An open admissions university, UHD has a very diverse undergraduate population that is majority Hispanic and African-American.

3. The week of February 17-21, 2003.

4. University of Houston Downtown Office of Institutional Research and Planning, "Spring 2003 Semester: 20th Day Preliminary Reports Fact Sheet," (*http://www.uhd.edu/about/irp/*), accessed June 9, 2003.

5. Originally attributed to African-American civil rights activist Malcolm X, from *The Autobiography of Malcolm X*. (1965).

About the Contributors

Michael Baum is Associate Professor of Political Science at the University of Massachusetts–Dartmouth, Executive Board Member of the University's Center for Portuguese Studies and Culture, and co-chair of the Iberian Study Group at Harvard University's Center for European Studies. He is a specialist in comparative politics and published articles in *South European Politics & Society*, the *European Journal of Political Research*, and other journals. Every summer he leads a study abroad program in Lisbon, Portugal, with students from all over North America.

Ron Belair retired in 2002 as assistant director of finance and management for the Rhode Island Department of Children, Youths, and Families. He was a co-founder of and is a charter member of the Rhode Island chapter of the American Society for Public Administration. Belair holds a Doctor of Public Administration degree and has taught at Roger Williams University, Johnson and Wales University, and the University of Massachusetts–Dartmouth.

Joel R. Campbell is Associate Professor of Economics at Kansai Gaidai University, Osaka, Japan. He specializes in globalization, global security issues, and foreign policy.

John Carroll is Chancellor Professor of Political Science at the University of Massachusetts–Dartmouth. His areas of research interest are state politics and constitutional law, especially church-state relations. Carroll's most recent publications have been studies of Indian constitutional law, and he is currently working on a comparative study of state lobbyists. His research has been published in *Comparative State Politics* and the *Journal of Palestinian Studies*.

Kevin Curow is a Visiting Lecturer in Political Science at the University of Massachusetts–Dartmouth. His research interests include the consequences of American hegemony, post–Cold War alliance politics, German-American relations, the effects of populist discourse on democracy, and democratization in the post-Communist world. Curow has also lived and taught in Germany.

Art English is Professor of Political Science at the University of Arkansas at Little Rock. His teaching and scholarly interests are in American government, state politics, and constitutional law, and his research has been published in numerous journals, including *Legislative Politics Quarterly*, the *American Review of Politics*, the *Arkansas Journal of Political Science*, *The Arkansas Lawyer*, *Comparative State Politics*, and the *Journal of Politics*. English is the recipient of University and College Awards for Public Service.

John Fobanjong is Professor of Political Science and Director of the African & African American Studies program at the University of Massachusetts–Dartmouth. His areas of academic expertise are in public administration and public policy, international relations, comparative politics, and ethnic politics. Fobanjong has published in a variety of academic journals, and he recently authored a book entitled *Understanding the Backlash Against Affirmative Action* (Nova Science Publishers).

Craig Goodman is a Ph.D. candidate in the Department of Political Science at the University of Houston and a visiting lecturer at Rice University. Goodman's research focuses upon Congressional politics, and his dissertation examines whether election results serve as a constraint on the observed roll call behavior of members of Congress.

Mark Hyde is a Professor of Political Science at Providence College. His research and teaching interests are in the areas of state politics and policy, interest groups, political parties, and research methodology. Hyde has published articles in a variety of journals, including *Journal of Politics, Polity,* and *Western Political Quarterly,* and he is co-author of *Doing Empirical Political Research* (Houghton Mifflin, 2003).

Leena Thacker-Kumar is Associate Professor of Political Science at University of Houston–Downtown. Her teaching and research interests are in the areas of international relations, comparative politics, and women in politics. Thacker-Kumar provides frequent commentary to the news media on international affairs and recently co-authored an article entitled "Fostering Inter-European Cooperation: Technological Collaboration among Nations of the EU" in the *Social Science Journal.*

John Linantud is Assistant Professor of Political Science at the University of Houston–Downtown. He specializes in global politics and U.S. foreign policy. His co-authors, **Raymond Johnson** and **Scott McClary,** are undergraduate political science majors at the University of Houston–Downtown.

Kenneth L. Manning is Assistant Professor of Political Science and University Pre-Law Advisor at the University of Massachusetts–Dartmouth. Manning's research focuses upon American politics broadly, with a particular emphasis upon judicial politics. He recently co-authored an article entitled "George W. Bush's Potential Supreme Court Nominees: What Impact Might They Have?" in *Judicature,* and he is co-author of the forthcoming book *Judicial Process in America,* 6th ed. (CQ Press, 2004).

Frank Niles is Assistant Professor of Political Science at John Brown University. His research focuses on religion and politics, and he is currently studying the causes and consequences of political information flow in religious communities. Niles serves on the Executive Council of the Religion and Politics Section of the American Political Science Association, and is author of a forthcoming chapter entitled, "Unity in the Face of the Faceless: Northwest Arkansas Clergy and the Klan," in *Religious Interests in Community Conflict.*

Dave Prentiss is a Visiting Lecturer in Political Science at the University of Massachusetts–Dartmouth and Ph.D. Candidate in Political Science at Boston College. His academic and research interests are primarily in the area of American constitutional theory and history, political institutions, and public opinion.

Adolfo Santos is Assistant Chair of Political Science at the University of Houston–Downtown. He teaches courses in the area of American politics and his research interests have focused upon congressional retirement patterns, Hispanic representation, affirmative action, and state and local politics.